LOST TO TIME

LOST TO TIME

UNFORGETTABLE STORIES
THAT HISTORY FORGOT

MARTIN W. SANDLER

STERLING

New York / London
www.sterlingpublishing.com

STERLING and the distinctive Sterling logo are registered trademarks of
Sterling Publishing Co., Inc.

Library of Congress Cataloging-in-Publication Data
Sandler, Martin W.
  Lost to time : unforgettable stories that history forgot / Martin W. Sandler.
    p. cm.
  Includes bibliographical references and index.
  ISBN 978-1-4027-2958-4
  1. History—Miscellanea. I. Title.
  D10.S313 2010
  904—dc22
                                    2009048992
10 9 8 7 6 5 4 3 2

Published by Sterling Publishing Co., Inc.
387 Park Avenue South, New York, NY 10016
© 2010 by Martin W. Sandler
Distributed in Canada by Sterling Publishing
ᶜ/ₒ Canadian Manda Group, 165 Dufferin Street
Toronto, Ontario, Canada M6K 3H6
Distributed in the United Kingdom by GMC Distribution Services
Castle Place, 166 High Street, Lewes, East Sussex, England BN7 1XU
Distributed in Australia by Capricorn Link (Australia) Pty. Ltd.
P.O. Box 704, Windsor, NSW 2756, Australia

Please see picture credits on page 290 for image copyright information.

Sterling ISBN 978-1-4027-2958-4

For information about custom editions, special sales, premium and
corporate purchases, please contact Sterling Special Sales
Department at 800-805-5489 or specialsales@sterlingpublishing.com.

FRONTISPIECE: THE GREAT CLOCK ABOVE the entrance to the rotunda of the Library
of Congress Thomas Jefferson Building in Washington, D.C., was sculpted by
John Flanagan in 1896. Above the clockface, Father Time strides forward,
holding his scythe.

For Carol, who makes it all worthwhile.

CONTENTS

"The only thing new in the world," Harry S. Truman said, "is the history you don't know." Arctic historian Russell Potter has stated that "history can only live if one recovers its strangeness, its singularity, even its shock." These two statements encapsulate much of what this book is all about. Its purpose is to inform, captivate, and surprise through stories that reveal and recover people, events, and developments that have been lost to history.

What is amazing is that all of the stories you are about to read are not only compelling and true, but also the furthest thing from trivia. They are important stories—tales from throughout history (even prehistory) and from throughout the world—of unknown or little-known personalities, achievements, ingenuity, heroics, blunders, and outright disasters that changed the world and still resonate today.

Here you will find the story of a man who is likely the most famous person you've never heard of, a man who during his all-too-brief lifetime became America's greatest hero, a man whose death elicited the greatest outpouring of grief the nation had ever witnessed, and a man whose extraordinary adventures in the Arctic signaled the beginning of the exploration of that region and led directly to historic discoveries. Here you also will encounter the forgotten story of a much earlier explorer, the man who accomplished nothing less than completing the world's first great voyage of discovery. And here as well you will meet the ninth-century black slave who not only revolutionized the world of music, but who also transformed cuisine, fashion, and manners in ways that remain with us today.

Surprise is a key ingredient of this book, and you should be prepared to have several of your long-held historical notions challenged—perhaps even disproved. Were the Wright brothers the first to achieve manned, powered flight? Did Paul Revere make the most important gallop during the American Revolution? Was the *Titanic* tragedy the greatest of all peacetime maritime disasters? Indeed, was the Chicago Fire of 1871 the greatest conflagration of its time or even of the very day on which it took place? Not according to what you'll find within these pages.

There are other astounding but true stories here as well, including the largely unknown saga of one of the most unique rescues in world history; the story of the building of America's first subway, totally in secret; the story of the sophisticated city of some thirty thousand people that flourished in the heart of what is now the United States some 350 years before Columbus; and the saga of one of World War II's greatest military disasters, purposely kept hidden for more than thirty years by the government.

They are all remarkable stories, but even more extraordinary perhaps is that they have, for so long, been either lost or neglected. It is time for them to take their place in history.

LOST TO TIME

UNFORGETTABLE STORIES
THAT HISTORY FORGOT

ONE

ZIRYAB

The Slave Who Changed Society
(Ninth Century)

In a world that is deeply troubled by religious antagonism and division, it is difficult to comprehend that there was a time in medieval Spain when Muslims, Christians, and Jews lived side by side in freedom and tolerance and together created a golden age of culture, commerce, music, and architecture that prefigured the Renaissance, separated Spain from the rest of Europe, and forever changed the West.

Of all the individuals responsible for bringing about this astounding multicultural civilization, none was more important than a Moorish liberated black slave known as Ziryab, a man about whom the seventeenth-century Arab historian Ahmad ibn Muhammad al-Makkari wrote, "There never was, either before or after him, a man of his profession who was more generally beloved and admired." The accomplishments of this one man and his lasting influence on much of the world were so great as to be practically inconceivable, so much so that the twentieth-century French scholar Henry Terrasse was compelled to write that "undoubtedly one person alone cannot change a society so deeply." But the man called Ziryab did. Perhaps even more remarkably, his name and what he accomplished have been lost to time.

❖ COURT MUSICIANS PLAY THE OUD and other instruments in this fresco, which decorates one of the walls in Chehel Sotoun, a royal pavilion in Esfahān, Iran. The pavilion was built in the mid-seventeenth century by Shah Abbas II to entertain guests.

He was born in Mesopotamia in 789 and was raised and educated in Baghdad. His birth name was Abu al-Hasan but, according to al-Makkari, because of his dark complexion, the eloquence of his speech, and his amiable personality, he was called Ziryab, meaning "blackbird."

As Guyanese author, playwright, and educator Jan Carew pointed out, Ziryab's rise from slavery to extraordinary fame, fortune, and influence provides a prime example of the striking difference between slavery in the Islamic world and slavery during the Columbian era. During Ziryab's time, all races, colors, and creeds were apt to find themselves enslaved. "A Black slave," wrote Carew, "endowed by nature with genius, wit, and good luck could rise to unbelievable heights during his or her lifetime."

ZIRYAB'S ASCENSION TO "UNBELIEVABLE HEIGHTS" began as a young man at the Baghdad court of Caliph Harun al-Rashid. Here, Ziryab, who had already displayed an outstanding singing voice, studied music under the celebrated royal court musician Ishaq al-Mawsili. According to the following account by al-Makkari as related by Yusef Ali, Ziryab progressed with his lessons so well that he soon surpassed the talents of his famous teacher, so much so that those who listened to him began to prefer his music and his singing to that of his professor.

Al-Mawsili, however, seemed to be unaware of the way in which Ziryab had surpassed him until the day the caliph asked him if any of his pupils were showing particular promise. Ishaq then mentioned Ziryab, saying, "He is a freeman of thy family: I once heard him sing in so tender a strain and with so much soul, that I did not hesitate to take him with me, and make him my disciple; he has since very much improved, and whatever he knows he owes to me, who found out his talents, and brought them to light. So great has been his improvement under my discipline, that I have predicted that he will live to be a famous musician."

The caliph then asked al-Mawsili to produce this talented pupil, and when Ziryab appeared, al-Rashid asked if he would play a song for him. Ziryab responded by stating that he would not only be honored to do so but also would play one that he had purposely reserved for the ears of the caliph, a song that no one else had ever heard. Al-Rashid immediately sent for al-Mawsili's lute, but when the instrument was handed to Ziryab, he respectfully declined it, saying, "I have a lute of my own hands, and finished according to my method, and I never play any other instrument; if thou allow me I will send for it."

After Ziryab's lute was hastily fetched, al-Rashid was puzzled. "What difference is there," he asked, "between thy instrument and thy master's? For me, I see none: they seem to me perfectly alike." "So they are in appearance," responded Ziryab, "but they are very different in voice; for although mine is equal in size, and made of the same wood, yet the weight of it is greater by nearly one-third, and the strings are made of silk, not spun with hot water, while the second, third, and fourth strings are made of the entrails of a young lion, which are known to be far superior to those of any other animal in point of strength, deepness of tone, and clearness of sound; besides, they will bear much longer pulsation without being injured and are not so easily affected by the changes of temperature."

Impressed with Ziryab's description of the nature of his lute, the caliph then asked him to play. Ziryab was only through the first verse of his song when al-Rashid interrupted him and began to repeat the melody. According to al-Makkari, he then turned to al-Mawsili and said, "By Allah! Were it not that I consider thee a veracious man, and that I believe that the talents of this youth were entirely unknown to thee; were it not for protestations that thou has never heard this song from him, I would have thee punished immediately for not acquainting me with his abilities."

Al-Mawsili was both shocked and alarmed by the caliph's statements. Summoning Ziryab, he astounded his pupil by stating:

Envy is one of the basest vices, and yet one of the most common in this world, and principally among people following the same

3

profession. It is in vain that men struggle against it; they never can conquer it. I cannot but confess that I am myself the victim of its attacks. I feel envious of thy talents, and the high estimation in which thou art held by the Khalif; and I see no way to free myself from it unless it be by depreciating thee and denying thy abilities; but in a short time hence thy reputation will increase, and mine will gradually vanish, until thou art considered my superior by everybody. This, by Allah! I will never suffer even from my own son, much less be the instrument of it. On the other side, thou art aware that if thou possess any abilities, it is allowing to my having taken care of thy education, and fostered thy talents; had I not taught thee all my secrets, thou wouldst never have arrived by thyself at thy present eminence. I have, therefore, to propose to thee two expedients—either to leave this country immediately and go and settle in distant lands, whence the fame of thy name may never arrive here—or to remain in this city against my will, living upon thy own resources, having me for thy implacable enemy, and being in perpetual fear and anguish at my enmity. If thou decide for the first, and engage thy word never to return to his country as long as I am alive, I promise to provide thee with every necessary for thy journey, and give thee, besides, whatever sum of money and other articles thou mayest ask from me; if, on the contrary, thou resolve upon staying, beware! I shall not cease one moment attacking and harassing thee with all my might, and I shall spare no trouble or expense to obtain thy perdition; nay, I will risk my life and my property to ensure it. Now, consider, and choose.

Given the ultimatum, Ziryab felt that he had no choice but to leave Baghdad. He traveled first to Sham (Syria), and then to Ifrīqiyyah (present-day Tunisia), and then across North Africa to the Strait of Gibraltar. As for the caliph, when he inquired of what had happened to the brilliant young musician, al-Mawsili told him that Ziryab had gone insane, that he imagined himself talking to the deities, that he had actually had come to dislike music, and that he had abruptly left al-Mawsili without a word of where he was headed.

None of it was true, of course, although Ziryab did have a final destination in mind. It is not known exactly when Ziryab first set foot in Spain. What *is* known is that he wrote to al-Hakam I, the ruler of the emirate of Al-Andalus in Spain, offering his musical talents to the royal court. Al-Hakam, anxious to add a Baghdad musician to his court, responded by inviting Ziryab to come to Córdoba, where he would be well paid. However, when Ziryab arrived in Spain in 822, he was shocked to learn that al-Hakam had died. He was actually preparing to return to North Africa when he received word that al-Hakam's son and successor, Abd ar-Rahman II, at the urging of Abu al-Nasr Mansur, a Jewish Cordoban royal court musician, wished to renew his father's invitation.

The Muslim Spain in which Ziryab found himself, which was to be his home for the rest of his life, dated back to the early eighth century, when Muslim armies crossed the Strait of Gibraltar and conquered the Visigoths who had established a kingdom there. The Muslims called these new Islamic territories Al-Andalus. In 822, Al-Andalus's crowning jewel was its capital city, Córdoba. At a time when most of the cities of Europe were little more than a collection of crude wooden shacks clustered around a cathedral, Córdoba was a haven of learning, commerce, science, and culture. Córdoba citizens were understandably proud of their city's paved and lighted streets, running water, and sewage systems. They lived in stone and stucco houses surrounded by shady trees and lush gardens. The city itself boasted more than three hundred libraries and mosques and more than seven hundred bathhouses. It was here that Ziryab would realize achievements that would not only further enhance the culture and lifestyle of Al-Andalus, but also in time that of France, the rest of Europe, and eventually the Americas.

Ar-Rahman's motives in inviting Ziryab to Córdoba were very clear. Like his father before him, the new ruler had a burning desire to enhance the glory of Al-Andalus and to help the city surpass Baghdad as the leading center of culture and refinement. When he finally met the thirty-three-year-old Ziryab and heard his songs, he was captivated beyond his imagination, so much so that he invited the musician to be

❖ The Mezquita de Córdoba—the Great Mosque of Córdoba—was the second-largest mosque in the world when Islamic rule governed much of the Iberian peninsula. Built from the eighth century to 987, the mosque is now a Roman Catholic church. Shown here is the immense prayer hall, which has 856 columns.

his constant companion at court and bestowed upon him and his family (it is not known when he was married) an extraordinary honorarium. Ziryab was given a furnished mansion, a salary of two hundred dinars per month for himself, twenty dinars per month for each of his four sons, plus three thousand dinars annually—one thousand on each Muslim festival and five hundred on two other special celebrations. In addition, Ziryab was granted two hundred bushels of barley and one hundred bushels of wheat per year along with farmhouses and productive farmland in the Córdoba countryside.

It was a payment almost beyond belief, and it was well earned: over the next thirty years, Ziryab personally brought about transformations upon which no price could be put. He began with music, but before his work was done, he profoundly altered, first in Muslim Spain and then throughout the world, what people ate, how they ate it, how they dressed, how they took care of their bodies, and how they behaved.

As al-Makkari has documented, by the time the wunderkind from Baghdad arrived in Córdoba, "he was deeply versed in every branch of art connected with music; and was moreover gifted with such a prodigious memory that he knew by heart upwards of one thousand songs with their appropriate airs."

Along with his musical knowledge, Ziryab brought with him the lute that had so impressed the caliph in Baghdad. Since that day, he had made continual improvements to the instrument, improvements that revolutionized stringed instrumentation and ultimately led to one of the world's most popular instruments of all: the guitar.

Before Ziryab, the lute (or oud, as it is known in the Arabic world), an instrument that dates back as far as 1500 BCE, had four pairs of strings. Historian Titus Burckhardt wrote that these strings "answered to the four elementary principles of the body [the four humors] and expressed the four natural sounds." Ziryab's great innovation was to add a fifth pair of strings to the middle of his lute, which gave the instrument greater delicacy of expression, improved its sound, and endowed it with a range far greater than had been attainable with any previous instrument of its kind. In addition to his technical genius, Ziryab was a deeply spiritual man who had faith in the interconnectedness of all things natural and human. Along with believing that music plays a vital role in the psychological relationships between individuals, he ascribed to the theory put forth by Arab physicians that one of the great goals of music is to "restore the equilibrium of the soul the same way that medicine restores the equilibrium of the body." Medieval Islamic medicine was based on Greco-Roman medical philosophy, which supposed that the human body was made up of four elemental substances called humors, which when unbalanced caused a breakdown in metabolic function, resulting in illness.

The lute before Ziryab represented these four humors. The first pair of strings was yellow, symbolizing yellow bile; the second pair was red, representing blood; the third was white for phlegm; and the fourth, the bass pair, was black for black bile. Ziryab placed his new strings, another red pair, between the second and third pairs. Not only did this addition revolutionize the sound of the instrument, but it also represented another human element as well. Ziryab had given the lute a soul.

Always seeking to further improve the quality of his lute, Ziryab also heightened the instrument's sensitivity by abandoning the traditional wooden pick with which it was played, using instead a flexible eagle's talon. Their hands guided, as historian Chris Lowney wrote, "by the soft down which covers the claw of that bird," Ziryab and the generations of musical students he taught found that this type of pick enabled them to maintain a lighter touch on the instrument than had previously been possible.

Under Ziryab's enormous influence, instrument making in Moorish Spain reached an unprecedented height of development. Some of these new instruments included the *carrizo* (reed), the *kanun* (harp), the *quinera* (a type of zither), the *zolami* (oboe), as well as the tambourine, brass rattles, castanets, the lutelike *rabal* (rebec), the *shokra* (baritone flute), and the *mura* (soprano flute). Other wind instruments included the pastoral flute and the Moorish pipes.

Along with his achievement in instrumentation, Ziryab introduced first Moorish Spain, then North Africa, and then much of Europe to

❖ WOMEN PLAY TRADITIONAL Persian musical instruments, including the lute, in this seventeenth-century mural from the Hasht Behesht palace in Esfahān, Iran.

whole new forms of musical composition, in the process rearranging musical theory completely. Based on his conviction that musical composition should be based on the three fundamental elements of rhythm (the marriage between music and words), melody (the fabric of beauty and emotion), and understanding (the marriage of melody and rhythm), Ziryab and those he influenced created the rules governing the performance of what became the most important form of Andalusian music, known as the *nuba* (or *nubah* or *newbah*).

As Spanish cultural historian Fernando Valderrama Martinez has defined it, the *nuba* (or suite) is

> a complete musical work, composed of various airs and melodies. It also appears like an assembly of independent songs though all relate to a single theme. They are songs gathered by the thread of time to give us an anonymous composition, like the great cathedrals which required the efforts of generations, a heritage bequeathed to our times by unknown great geniuses.

As first developed by Ziryab and his followers, each *nuba* is divided into five separate movements. At times these movements are exclusively music; at other times they are a combination of music and singing. The verses of the songs vary considerably, focusing on such subjects as love, nature, and other common topics. In its time one of the most popular of all these compositions was Ziryab's twenty-four-section creation titled *Nobeh*.

As important as all these far-reaching accomplishments were, Ziryab's greatest contributions to music, according to the ancient historians who were aware of him, were in the field of instruction. One of his first projects in Córdoba was the founding of Spain's first music conservatory. Established at a time when music had always been taught one-on-one, Ziryab opened the school's doors not only to the sons and daughters of the upper classes but also to pupils from families of much lesser means.

Groundbreaking also was the way in which Ziryab's conservatory provided instruction in a methodical and systematic fashion. Among other subjects, students were taught rhythm, meter, singing to the accompaniment of musical instruments, and the mastery of melody, all while being prodded to pay the closest possible attention to syllables and the clear and correct pronunciation of lyrics. It was an approach that was eventually emulated by music education institutions throughout Europe.

The master musician's approach to teaching students was as innovative as his curriculum. As Ivan Van Sertima recounts, when teaching singing,

Ziryab always began by testing a new pupil's voice. The student was required to sit as straight as possible and to shout at the top of his lungs. This enabled Ziryab to determine the power of the student's voice, and to discover whether or not there was a breathing problem. If the voice was acceptable to Ziryab, the student was allowed to commence his studies. If it was found wanting, Ziryab ordered the pupil to tie a turban around his stomach in order to compress the middle of his body and help him attain proper voice projection. For those students who had difficulty opening their mouths enough, Ziryab had a special remedy. They were advised to clench a three-inch-wide piece of wood between their jaws and to keep it there continually until their jaws were properly loosened.

Ziryab's conservatory would endure for more than five hundred years, and along with introducing the world to the new science of musicology, it introduced many innovations in instrumentation and composition. He created an orchestra that revolutionized orchestral organization, including the first wedding of orchestra to chorus. Ziryab unequivocally established his reputation as "the founder of the musical traditions of Muslim Spain."

It was a tradition that would have widespread effect. G. Talebzadeh writes, "Ziryab's music influenced all neighboring countries. In Morocco it was called *Gornati* and in Tunisia, *Aulof,* but regardless of the names, all these musical traditions found their roots in Ziryab's methods." The famous fourteenth-century historian, scholar, and theologian Ibn Khaldoon, as quoted in Talebzadeh's essay, wrote that "Andalusian music was advanced by Ziryab and passed onto generation after generation. His influence was an ocean that swept over all of Africa and left us an eternal legacy." And as Van Sertima noted, "Even when the Moors had been defeated and Christians had reconquered the territory once occupied by these people the music was imitated by a great number of Christian Europeans and the Christian kings still kept Moorish musicians in their employ even as had the Moorish kings before them."

Perhaps the greatest testimony to the enduring musical legacy of Ziryab and those he taught and influenced was written by Spanish musicologist Julian Ribera:

The artistic Spain of olden times thus becomes the central bond which ties ancient art to modern. The great musicians of Andalusia knew not only how to preserve their inherited art but also how to transform and renovate it by creating a popular form through which their compositions were broadcast, thus spreading it all over Europe. There it still lives because the people have loved it and adopted it. Europe therefore owes a debt of gratitude to the Andalusian Moors, who maintained and passed on a rich fund of music, a perennial spring to which all European composers have come to renew their inspiration, but without seeking its unknown sources.

IF ZIRYAB'S ACCOMPLISHMENTS HAD BEEN confined solely to music, his would have been a remarkable life. But his contributions far transcended music alone. By becoming the Cordoban court's arbiter of food, fashion, grooming, and more, he accomplished nothing less than changing lifestyle customs that endure today.

Before Ziryab, for example, people wore the same type of clothing year-round, adjusting to the changing seasons by either adding or subtracting layers of garments. A well-dressed man himself, it was Ziryab who submitted fashion to the changing seasons. As al-Makkari chronicled, "The tradition of changing clothes according to seasons of the year was another of [Ziryab's] improvements. He suggested wearing certain garments in the season intervening between summer and winter and likewise other garments to be worn toward the end of summer and the beginning of autumn."

It was also Ziryab who persuaded those of his time to replace the traditional dark, drab Moorish clothing with vibrantly colored garments. As Jan Read wrote, "A vogue for brightly colored clothes began with the arrival from Baghdad of the musician and singer Ziryab, sometimes described as an Arab Beau Brummel, during the reign of Abdu'r-Rahman II. He started fashions for the different seasons: light silk robes and vivid colors for the spring . . . and quilted gowns and furs for winter."

Having profoundly changed the nature of the clothing that the people of Moorish Spain wore, Ziryab also taught them how to keep their garments clean. Before Ziryab, those who could afford it had their clothing rinsed in rose water and garden flowers, the result of which was that their garments never looked truly clean. Ziryab invented a process in which salts were added to the traditional mixture of water and flowers, which improved the cleaning process.

Ziryab's innovations in fashion extended to changes in the way that women wore their hair. As al-Makkari described, before Ziryab, "both men and women wore the hair over the upper part of the forehead, and hanging down between the temples and the eye." But, according to al-Makkari, "when people of fashion saw Ziryab, his wives, and sons wearing their foreheads uncovered, with the hair trimmed level over the eyebrows and slanting toward the ears, they imitated him." Historian Chris Lowney put it precisely: "Bangs," he wrote, "were out; the swept-back look was in." Impressed with the way in which his new hairstyle had been adopted, the entrepreneurial Ziryab opened a beauty parlor and cosmetology school. There, along with introducing even more daring hairstyles, he taught women how to shape their eyebrows and how, through the use of depilatories, to remove unwanted hair from their bodies. It was in this facility also that Ziryab introduced women to new perfumes and new cosmetics.

It was not surprising that the elegant Ziryab also turned his attention to reforms in hygiene. Before his time, the most common form of deodorant was composed of powdered rose, basil, and myrtle. It was highly ineffective at removing body odor, and it also left stains on the user's clothing. Ziryab remedied the situation by introducing a new type of deodorant whose main ingredient was a lead extract that, according to al-Makkari, removed "the fetid smell of the armpits."

Care of the teeth did not escape Ziryab's attention either. The earliest mention of toothpaste is found in a fourth-century Egyptian manuscript, which prescribes a mixture of powered salt, pepper, mint leaves, and iris flowers. It is also known that the Romans used a type of toothpaste based on human urine (because of its ammonia content). Although the exact ingredients of the toothpaste that Ziryab created have remained unknown, it was, according to Van Sertima, a vast improvement over anything that had been previously introduced, and it became popular throughout Islamic Spain. .

Al-Makkari and others tell us that Ziryab loved well-prepared food almost as much as he did music, and it was he who brought about enduring changes in the types of food that were eaten and the way it was served. Ziryab was the first to gather the wild weed called *asfaraj* and to elevate it to the status of a dinner vegetable that we now call asparagus. He invented a dish called *al-Tafaya*, made of meatballs and pieces of dough fried in oil, a delicacy that under the name *takalliyah Ziryab* ("the fried dish of Ziryab") is still popular in Andalusia and other parts of Spain today. He was obviously a man with a sweet tooth, and among the various other dishes he created were a variety of desserts including *zalabia*, fried dough soaked in orange syrup, and various combinations of walnuts and honey that are still served today throughout North Africa and the Mediterranean world.

Even more important was the way in which Ziryab revolutionized the manner in which meals were organized. Before he appeared in Córdoba, Moorish dining, like that of the Romans, Vandals, and Visigoths, was a crude affair. Every type of food, from savories to sweets, from fruits to meats, was piled together on bare wooden tables. There was no such thing as table manners. Ziryab changed that.

With his ruler's approval, Ziryab decreed that palace dinners would be served in sequential courses, starting with soups; followed by fish, fowl, or meats; and ending with sweet desserts, fruits, and nuts. It was a manner of eating unknown even in Baghdad, and it quickly gained popularity, first with the upper and middle classes and then with the peasantry. Eventually the three-course meal became standard practice throughout Europe, giving rise to the expression "soup to nuts," the origins of which can be traced directly back to Ziryab's major innovations.

Always seeking elegance, Ziryab looked to reform the accoutrements of dining as well. He enhanced the plain wooden dinner table by teaching local craftsmen how to fashion tooled and fitted leather table coverings.

❖ IT IS BELIEVED THAT ZIRYAB introduced the game of chess to Europe by asking Indians at the royal court to teach the game to the courtiers. This illustration is *The Game and Playe of the Chesse* (1474) by the English printer William Caxton.

He did away with the heavy gold and silver drinking goblets that had been used by the upper class since Roman times and replaced them with fine crystal. He even redesigned the heavy wooden soupspoon and created a trimmer model that was lighter in weight.

The innovations of this one man seemed endless. It was he who taught those in Moorish Spain who could afford it to sleep on a soft leather couch instead of cotton blankets. It was he who introduced to Al-Andalus the New Year celebration based on the Iranian holiday Nowruz, establishing a tradition that spread across Europe. And it was Ziryab who brought in astrologers from India and Jewish doctors from North

Africa and Iraq, which led to the diffusion of their knowledge throughout Spain. He even taught his countrymen how to play chess.

ZIRYAB DIED IN 857, FIVE YEARS after the passing of Abd ar-Rahman II, the man who had encouraged and applauded his remarkable innovations for thirty years. Although Arabian historians disagree as to the number of children he left behind (some claim there were as many as twelve sons and three daughters), what has been documented is that all of his offspring were musicians and singers. What we also know is that his second daughter, Hamdouneh, with the help of her brother-in-law collected and published her father's compositions and songs in a book titled *Al-Aghâni Ziryâb*. Tragically, the book was lost during the Moroccan siege of Córdoba in 1100.

What was never lost were Ziryab's pivotal contributions in helping make the seven-hundred-year Islamic reign in Spain one of the most magnificent periods of tolerance and multicultural development in history. What should also be remembered is that well after this unique reign ended, students from France, England, and all of Europe as late as the year 1000 continued to gather in Córdoba to study in its immense library. When they returned to their native countries, they took back with them not only the book knowledge they had gained, but also a newly acquired sense of music, cuisine, fashion, and manners, much of which had been initiated centuries earlier by a man born a slave named Ziryab.

His greatest tribute came from al-Makkari, the seventeenth-century historian who uncovered most of what we know about him. Al-Makkari wrote:

> [Ziryab] was fitted with so much penetration and wit; he had so deep an acquaintance with the various branches of polite literature; he possessed in so eminent a degree the charms of conversation, and

the talents requisite to entertain an audience, he could repeat such a number of entertaining stories; he was so acute and ingenious in guessing of the wants of his royal master, that there never was either before or after him a man of his profession who was more generally beloved and admired. Kings and great people took him for a pattern of manners and education, and his name became forever celebrated among the inhabitants of Andalus.

How remarkable it is that his name remains virtually unknown and that his extraordinary achievements have, in such great measure, been lost to time.

TWO

CAHOKIA
The Forgotten Rome of the Americas
(Twelfth Century)

The history of every nation is filled with myths, some more serious than others. Generations of schoolchildren, for example, have been taught that at the time Christopher Columbus set foot in the Americas, those people to whom he gave the name "Indians" lived mostly in small nomadic tribes and that the Americas were mostly a vast wilderness. It is a serious misconception, fostered and perpetuated for generations by some of the nation's most respected historians, anthropologists, and scholars.

For example, Alfred L. Kroeber, one of the pioneers of American anthropology, argued that the Indians in North America spent so much of their time in "warfare that was insane, unending, continuously attritional" that there was no time for substantial communities to be developed or for a sophisticated agricultural system to take hold. The result, Kroeber concluded, was that "ninety-nine per cent or more of what [land] might have been developed remained virgin."

And as late as 1995, *American History: A Survey*, one of the most widely used high school textbooks in the nation, presented its view of Indian history by declaring, "For thousands of centuries—centuries in

❖ The Birdman Tablet: Cahokians engraved this sandstone tablet, which depicts a man wearing a mask and dressed in eagle (or falcon) regalia.

which human races were evolving, forming communities, and building the beginnings of national civilizations in Africa, Asia, and Europe—the continents we know as the Americas stood empty of mankind and its works."

Today, we are increasingly learning that all of these statements and long-held assumptions are the furthest thing from the truth. Over the past thirty years, archaeologists, anthropologists, historians, and other scholars, aided by advanced new technologies and scientific techniques such as relative dating (stratigraphy, seriation, and cross-dating) and chronometric dating (including radiocarbon, archaeomagnetism, fission track, and thermoluminescence) have given us a whole new and startling picture of life in the Americas before Columbus. Their investigations have revealed, for example, that in the years just prior to Columbus's arrival, there were, in all probability, more people living in the Americas than in Europe. The experts have discovered that hundreds of thousands of these people were living in cities, such as the Aztec capital Tenochtitlan, which had far greater populations than any European city, ancient municipalities that had running water, clean streets, and magnificent botanical gardens. As Charles C. Mann has stated, "Native Americans transformed their land so completely that Europeans arrived in a hemisphere already massively 'landscaped' by human beings." According to Mann, this pre-Columbian Western Hemisphere was, thanks to the Indians,

> a thriving, stunningly diverse place, a tumult of languages, trade, and culture, a region where tens of millions of people loved and hated and worshipped as people do everywhere. Much of this world vanished after Columbus, swept away by disease and subjugation. So thorough was the erasure that within a few generations neither conqueror nor conquered knew that this world had existed.

The majority of natives who lived in the prehistoric Americas that Mann described dwelled south of the Rio Grande. But there was one remarkable community north of the Rio Grande, a city that by 1150 CE had become the largest urban center north of Mexico, a record that would stand until Philadelphia surpassed it in the late 1700s. It is difficult to imagine a city covering more than six square miles flourishing in the Mississippi Valley some 350 years before Columbus reached the New World, a city, which at its zenith in about 1150 contained a population estimated by some experts to have been as high as thirty thousand, more inhabitants than any contemporary European city, including London. Its people constructed enormous pyramid-shaped earthen mounds (the largest, Monks Mound, has a base larger than that of the Great Pyramid of Giza in Egypt), designed and built solar observatories, and carried out a far-flung trade. Its name was Cahokia.

CAHOKIA WAS LOCATED IN THE AMERICAN BOTTOM, an exceptionally fertile and expansive flood plain created ten thousand years ago at the end of the last Ice Age. When the glaciers melted, an eight-mile-wide torrent of water rushed southwest, creating the Mississippi, Illinois, and Missouri Rivers. When these waters eventually receded, the vast American Bottom was exposed.

Beginning sometime between 700 and 800, various groups of Native Americans who came to be known as Mississippians began to settle this rich land. And incredibly rich it was. The forest-filled Ozark Mountains that lay to the southwest of the Bottom contained granite, limestone, sandstone, and other rocks and minerals, particularly chert (a fine-grained, silica-rich microcrystalline rock), that could be used for making tools. The Ozarks were also filled with white-tailed deer, which became the Mississippians' main source of meat. To the north and west lay the great American prairie, which offered a seemingly never-ending supply of tall grasses that could be used for constructing houses and other buildings.

The woodlands east of the American Bottom also abounded in natural resources. Along with white-tailed deer, there were such food sources as turkey, squirrel, possum, and raccoon. The oaks, hickories, and other deciduous trees that characterized the woodlands not only provided nuts and berries, but also supplied the hardwood used in the building of canoes, tool handles, bows, and arrows. Finally, there was the Mississippi Valley itself, which not only gave the Mississippians their rich soil, but also abounded in fish as well as ducks, geese, and other waterfowl.

Of all the various and widespread Native American settlements that took advantage of these natural benefits, Cahokia—situated in present-day Collinsville, Illinois, near St. Louis—far outdistanced them all. According to the Web site of the Cahokia Mounds State Historic Site, it was "named for the Cahokia subtribe of the Illiniwek (or Illinois tribe, a loose confederacy of related peoples), who moved into the area in the 1600s." Their location at the confluence of the Mississippi, Illinois, and Missouri Rivers was essential to their success. As archaeologists have learned, these rivers and their extensive network of tributaries gave the people who came to known Cahokians access to distant areas where they traded, hunted, and benefited from contact with other cultures. As Claudia G. Mink wrote,

> From their central location, [the Cahokians] traveled vast distances, walking, running, and canoeing along trade routes already established by the Woodland Indians and, to some extent, the Archaic peoples. They got copper from the Great Lakes, mica from the southern Appalachians, and seashells from the Gulf of Mexico. And in the process of obtaining these exotic materials, they observed traditions and lifestyles they would incorporate into their own.

As essential as trade was to Cahokia's rise to predominance among the Mississippian cultures, so too was the cultivation of a crop that had originated in Mexico some four thousand years earlier. By 800, the Cahokians acquired the knowledge of growing corn (maize), which proved vital in feeding the huge population that the city would attain. As Sidney G. Denny and Ernest Lester Schusky wrote, "As years passed, people learned to cultivate corn intensively and it became a basic part of the diet. Intensive agriculture at the mouths of [the] Missouri, Illinois, and Ohio Rivers laid the basis for [the] growth of Cahokia."

As Mississippians, the Cahokians were part of a four-thousand-year-old Native American tradition of mound building. And the Cahokians were the greatest mound builders of all. For hundreds of years, those who came upon the 120 mounds at what had once been Cahokia were not only amazed but also mystified by them. Many of the earthen structures were enormous flat-topped, square-bottomed pyramids. The largest rose more than one hundred feet into the air. One early observer was the American lawyer, judge, author, and Pennsylvania congressman Henry Marie Brackenridge who, after first seeing the mounds in 1811, immediately conveyed his impressions to Thomas Jefferson. "When I reached the foot of the principal mound," Brackenridge wrote,

> I was struck with a degree of astonishment not unlike that which is experienced in contemplating the Egyptian pyramids. What a stupendous pile of earth! To heap up such a mass must have required years, and the labors of thousands. . . . Were it not for the regularity and design which it manifests, the circumstances of it being on alluvial ground, and the other mounds scattered around it, we could scarcely believe it the work of human hands.

"The labors of thousands"—who could these "thousands" have been? Well into the twentieth century, speculation abounded. One theory was that the mounds were built by a lost tribe of Israel. Another attributed the structures to the Vikings. In the 1860s, Minnesota congressman Ignatius Donnelly insisted that the mound builders were survivors of the lost colony of Atlantis. As Mann noted, other accounts credited the Chinese or the Welsh or the Phoenicians. One of the most widely spread speculations claimed that the builders were Scandinavian émigrés who, after moving to Mexico, became the Toltecs.

In an era of extreme prejudice, few even considered crediting Native Americans. In 1871 J. D. Baldwin wrote, "It is absurd to suppose a relationship of any kind, or connection, between the original barbarism of these Indians and the civilization of the Mound-Builders." No less a personage than J. W. Foster, president of the Chicago Academy of Sciences, stated that to imply that the Indians, who he characterized as a people "signalized by treachery and cruelty," had constructed the mounds "is as preposterous almost, as to suppose they built the pyramids of Egypt." He declared:

> The Indian repels all efforts to raise him from his degraded position and whilst he has not the moral nature to adopt the virtues of civilization, his brutal instincts lead him to welcome its vices. He has never been known voluntarily to engage in an enterprise requiring methodical labor.

❖ A BIRD'S-EYE-VIEW PAINTING by Cahokia mounds expert William R. Iseminger reveals a city aligned with the cosmos: strategically sited mounds, four plazas marking the cardinal directions, and equinox-predicting structures.

In his 1834 poem "The Prairies," American poet William Cullen Bryant expressed the cruelest opinion of all: poetically proclaiming that whoever had built the mounds had been wiped out by "the red man."

> *. . . Let the mighty mounds*
> *That overlook the rivers, or that rise*
> *In the dim forest crowded with old oaks,*
> *Answer. A race, that long has passed away,*
> *Built them;—a disciplined and populous race*
> *Heaped, with long toil, the earth, while yet the Greek*
> *Was hewing the Pentelicus to forms*
> *Of symmetry, and rearing on its rock*
> *The glittering Parthenon. These ample fields*
> *Nourished their harvests, here their herds were fed,*
> *When haply by their stalls the bison lowed,*
> *And bowed his maned shoulder to the yoke.*
> *All day this desert murmured with their toils,*
> *Till twilight blushed, and lovers walked, and wooed*
> *In a forgotten language, and old tunes,*
> *From instruments of unremembered form,*
> *Gave the soft winds a voice. The red man came—*
> *The roaming hunter tribes, warlike and fierce,*
> *And the mound-builders vanished from the earth . . .*

Today, thanks to the excavations and investigations of archaeologists and anthropologists, we know that without question the mounds were built by the Mississippians.

THE CITY OF CAHOKIA WAS PHYSICALLY DOMINATED by the Monks Mound, named for French Trappist monks who lived in a monastery nearby in the early 1800s and gardened on the mound. Cahokia was built in a dozen or more phases beginning in about 900 CE, a time described by archeologists as the "Big Bang," a period in which, for still unknown reasons, thousands of Native Americans from surrounding regions poured into Cahokia and the city experienced as much as a tenfold increase in its population.

Covering an area of fourteen acres, making it larger than the Great Pyramid of Giza, the clay slab that serves as the base of Monks Mound is about 954 feet long and 774 feet wide. The enormous structure stretches 100 feet from its base to its top. Archeologists and geographers such as William I. Woods of the University of Kansas, who has spent two decades excavating the mound, have discovered that the structure contained four terraces: a large terrace at the front, a second terrace on the east, and two terraces on top. Excavations have made it clear that a massive ceremonial building, perhaps a temple or a palace (where, it is thought, the Cahokian leaders lived), stood at the top of the mound and measured approximately 108 feet long, 48 feet wide, and some 50 feet high. Smaller buildings were constructed on the lower terraces.

Most archaeologists who have worked the site are in agreement that the temple or palace atop Monks Mound was the focal point from which Cahokia's rulers carried out various political and religious rituals, including prayers for favorable weather to nurture the acres of maize that stretched out from the city as far as the eye could see. Excavations have also revealed that at some point in the mound's various phases of construction a low platform was extended out from one of its sides, creating a stage from which priests could perform ceremonies in full view of the public.

What is perhaps most intriguing of all is the question of how Monks Mound was constructed. Archaeologists calculate that the structure contains twenty-two million cubic feet of earth, which was dug with stone tools and carried out in baskets on people's backs to the ever-growing mound.

Sally A. Kitt Chappell provided a graphic calculation of the enormous effort that went into building Monks Mound:

> This pharaonic enterprise required carrying 14,666,666 baskets, each filled with 1.5 cubic feet, of dirt weighing about fifty-five pounds

each, for a total of 22 million cubic feet. For comparison, an average pickup truck holds 96 cubic feet, so it would take 229,166 pickup loads to bring the dirt to the site. If thirty people each carried eight baskets of earth a day, the job would take 167 years.

As Mann documented, aside from the sheer enormity of digging and transporting such an astounding amount of dirt, the construction of Monks Mound presented other significant challenges. The huge slab that serves as the base of the mound was constructed of clay. To minimize instability, the Cahokians kept the slab at a constant moisture level by sealing it off from the air, surrounding it with alternating layers of sand and clay. They also used soil of varying textures to build different parts of the mound and constructed various drains on its sides to ensure proper drainage and structural integrity. Excavations have also revealed the presence of retaining buttresses, inserted throughout the mound to fortify its internal structure.

As these building methods indicate, the building of Monks Mound was far from a matter of creating an enormous pile of dirt and then adding on to it over the years. They infer the presence of individuals with specialized knowledge of soils and earthen construction. Despite the instability of the materials they had on hand and the fact that they built their enormous structure on a floodplain, these ancient engineers achieved nothing less than the largest prehistoric construction in the Americas, and there it has stood for more than one thousand years.

Although Monks Mound is the major structure at Cahokia, it is another earthen structure known as Mound 72 that has disclosed the most about the prehistoric city while at the same time raising perplexing questions. Mound 72 is less than seven feet high, yet what scientists— particularly esteemed archaeologist Melvin L. Fowler—have discovered underneath the mound has revealed both the grisly and the spiritual nature of life in Cahokia.

As documented in several sources, beneath Mound 72 were found the remains of a man buried in about 1050. Estimated to be in his early forties, he was laid to rest on a bed of about twenty thousand shell beads and more than eight hundred seemingly unused arrows with finely crafted heads. Surrounding the corpse were the bodies of three men and three women, all richly adorned; it is surmised that they were probably close relatives. As anthropologists Thomas E. Emerson and R. Barry Lewis noted, "Only a person of central importance would have been buried with such an expenditure of life and effort." The leader and his relatives were far from alone in the grave. Interred with him were the bodies of four men with their heads and hands cut off—probably, according to some archaeologists, prisoners of war. And that was not all. Also in the grave were the corpses of fifty-three young women between the ages of fifteen and twenty-five who had been either buried alive or strangled, sacrificed perhaps to serve the deceased leader in his next life. As Fowler and those who assisted him kept excavating, they found other burial pits, one containing the bodies of fourteen people, obviously elites, who had been carried to their graves on litters. Another pit contained the corpses of forty individuals who had been thrown haphazardly into the mass grave and the bodies of more than another one hundred young women who had apparently been sacrificed.

The discoveries made beneath Mound 72 reveal what archaeological anthropologist George R. Milner has described as the clear distinction between two groups of people: the principal members of Cahokian society, along with their close relatives, and everybody else. And while mysteries remain about the remains found in Mound 72 and their placement, there are specific conclusions on which most anthropologists and archaeologists agree. In *Envisioning Cahokia*, Rinita A. Dalan and her coauthors concur with many other experts that the four men were deliberately placed in graves to represent the four cardinal directions. And Denny and Schusky agree that the fifty-three women were, in all probability, sacrificed to accompany their leader to eternity. On the other hand, while some experts have speculated that the number of men in the grave without heads or hands were prisoners of war, this theory is refuted by Emerson and Lewis.

Cahokia

WHILE THERE WILL UNDOUBTEDLY always be disagreement over the meaning of what has and what will be found, there is one thing about which the experts are in agreement: evidence makes it clear that Cahokia was a deliberately planned and designed city. From the top of Monks Mound one could see scores of other mounds arranged around plazas. Around these plazas were houses, arranged in neat rows. Pathways connected open public markets, community buildings, and exclusive neighborhoods for the elite. Outside the city lay the main agricultural fields. That the Cahokians centered much of their urban design around plazas is not a surprise. Cleared areas in which games, dances, planting and harvesting ceremonies, and other public events were held were commonplace in late prehistoric Native American communities. What truly surprised the experts, however, was not only the extraordinary size of the plaza—approximately fifty acres, or thirty-eight football fields end to end—that extended southward from Monks Mound, but also how it came into being.

From the time that archaeologists and anthropologists first began examining the Cahokian site, they assumed that the enormous, almost perfectly level stretch of land that extended southward from Monks Mound and served as the Cahokians' Grand Plaza was a natural result of the city's location on a flat alluvial plain. Investigations conducted in the 1960s, however, dramatically changed this assumption. Soil samples revealed that originally the landscape was not flat at all but multileveled in many places, filled with ridges in others, and deeply rutted as well. There was only one conclusion: the Cahokians possessed the knowledge of surveying surfaces and grading and filling even the largest and most difficult terrain. They not only built the largest structure north of Mexico; they created one of the largest artificial landforms in North America.

In the process the Cahokians created not only a well-planned city but also, in keeping with their beliefs, a city aligned with the cosmos. The four plazas they constructed, stretching out north, south, east, and west from Monks Mound, honored the four cardinal directions. The very shape of the 120 Cahokian mounds—some squared or platform-shaped, others circular or conical-shaped—had cosmic significance as well. Cahokians believed, as did other Mississippian cultures, that there

❖ A MURAL BY LLOYD TOWNSEND re-creates the Grand Plaza of Cahokia as it may have looked in the twelfth century.

was a division between the world above and the world below. To them, the upper world represented order, the world below disorder, and the middle world, the world in which they lived, a mix of the two. Through their investigations, archaeologists and anthropologists have deduced that the square or platform-shaped mounds were deliberately shaped so as to be symbolically tied to chiefs, warriors, and the upper world, whereas the circular or conical-shaped mounds tied the earth to the underworld. Thus, through this pairing, the upper world, the earth, and the lower world were connected, symbolizing a cycle of birth, death, and regeneration. Together, the placement of the plazas, the shapes of the mounds, and a large circular area featuring enormous red cedar posts endowed Cahokia with what Kitt Chappell termed a "sacred geography."

OF ALL THAT HAS BEEN UNCOVERED at the Cahokia site, the discovery in the 1960s of four large circles of pits west of Monks Mound represents one of the archaeologists' most dramatic finds. The pits once contained red cedar posts. Named "Woodhenge" by those who discovered it, in honor of England's solar calendar Stonehenge, each circle contained between twelve and forty-eight evenly spaced posts about twenty feet long and fifteen to twenty inches in diameter. After intense investigations, archaeologists discovered that one post within each circle pointed toward the horizon at the exact spot where the sun rises at the spring and fall equinoxes, while two posts aligned with the summer and winter solstices.

Some experts believe that Woodhenge, which was rebuilt at least five times over the years, was constructed to aid Cahokia's huge farming population by accurately predicting the changing seasons. In addition, since at the equinoxes the sun rises due east directly over the top of Monks Mound and constitutes a spectacular sight, Cahokia's chiefs and priests—standing at the top of the mound—may have used the occasions to demonstrate to their subjects that it was they who were giving birth to the sun. Smithsonian curator Bruce Smith has speculated that "through Woodhenge and dealing with the sun, [the chiefs] could solidify their position . . . and show the general populace how the sun moved and predict it." Other investigators think that Woodhenge may have also been used as a land-surveying device, a valuable tool in helping Cahokia's leaders and engineers align monuments, residential districts, public buildings, and other parts of the community as they designed and built their planned city.

Ironically, one of the most ambitious and most arduous of all the Cahokians' endeavors was not part of the original designers' plans. Excavations have revealed that sometime in the early 1100s, the Cahokians constructed a nearly two-mile-long palisade around the center of their city and that, over the next two hundred years, they replaced it four times. It is thought that the Cahokian palisades may have set a precedent for Native American Mississippi Valley defensive walls for the next four hundred years. Young and Fowler relate an account by sixteenth-century Spanish conquistador and poet Garcilaso de la Vega about a similar wall. De la Vega interviewed members of explorer Hernando de Soto's party about the impressive palisade constructed in the Mississippian Indian fortress known as Mauvila (or Mabila), in Alabama:

> Situated upon a very beautiful plain, the town of Mauvila was
> surrounded by a wall as high as three men and constructed of

wooden beams as thick as oxen. These beams were driven into the ground so close together that each was wedged to the other; and across them on both the outside and inside were laid additional pieces, not so thick but longer, which were bound together with strips of split cane and strong ropes. Plastered over the smaller pieces was a mixture of thick mud tamped down with long straw, filling up all of the holes and crevices in the wood and its fastenings, so that properly speaking, the wall appeared to be coated with a hard finish such as one might apply with a mason's trowel. At every fifty feet there was a tower capable of holding seven or eight persons who might fight within it, and the lower part of the wall up to the height of a man, was filled with the embrasures of a battery designed for shooting arrows at those outside.

Whether or not the palisades that were built at Cahokia became the actual models for future Native American settlements, it is difficult to imagine that they could have been surpassed in sheer size or in the effort it took to build them. Archaeologist William R. Iseminger, who was a key member of the team that excavated the Cahokian palisades in 1968, estimated that the construction of each of the two-mile-long palisades required 20,000 logs, each one the size of a full-grown tree. This, according to Iseminger, would have included 9,800 logs for the main wall, 5,880 logs to build the 112 fortified positions on each palisade, 750 logs for each of the thirty gates, and at least 1,120 logs to make the horizontal lash tied to the top of the posts to hold them together. Calculating how long it probably took for a Cahokian with a stone ax to fell and trim a tree, how long it would take to dig the deep trenches to hold the logs, how much time would be required to transport the fallen logs to the construction site, and how long it probably took to erect the posts, backfill them, tie them together, and then plaster the entire construction (probably with mud), Iseminger came to the conclusion that the building of each Cahokian palisade took at least 190,000 hours or 23,750 eight-hour days (approximately sixty-seven years). Fowler, who documented Iseminger's calculations in *Cahokia*, stated, however, that since his fellow archaeologist allowed no time for the planning or the organizing of each palisade project or for making what would probably have been increasingly longer trips to find large enough logs, the construction of each palisade could easily have taken twice the amount of time that Iseminger estimated.

However long it took, another question needs to be raised, one that has spawned disagreement among the experts. Why was each palisade built in the first place? According to the experts at the Cahokia Mounds State Historical Site:

> Three things lead most archaeologists to believe that it was primarily a defensive structure. The great height of the wall, the presence of evenly spaced bastions, projections from which archers could shoot arrows; and evidence that portions of the wall were hurriedly built, cutting through residential areas, as if danger was imminent.

That explanation, however, raises yet another question. Why was such an elaborate and costly defensive structure needed, particularly when there is no evidence that Cahokia ever came under armed assault? Most of those who doubt that the palisades were built for defensive purposes are convinced that they were constructed purely for social reasons.

As Mann wrote, "Cahokia being the biggest city around, it seems unlikely that the palisade was needed to deter enemy attack. . . . Instead it was probably created to separate elite from hoi polloi, with the goal of emphasizing the priestly rulers' separate, superior, socially critical connection to the divine." Young and Fowler, while emphasizing that the palisades were "evidence of Cahokia's response to its uneasy relations with the leaders of other mound centers," also came to the conclusion that the palisades were built as much for social reasons as for military purposes. "It surrounded the central core of the community," they noted, "[and] . . . set apart the most impressive and influential part of the community."

WHILE THERE MIGHT BE DISAGREEMENT over the main reason for building the palisades, experts have no doubts concerning what made such undertakings possible. Like Monks Mound, such a mammoth endeavor would never have been possible without Cahokian rulers who could envision monumental architecture and who had the ability and power to convey the need for such structures to the enormous number of people needed to build them.

Research has shown that these Cahokian rulers operated under what is known as a theocratic chieftainship. Supreme power lay in the hands of the chief, who was thought to be the brother of the sun. The chief's relatives and favored associates formed an elite class and, acting as subchiefs, had control over the heads of family clans, who in turn directed the commoners. In a society where there was no money and all commerce was carried on by barter, Milner believes that the chiefs consolidated their power by giving away goods to their followers, thereby gaining and maintaining their loyalty. This giving away of wealth in the form of copper, mica, chert, hematite, whelk shell, and ritual artifacts extended to the chiefs of other tribes throughout the American Bottom. It was a practice that enabled Cahokia's rulers to obtain needed outside labor for the building of the mounds and palisades and even, according to researchers, to acquire maidens for sacrifice.

The chiefs gave away wealth in return for favors, but they also presided over a commercial network so extensive and far-flung that Cahokian merchants acquired copper from mines along the Great Lakes, shells from the Gulf of Mexico, chert from quarries as far away as Oklahoma, and mica from the Carolinas. The Cahokians left no written records, but it is these materials and others that they acquired through trade, and the products they made from them, that give us some of the best clues as to how they lived. Investigations have revealed the great many different items that Cahokians made from copper, including bracelets, rings, and many of the tools that were not made of stone. Excavations both at the Cahokia site and throughout the American Bottom have also disclosed their affinity for ornamentation, particularly for beads made from seashells collected more than a thousand miles away.

Of all their arts, however, it was pottery making in which the Cahokians truly excelled. Created mostly by women who dug clay from the riverbanks, shaped it, and fired it over open flames, Cahokian pottery was used for practical, artistic, and ceremonial purposes. As the potters became more skillful, they incorporated motifs symbolizing their religious beliefs. Depictions of creatures such as snakes, spiders, and amphibians on bowls, pots, plates, and other pottery represented the chaos of the Below World. Representations of birds symbolized the harmony of the Above World, while figures of humans and various woodland animals represented the Middle World—the earth and its inhabitants. These symbolic motifs appeared not only on pottery, but also on other objects such as embossed copper sheets, engraved shell pendants and cups, and clay statuary.

Excavations at Cahokia did not begin in earnest until the 1960s. Yet, thanks to modern discovery and dating technology and techniques, much has been learned about what the Cahokians grew, what they ate, and how they spent some of their leisure time. Along with corn, which was by far the most abundant staple item of their diet, the Cahokians grew squash, pumpkins, beans, and sunflowers. They also cultivated such ancient food plants as goosefoot, amaranth, canary grass, and other starchy crops. They fished in the rivers running throughout their valley and hunted in the adjoining woodlands.

Cahokians relied on the animals that dwelled in their region for much more than food. Many of the garments they wore were fashioned from deer skins and the needles they used in weaving were created from animal bones. The anthropologists who have excavated the site also found that the Cahokians used turtle shells to make dishware and combs and fashioned the feathers and bones of turkeys and hawks into such items as headdresses, necklaces, and capes.

Excavations have also revealed that Cahokians found time for leisure activities, particularly games. They gambled with dice and engaged in shell-guessing contests. Their premier sport by far was a game called *chunkey*. In one version of this contest, two men would stand in what amounted to an outdoor bowling alley. One man would roll a stone down the line, and both would race alongside it, each of them throwing a spear where he believed the stone would stop. In another version of *chunkey*, players threw spears in an attempt to knock over the rolling stone.

Invented by Cahokians, *chunkey* became so popular that each contest attracted thousands of onlookers. As archaeologist Timothy Pauketat documented, gambling was frequently associated with the game, with some players actually betting everything they owned on its outcome. According to Pauketat, some losers were known to have committed suicide. Long after the fall of the Mississippian culture around 1500, *chunkey* continued to be played by Indians throughout North America.

By the 1100s, Cahokia had become an extraordinary place. It had developed into what Emerson and Lewis describe as "the largest population center with probably the most complex social organization and most expansive political influence ever seen in the United States."

By 1200, Cahokia's vast superiority in population, the large number of warriors it could call upon if needed, and its bustling trade had enabled the city's ruler to become the paramount chief of the various other Native American communities in the region, leading to what has been termed a Cahokia-area society. The result, according to Emerson, was that Cahokia became "the seat of the largest political chiefdom and probably the most complex socially ranked society in North America, a city-state in the making." In *Cahokia,* Young and Fowler quote Emerson, who said,

> Cahokia is unique. . . . I still can't say it is a state but [it] sure as hell is a different kind of chiefdom. Cahokia was much more complexly organized than we ever had any idea . . . they had a form of bureaucracy; they exported their philosophy; they exerted

authority over the America Bottom. That is not what you typically read about chiefdoms. Cahokia was in some sort of intermediate stage. Clearly, hundreds of thousands of chiefdoms died without reaching statehood. Cahokia never made the jump but it was really close to making it.

FOR FIVE CENTURIES, CAHOKIANS FASHIONED an extraordinary society. Then, as abruptly as it had begun, it all ended. By about 1350, the entire site of the greatest prehistoric city north of Mexico had been almost completely abandoned. It was a remarkable development, yet no one is certain why it happened, and it has led to scores of speculations among the experts. Pointing to the fact that other Mississippian cultures—although much smaller than Cahokia—developed similar ranked societies and that none of them stayed together for more than 150 years, Pauketat has suggested that the citizens of Cahokia may have grown weary of life at the bottom of the social scale and searched for "greener pastures" elsewhere.

Archaeologist Robert Hall has raised the possibility that the introduction into the Mississippi Valley of enormous numbers of buffalo from the west in the 1200s may have led Cahokians, tired of the bustle of "urban" life, to become nomadic, following migrating buffalo just as millions of other Native Americans did in the centuries that followed. Other archaeologists theorize that as other Native American settlements in the American Bottom grew more prosperous—ironically, often through trade with Cahokia—they began to attract an increasing number of Cahokians.

The most commonly held theory regarding Cahokia's decline and eventual abandonment, however, has to do with what many experts believe was its citizens' disregard of the environment. There is much evidence to support the fact that the enormous quantities of wood used by Cahokians over the centuries for fuel, for building homes and public edifices, and especially for their monumental projects

❖ MONKS MOUND as it looks today.

(for example, the palisades) resulted in the depletion of the forests within a fifteen-mile radius of the city. This wanton tree cutting likely caused unchecked erosion, resulting in the destruction of the life-sustaining maize crop when the inevitable Mississippi floods struck the region. These floods would have had dual catastrophic effects: not only would they have destroyed the main source of the Cahokians' diet, they also would have seriously eroded the power of the city's rulers, who derived much of their legitimacy from their claims that they could control the weather.

Whether it was a long series of developments or a simple catastrophe, we will probably never know exactly what caused Cahokia's demise. Most experts, however, do agree with the assessment given by Emerson and Lewis: "The primary facts now seem to indicate that

Cahokia was a very short-lived entity that climaxed for a moment in the eleventh and twelfth centuries and then faded from the picture by the end of the thirteenth century." According to them, "Cahokia did not go out with a bang, but a fizzle." What is most important to remember is that, long before Columbus, the extraordinary city called Cahokia did exist, and compelled us to reexamine our entire notion of the ancient history of the Americas.

SAGRES

THREE

GIL EANES

Conquering the Point of No Return (1434)

In his 1934 book *Mensagem* (Message), a work comprising forty-four short poems, Portuguese poet and writer Fernando Pessoa (1888–1935) paid tribute to the Portuguese mariners who ushered in the golden age of exploration. In one of the poems, "Portuguese Sea," he writes that "Whoever wants to go beyond (cape) Bojador/Has to go beyond pain." Pessoa was careful to mention Cape Bojador, that treacherous locale on the coast of the western Sahara, in present-day Morocco. Well into the fifteenth century, Bojador remained the greatest obstacle to be surmounted by those who dared to venture far out into the unknown seas. One name, however, is missing from Pessoa's tribute. It is Gil Eanes, a man who remains largely lost to time. Yet it was Eanes who, by passing the point of no return at Cape Bojador, allayed fears that had haunted captains and sailors for centuries, and completed what, in many ways, can be regarded as the world's first great voyage of discovery.

Eanes's story has its beginnings in Portugal's desire to attain spices and other treasures of the East, riches that had been so eloquently described by such early travelers as Marco Polo and the Italian friar Odoric of Pordenone. In the late fourteenth century, with Muslims blocking

❖ IN THIS 1922 PANEL OF GLAZED TILES, Portuguese artist Jorge Colaço paid tribute to Prince Henry the Navigator by showing the regent standing at Sagres before the mysterious and threatening ocean, while envisioning the lands and opportunities that lay beyond once the seas could be conquered.

the overland trade routes to these coveted goods, the Portuguese began seeking a water route to India and beyond by exploring the uncharted and foreboding waters off the west coast of Africa. The Portuguese had another agenda as well. Since the early Middle Ages, gold dust from the rivers and streams of the Sahara had been shipped to Spain and other European regions for trade. Now Portugal wished to satisfy its own gold lust. In seeking to lead the way not only to the riches of the East but also to what might lay far beyond, Portugal had several advantages over its European rivals. In the late fourteenth century and throughout most of the fifteenth century, it was a nation devoid of civil wars. Geographically, Portugal's deep harbors and its several long rivers that flowed into the Atlantic provided a natural backdrop for exploration beyond its shores. Most important of all, there was, within the nation, a man with the vision and ultimately the power to make the dream of far-off discovery a reality.

BORN IN 1394, INFANTE DOM HENRIQUE was the son of Portugal's King John I and Phillipa of Lancaster, daughter of King Henry IV of England. He became known to history as Prince Henry the Navigator.

The most detailed description of him comes from the fifteenth-century chronicler Gomes Eanes de Zurara, whose 1453 *Crónica dos Feitos da Guiné* (The Chronicle of the Discovery and Conquest of Guinea) remains the authority for the early Portuguese voyages of discovery. Zurara described Prince Henry as

> big and strong of limb, his hair . . . of a color natural fair, but by which constant toil and exposure had become dark. His expression at first sight inspired fear in those who did not know him and when wroth, though such times were rare, his countenance was harsh. Strength of heart and keenness of mind were in him to an excellent degree and beyond comparison, he was ambitious of achieving great and lofty deeds.

Prince Henry never took part in a single voyage of exploration, but he earned the title of "father of modern exploration" through both his organizational skills and his ability to motivate the many mariners he assembled to carry out the risky and often precedent-setting voyages he launched. He was also a deeply religious man who, at the same time, placed great faith in astrologers. Zurara reported that the prince's court astrologers had foreseen that Henry was "bound to engage in great and noble conquests, and above all was he bound to attempt the discovery of things which were hidden from other men and secret." The prediction could not have been more accurate. In Prince Henry's lifetime, his navigators, including the unlikely Gil Eanes, would explore the "great seas of darkness" along the foreboding African coast and lead the world into a bold new age.

Before exploring the world, the prince embarked on a crusade as his first "great and noble conquest." In 1413, when he was only nineteen years old, he convinced his father that a military assault on the Moroccan trading center of Cuerta would give them an opportunity to win the souls of "unbelievers" while driving the infidel Muslims from their strongholds. The king agreed, and he put his son in charge of helping to both plan the attack and build a fleet. When, on August 14, 1415, the Portuguese forces scored a complete, one-day victory, Prince Henry returned home covered in glory—so much so that he immediately began embarking on an even more ambitious military venture: an attack on the Muslim stronghold of Gibraltar. But this time the king refused to back the plan. Bitterly disappointed—particularly because his adventure in Cuerta had permitted him to see firsthand the extraordinary treasures that lay there—Henry was determined to unlock a water route to the East. He decided to leave his father's court and to take up residency on Portugal's Cape Saint Vincent in a village called Sagres.

Contrary to what was long believed, Prince Henry did not establish a school for navigators at Sagres. What he did do, however, was assemble and train a host of mariners and develop a succession of different types of ships that would prove essential in the discovery of whole new worlds.

These were vital achievements, but the greatest of all the challenges that Prince Henry faced was overcoming his sailors' fears of the perceived horrors lurking in the waters in which he was asking them to sail. This was particularly true of Cape Bojador, approximately 850 miles south of Sagres, for it was at Bojador that geographical knowledge stopped and mythical terrors took over.

Located about 140 miles southeast of the Canary Islands and jutting out into the Atlantic Ocean, human civilization's first exposure to Cape Bojador is believed to have taken place about 600 BCE, when, according to the ancient Greek historian Herodotus (ca. 484–425 BCE), Egypt's pharaoh Necho II sent a group of Phoenician mariners to circumnavigate the African continent. Some maritime historians also believe that further contact may have occurred about 530 BCE during a voyage made by the Carthaginian explorer Hanno the Navigator.

Cape Bojador's name in Arabic is Abu Khatar, meaning "father of danger." It is an appropriate appellation. As Peter D. Jeans wrote,

> Beneath the huge red sandstone cliffs of Cape Bojador . . . the Atlantic Ocean erupts in an almost constant fury, the sea crashing into the clefts and gullies of the cliffs and exploding into huge columns of compressed water; it is a place where the water looks like molten metal because of the schools of sardines turning and flashing in the turbulent sea. Fearsome water spouts savage the sand-laden sea and dust storms howl off the cliff tops in the constant northeasterlies.

No one could deny that these were very real challenges to any mariner, but as far as Prince Henry's navigators were concerned, they were nothing compared to the terrors believed to exist in all distant uncharted waters, nightmarish creatures and evil supernatural forces about which medieval scholars had written with such relish.

Their books and treatises had been filled with accounts of giant sea monsters waiting to devour any mariner who set so far out into the sea. As for Cape Bojador, it was the locus, according to common belief, of all fear. The cliffs along Cape Bojador's coast were said to contain a lodestone so powerful that it pulled out a ship's metal rivets, sending the vessel and all aboard to the bottom of the sea. Just as frightening were the stories of how these same cliffs also rained down sheets of fire upon any vessel that dared sail by them. Still other writings proclaimed that once the water off the cape was entered, the white sailors aboard would immediately turn black.

Just as petrifying were the stories about what would happen to a vessel if, by some miracle, it made its way around the cape. During Prince Henry's time, for example, it was widely believed that the sun was boiling hot at the equator. Thus even if a vessel got past the cape, the equatorial sun would burn it to powder. Those who ascribed to this theory also had a special belief concerning the specific type of monsters that a ship and its crew would encounter in the unlikely event the equator was crossed, a belief historians have attributed to "impeccable medieval logic." It went this way: since all men were descended from Adam and Eve, and since it was impossible to cross the equator, all creatures in the subequatorial region known as the antipodes must be something other than human, something particularly monstrous.

The most commonly held belief was far more simple. In labeling the waters beyond Cape Bojador as the "Green Sea of Darkness," geographers and other sages stated with certainty that not only were these seas inhabited by terrible monsters and the spirits of dead sailors, but they also represented a point of no return, a place where, once entered, ships and their crews fell off the edge of the world and into the pits of hell.

Prince Henry would have none of it. Those were superstitions and myths, not truths, he told his mariners. Their fears had to be put aside. Cape Bojador had to be rounded. Between 1421 and 1433 the determined prince sent out no less than fourteen expeditions, each of whose main purpose was to round the cape and set the stage for further, more ambitious exploration. Describing these attempts and the frightened mariners who undertook them, Zurara wrote:

> So the Infant [prince] . . . began to make ready his ships and his people, as the needs of the case required; but this much you may learn, that although he sent out many times, not only ordinary men, but such as by their experience in great deeds of war were of foremost

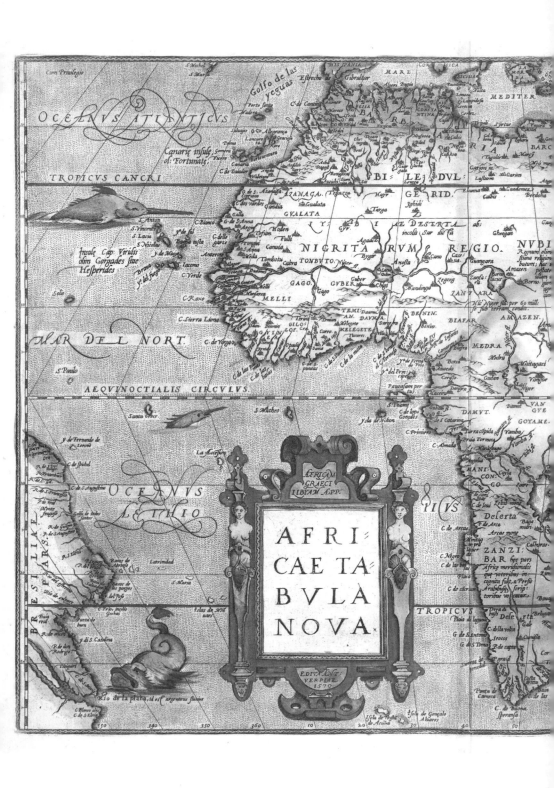

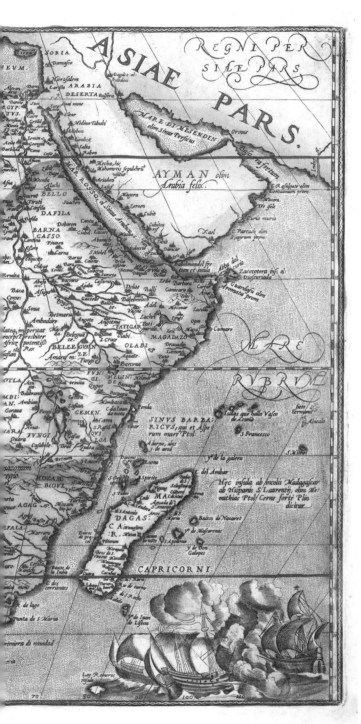

❖ This map, drawn in 1570 by famed Belgian cartographer Abraham Ortelius, shows Cape Bojador jutting out above the Tropic of Cancer into the Atlantic from the northwestern coast of Africa. A fierce leviathan is depicted to the southwest of the cape.

name in the profession of arms, yet there was not one who dared to pass that Cape Bojador and learn about the land beyond it, as the Infant wished. And to say the truth, this was not from cowardice or want of good will, but from the novelty of the thing and the widespread and ancient rumour about this Cape, that had been cherished by the mariners of Spain from generation to generation. And although this proved to be deceitful, yet since the hazarding of this attempt seemed to threaten the last evil of all, there was great doubt as to who would be the first to risk his life in such a venture. How are we, men said, to pass the bounds that our fathers set up, or what profit can result to the Infant from the perdition of our souls as well as of our bodies. . . . But being satisfied of the peril, and seeing no hope of honour or profit, they left off the attempt. For, said the mariners, this much is clear, that beyond this Cape there is no race of men nor place of inhabitants; nor is the land less sandy than the deserts of Libya, where there is no water, no tree, no green herb—and the sea so shallow that a whole league from land it is only a fathom deep, while the currents are so terrible that no ship having once passed the Cape, will ever be able to return.

. . . during twelve years the Infant continued steadily at this labour of his, ordering out his ships every year to those parts, not without great loss of revenue, and never finding any who dared to make that passage. Yet they did not return wholly without honour, for as an atonement for their failure to carry out more fully their Lord's wishes, some made descents upon the coast of Granada and other voyaged along the Levant Seas, where they took great booty of the Infidels, with which they returned to the Kingdom very honourably.

Booty—but not the great prize that Prince Henry sought. Yet, disappointed as he was with each failed expedition, he never lost sight of his goal. "Now," wrote Zurara, "the Infant always received home again with great patience those whom he had sent out . . . never upbraiding them with their failure, but with gracious countenance listening to the story of the events of their voyage, giving them such rewards as he was wont to give those who served him well, and then either sending them back to search again or despatching other picked men of his Household."

Still, gracious and patient as he was, Henry was growing increasingly frustrated. Surely there was someone among all his navigators who would not lose nerve and would bring home the prize. And then he made a startling decision. To lead his fifteenth attempt he chose someone who had no navigational experience. Instead, he selected a man who had served him loyally from boyhood as a squire and shield bearer. His name was Gil Eanes, and almost nothing is known about him prior to his attempt to round Cape Bojador. The little we do know is that he was born around 1415 in Lagos in the southern Algarve region of Portugal—and that he was totally devoted to his prince.

EANES SET OUT FOR CAPE BOJADOR IN 1433. As historian Hugh Thomas wrote, he "probably sailed in a simple square-rigged single-masted *barca*, partly decked if decked at all, only about thirty tons, flat-bottomed, with a shallow draft, and with a crew of about fifteen, who would have been expected to row much of the time—the same kind of ship that had been used often before in unsuccessful attempts to round the cape."

As inexperienced a seaman as he was, Eanes proved to be a natural leader and in good time landed successfully at Madeira Island. From there he sailed on to the Canary Islands, again without incident, where he captured some island natives. Then he headed for Cape Bojador. The closer he came to the feared spot, the more stories he began to hear about the horrors that might await them from his increasingly apprehensive crew. Then the cape came into sight.

Immediately there came a terrified cry from the lookout perched atop the masthead, warning of boiling waters dead ahead. Then the crew informed Eanes that they refused to go any farther. Eanes was a squire, not a pilot; a leader it seemed, but not a seaman. Having no explanation of the sea's strange behavior, he turned and headed back to Sagres.

Once again Prince Henry was called upon to exhibit graciousness in the face of disappointment, deeper disappointment perhaps than after hearing of most previous failed attempts. For despite Eanes's lack of seamanship, the prince had been convinced that his squire's loyalty and dedication to task gave him perhaps a greater chance of succeeding than the experienced mariners who had failed before him. Patiently he listened as Eanes swore that the seas off Cape Bojador had been boiling. Even more patiently the prince explained that the sea had not been boiling but had been racing at ebb tide over the shoals that surrounded the cape, something that took place commonly on Portugal's own coast. Then he asked Eanes if he would be willing to make a second attempt. The chagrined squire, more determined than ever to please his prince, agreed.

Less than a year later, in 1434, according to Zurara,

> The Infant made ready the same vessel, and calling Gil Eanes apart, charged him earnestly to strain every nerve to pass the Cape and even if he could do nothing else on that voyage, yet he should consider that to be enough. "You cannot find," said the Infant, "peril so great that the hope of reward will not be greater . . . Go forth then . . . make your voyage straightaway, in as much as with the grace of God you cannot but gain from this journey honour and profit.

So once again, Gil Eanes set out for one of the most feared places in the known world. Truth be told, he was prepared to sacrifice his life to fulfill his obligation to his prince. He was more than half-convinced that he was about to do so. His sailors, however, had no motivation to make such a sacrifice and, as Eanes's small vessel approached the cape for the second time in two years, stories of the horrors that awaited them spread throughout the ship. Soon, they were in open rebellion, demanding that the captain turn the ship around and head back to Sagres. Although Eanes was far from convinced that the sailors' fears were not justified, he summoned every ounce of his energy and persuasive powers and somehow convinced the men that they should sail on.

And then the miracle happened. As they entered the waters off Cape Bojador and gazed anxiously at the towering cliffs above, no liquid sheets of flame rained down on them. As they sailed on, the ship's metal fastenings did not fall out. And as they nervously looked upon one another, none of them turned black.

Now they were actually rounding the cape, about to become the first to enter the most feared waters of all. Again, a miracle! There were no monsters anywhere, only a calm sea. There was no edge of the world to fall off of. They did not descend into the pits of hell. After joining his men both in prayer and rejoicing, Eanes landed on a barren desert coast. He found no inhabitants; in fact, he discovered no living thing except for a plant that eventually became known as St. Mary's rose or the rose of Jericho (*Anastatica*, similar to tumbleweed) that he brought back to Sagres to prove to his prince that he had landed on the other side of the cape.

It had taken Prince Henry nineteen years and fifteen expeditions, but, thanks to Gil Eanes, Cape Bojador and all it symbolized had been conquered. Writing of Eanes's accomplishment, Zurara exclaimed, "and as he proposed, he performed, for in that voyage he doubled the Cape, despising all danger, and found the lands beyond quite contrary to what he, like others, had expected. And . . . on account of its daring it was reckoned great."

Great indeed—regarded by mid-nineteenth-century historian and English Privy Council member Sir Arthur Helps as "a great event in African history and one that in that day was considered equal to a labor of Hercules." It was actually an understatement. For by breaking the psychological barrier of fear that rounding Cape Bojador had represented, Gil Eanes had not only profoundly affected the future course of African history, he had opened the way to the world beyond Cape Bojador.

EANES HAD RETURNED HOME A HERO, showered with gifts and acclaim. And now the prince had another assignment for him. By rounding Cape Bojador, Eanes had paved the way for the discovery of new peoples, new avenues, and, most important, new opportunities for trade. As usual, Prince Henry acted quickly.

In 1435, Henry sent Eanes out again, this time on a larger vessel called a *barinel* (balinger) or oared galley, commanded by the prince's royal cupbearer Afonso Gonçalves Baldaya (also Baldaia). Sailing past Madeira and the Canaries, they reached a spot on the African coast about 150 miles south of Cape Bojador where they and their crew came upon footprints of both men and camels. They encountered no humans, but it was an important discovery nonetheless, dispelling the long-held notion that people couldn't live in what the ancient Greek philosopher Aristotle had dubbed the "Torrid Zone." For Eanes, it was yet another historic achievement. The man who had been the first to round Cape Bojador had now been present when the most southerly sign of life yet known to Europeans had been discovered.

Almost as soon as Eanes and Baldaya returned to Sagres, Prince

Henry sent Baldaya out again, ordering him to sail beyond the point that he and Eanes had reached until he found opportunity for trade. Baldaya reached a body of water that he called Rio de Ouro (River of Gold) in West Africa, but soon found that it was not a river but a bay and that there was no gold trading post. He then proceeded even farther south, where he collected thousands of seal skins, the first commercial cargo brought back from West Africa to Europe.

❖ THIS STATUE OF GIL EANES in Lagos, Portugal, pays tribute to one of the least known yet most important of all Portuguese mariners who led the world into the Great Age of Exploration.

As for Gil Eanes, records of his life after his voyage with Baldaya are fleeting. There are indications that he may have commanded one or two exploratory expeditions to West Africa sponsored by Portuguese merchants stationed in the port city of Lagos (Nigeria). What is known for certain is that on August 10, 1445, he sailed in an armada of fourteen caravels to the island of Tidra, off the coast of present-day Mauritania. There, under the command of Admiral Lanzarote Pessanha, the Portuguese, determined to conquer the island's largely Muslim population, won a resounding victory. The armada returned home with some sixty captives. It is here that Eanes disappears from the pages of history. Some unsubstantiated accounts claim that he was killed in the fighting on Tidra. Others simply state that he died at a young age around the year 1450.

It was a brief life, yet it was highlighted by an accomplishment that can be regarded as a turning point in history. Gil Eanes broke both the physical and psychological barriers of rounding Cape Bojador, a breakthrough that led to European trade with Africa and eventually with India as well.

As historian John Friske stated, "This achievement of Gil Eanes marks an era. It was the beginning of great things. When we think of the hesitation with which this step was taken, and the vociferous applause that greeted the successful captain, it is strange to reflect that babies were born in 1435 who were to live to hear of the prodigious voyages of Columbus and Gama, Vespucius and Magellan."

Gil Eanes's breakthrough was indeed followed by a succession of Portuguese voyages that, along with Christopher Columbus's journey in the opposite direction, changed the course of history. Despite the true progress it represented, not all of this course was positive. The commerce that developed as a result of Eanes's achievement included the capture, trade, and enslavement of a horrifying number of human beings. But, as John Fiske pointed out so long ago, there can be no denying the importance of what Gil Eanes accomplished. It is time for history to grant him the recognition he deserves.

Gen. JOSEPH WARREN

FOR WHOM
THE TOWN AND COUNTY
WERE NAMED
BORN AT ROXBURY MASS.
JUNE 11, 1741 KILLED AT
THE BATTLE OF BUNKER HILL
JUNE 17, 1775

54

FOUR

JOSEPH WARREN
Architect of a Revolution (1741–75)

He was regarded by many in his time as the true architect of the American Revolution. He was the key figure in one of history's most famous tea parties. He wrote a set of Resolves that served as the blueprint for the first autonomous American government. He delivered a speech that sparked the first battles of the Revolutionary War. He sent Paul Revere out on one of history's most famous rides. He was the only Patriot leader, prior to the Declaration of Independence, to risk his life against the British on the battlefield. His name was Joseph Warren, and, remarkably, he has been largely lost to history.

Warren was born in Roxbury, Massachusetts, on June 11, 1741. When he was fourteen, his father, a well-known farmer and respected member of the community, fell off a ladder while gathering fruit in his orchard and was killed. Fortunately, there was enough money in the family to pay for a superior education, and, after attending the prestigious Roxbury Latin School, Warren studied medicine at Harvard, graduating at the age of eighteen.

At a time when there was no formal medical school in North America and doctors received their practical training by serving an apprenticeship, Warren was taken in by James Lloyd, who had acquired much of his medical knowledge by studying in England with William

❖ A ca. 1912 statue of General Joseph Warren stands in General Joseph Warren Park in Warren, Pennsylvania.

Cheselden, one of Europe's greatest surgeons. Lloyd took a particular liking to the young Warren and not only passed on to him the most advanced knowledge of the European medical institutions, but also gave him a much freer hand in diagnosing and treating patients than was ordinarily granted apprentices.

In 1763, at the age of twenty-two, Warren became the youngest doctor in Boston. It was the beginning of an extraordinarily busy medical career, one in which he would become the best-known physician in the city. Hundreds of sailors, rope makers, pewterers, saddlers, and even slaves came to him for treatment. But it was another group of patients who would represent the turning point in Warren's life.

He started his practice at a momentous time in the history of the American colonies in general and of Boston in particular. England, after years of allowing its colonies across the Atlantic to do pretty much as they pleased, had reversed its course. Its new king, George III, and his ministers were determined to bring the policies of "salutary neglect" to an end. Acts would be passed designed to make the colonists pay their share of the costly French and Indian War that was being waged when George III ascended the throne in 1760. As far as England was concerned, the war had been fought for the colonists' protection. Most important, the British government would make it clear that it held supreme authority over the colonies.

The new king and parliament began their new policies not by instituting legislation, but by resurrecting and enforcing old laws that had not been enforced. Chief among them were the Navigation Acts, which restricted the use of foreign shipping for trade between England and its American colonies. Particularly onerous to the colonists was the reinstatement of writs of assistance, a measure designed to enforce the Navigation Acts. This law gave royal custom officials in America the authority to issue writs compelling local colonial authorities to assist them in identifying and capturing smugglers and others. Even more outrageous as far as the colonists were concerned, a writ of assistance permitted British officials to search warehouses and colonists' homes without a court order.

 GEORGE III is shown here as a young king in an engraving from 1762.

As WARREN'S REPUTATION AS A SKILLED physician grew, so did his reputation as a born leader and a well-read, highly articulate individual, always eager to express his opinions. He began to attract as patients many of those who would lead the way in opposing the new British policies, men such as John Adams, John Hancock, Samuel Adams, James Otis, and Josiah Quincy Jr. All of these men would soon become Warren's political allies as well as patients. He joined them as they gathered at the many clubs that were being formed throughout Boston. He joined others at the St. Andrew's Masonic Lodge, where his magnetic personality and strong convictions convinced fellow members—including the young silversmith Paul Revere—that he was a man ready to assume a leadership role in what could become a serious clash with the mother country.

They were right. In 1733, Parliament passed the Molasses Act, which levied prohibitive duties of six pence per gallon on molasses. In 1764, via the Sugar Act, Parliament reduced the duty on molasses but raised it on sugar. These were but two of numerous revived Navigation Acts and other acts of trade that England would impose on the colonies in the early eighteenth century. As these taxes were announced, Warren began to speak out openly against not only the levies themselves but also England's right to impose them upon a people who had no representation in the Parliament that was laying down the taxes. Other Patriots spoke out on the same issues, but Warren did so with extraordinary passion and eloquence.

Tensions escalated tremendously with the passage of the Stamp Act in 1765, a measure that imposed a direct tax on all legal documents, permits, newspapers, almanacs, wills, commercial contracts, pamphlets, and even playing cards, a tax that affected almost every colonist. Officers were appointed to collect stamp duties and ensure that all printed material was officially stamped or marked. In his first letter to the press, published in the *Boston Gazette* of October 7, 1765, Warren demonstrated the emotional style that would arouse and inspire his fellow citizens throughout the events to follow.

> Awake! Awake, my countrymen, and, by a regular and legal opposition, defeat the designs of those who would enslave us and our posterity. Nothing is wanting but your own resolution—For great is the authority, exalted the dignity, and powerful the majesty of the people . . . Ages remote, mortals yet unborn, will bless your generous effort, and revere the memory of the saviors of their country.

Spurred on by Warren, Samuel Adams and other colonial leaders in Boston (as well as outraged citizens in New York and Philadelphia) organized themselves into a secret society named the Sons of Liberty in opposition to the Stamp Act. The mob violence that followed included physical attacks on British tax collectors, the burning of the houses of

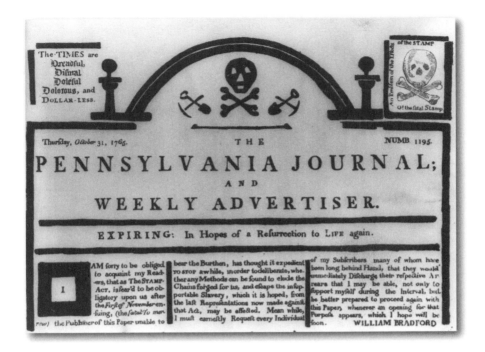

❖ The satiric masthead of the October 31, 1765, edition of the *Pennsylvania Journal and Weekly Advertiser*, with a skull and crossbones representation of the official stamp required by the Stamp Act of 1765 that reads: "An emblem of the effects of the STAMP— O! the fatal Stamp," and a note on the top left stating that "The TIMES are Dreadful, Dismal, Doleful, Dolorous, and Dollar-less." The article opens with a statement by the publisher, William Bradford, that reads "I am sorry to be obliged to acquaint my Readers, that as the STAMP Act, is fear'd to be obligatory upon us . . . the Publisher of this Paper unable to bear the Burthen, has thought it expedient to STOP awhile."

British tax collectors and other British officials, and the widespread destruction of the detested stamps. In the most effective protest of all, a boycott of all British goods was initiated.

The resulting loss of trade caused by the boycott hit British merchants squarely in their pocketbooks, so much so that, after a series of petitions from many of these merchants, Parliament was forced to repeal the act—but not before passing the Declaratory Act (1766), which stated that Parliament had the right to make laws for the colonies "in all cases whatsoever."

The repeal of the Stamp Act brought rejoicing throughout the colonies. Some spoke openly about the restoration of harmony between England and her American brethren. Harmony, however, was the last thing Warren wanted. By this time, particularly with England's latest declaration of its complete legal authority over the colonies, he was more convinced than ever that an irreconcilable rift with the mother country was inevitable.

Determined to keep the flames of agitation burning, within two weeks of the repeal of the Stamp Act, he began a written assault on the royal governor of Massachusetts, Francis Bernard. In a series of letters to the *Boston Gazette*, he charged the governor with "wantonly [sacrificing] the happiness of this Province" by enforcing unpopular laws and taxes, often, Warren charged, for his own selfish purposes. As historian John H. Cary wrote, Warren's ultimate aims were to drive Bernard out of office and to

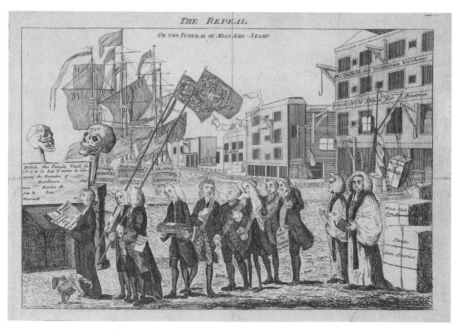

❖ A 1766 CARTOON DEPICTS a mock funeral for the Stamp Act. The caption under the cartoon read in part, "The hero of this print is the gentle Mr. Stamper, who is carrying to the family vault his favourite child, in a coffin, Miss Ame-Stamp, about 12 months old."

bring Warren, Samuel Adams, Hancock, and the other Patriots to power. "The former," Cary stated, "was accomplished by the close of the decade; the latter awaited the Revolution to achieve complete success. Warren's propaganda played an important role in preparing public opinion for both."

"Important" was an understatement. By this time, Warren was convinced that, despite the Stamp Act's repeal, other onerous measures would follow and that nothing short of rebellion would restore the liberty the colonists had for so long cherished. On March 19, 1766, in a letter to his friend Edward Dana, he wrote, "Never has there been a time, since the first settlement of America, in which the people had so much reason to be alarmed as the present. The whole continent is inflamed to the highest degree. . . . They can conceive of no liberty when they have lost the power of taxing themselves."

Warren then went on to describe a development that had arisen from measures such as the Stamp Act, a result that even "the most zealous colonist never could have expected," one that few on both sides of the Atlantic could have predicted less than a decade earlier. "The colonies, until now," he wrote, "were ever at variance, and foolishly jealous of each other. They are now, by [the new British policies] united for their common defense against what they believe to be oppression; nor will they soon forget the weight which this close union gives them."

Propaganda it might have been. But Warren was correct in stating that the new British policies had brought the once-divided colonies together as never before. And he also was correct in his conviction that the repeal of the Stamp Act did not signal an end to British "oppression."

HE DID NOT HAVE TO WAIT LONG. In 1767, a still-determined Parliament, urged on by King George III, passed the Townshend Acts, imposing taxes on such commodities as glass, paint, lead, paper, and tea. Once again boycotts of British imports were organized. On May 9, 1768, British officials in Boston responded by seizing the *Liberty*, one of Hancock's ships, and accusing Hancock of smuggling goods without paying taxes.

On the surface the seizure would not seem to be a pivotal incident on the road to the American Revolutionary War. But it came at a time when the captain of HMS *Romney*, the British ship involved in the seizure, had already outraged Bostonians by impressing colonial sailors in Boston Harbor into naval service. In response to the *Liberty* seizure, the already incensed mob became so violent that the customs officials sent a hasty message to London declaring that Boston was now in a state of rebellion.

Alarmed at the situation, England took its most dramatic step yet by sending four thousand British troops to restore order. Regarding the soldiers as nothing less than an army of occupation, Bostonians refused to house the troops as England had ordered. British military officers then commandeered public and private dwellings as lodgings for their men. The presence of four thousand armed troops brought tension in Boston to a boiling point, a pot that boiled over when, on March 5, 1770, a Bostonian, Edward Garrick, picked a fight with a young British sentry on guard at the customs office. The sentry hit Garrick in the face with his musket butt, which set off a mob that began throwing ice and snowballs at the sentry and a few other British soldiers. A small group of British officers and soldiers arrived to help protect their battered comrades as the mob grew larger and began to throw other small objects. Almost immediately a fight broke out, and in the scuffle a soldier named Montgomery, who had been hit with a club, suddenly fired into the crowd, although there had been no order to fire. His shot missed, but another soldier, named Kilroy, then discharged his weapon, killing one of the Bostonians. Other shots were then fired, and when the smoke cleared, three townspeople lay dead and two others had been mortally wounded.

Five unfortunate citizens was hardly a slaughter, and the unruly mob was probably as much to blame as the soldiers. But the incident would forever be known as the Boston Massacre, an event regarded with such importance by the Patriots that John Adams wrote, "On that night, the foundation of American independence was laid."

By that time, Warren had earned a full reputation as perhaps the most radical of the radical leaders—so much so that when, in 1772, he was chosen to deliver the second annual Boston Massacre commemorative

❖ ONE OF THE VERSIONS OF PAUL REVERE's now-famous print depicting the Boston Massacre, from 1770.

oration, even so staunch a Patriot as John Hancock expressed his concern that Warren's speech might be so incendiary as to remove any possibility of easing tensions with the mother country.

Hancock's fears were not unfounded. In an oration that Cary characterized as "one of the finest in American revolutionary literature," Warren delivered a speech that stopped just short of a call to arms. A state, he exclaimed in his opening remarks, remains happy and secure only as long as its people are willing to fight for their rights. Then, summoning all the passion within him, he used the commemoration of the "massacre" not only as a vehicle to remind his listeners of the "tyranny and oppression" of the present British government but also as a warning of the dire results that might well lay ahead.

> The fatal fifth of March, 1770, can never be forgotten. . . . The horrors of that dreadful night are but too deeply impressed upon our hearts. Language is too feeble to paint the emotions of our souls, when our streets were stained with the blood of our brethren; when our ears were wounded by the groans of the dying, and our eyes were tortured with the sight of the mangled bodies of the dead. When our alarmed imagination presented to our view our houses wrapt in flames, our children subjected to the barbarous caprice of the raging soldiery; our beauteous virgins exposed to all the insolence of unbridled passion.

After discussing the dangers of standing armies, Warren then, in his most vehement remarks, attacked the very notion of the British colonial system.

> By what figure of rhetoric can the inhabitants of Massachusetts be called free subjects, when they are obliged to obey implicitly such laws as are made for them by men three thousand miles off, whom they know not and whom they have never empowered to act for them. Or how can they be said to have property, if such a foreign body can oblige them to deliver a part or the whole of their substance without their consent. If in this way they may be taxed even in the smallest trifle, they may also, without their consent be deprived of everything they possess.

He was not done. In arguably the most incendiary remark yet made in the American colonies, he concluded by exclaiming, "May our land be a land of liberty, the seat of virtue, the asylum of the oppressed, a name and a praise in the whole earth, until the last shock of time shall bury the empires of the world in one common undistinguished ruin."

According to the *Boston Gazette*, Warren's oration was celebrated with "unanimous applause." Even Massachusetts's royal governor, Thomas Hutchinson, who had succeeded Bernard, admitted that the "fervor" of the speaker "could not fail in its effect on the minds of the great concourse of people present." Hutchinson's words proved prophetic later that year, when an event took place that greatly accelerated the movement toward the colonies' final split with Great Britain.

In April 1770, Parliament, in response to the furor caused by the Boston Massacre, repealed the Townshend Acts except for the tax it had imposed on the importation of tea. Warren, along with Samuel Adams, immediately saw in the retention of the tea tax another opportunity to let the British government know that *any* taxes would be vehemently opposed. But they also knew they had a problem. In order to aid one of England's largest businesses, the East India Company, Parliament had eliminated the duties that British tea merchants had previously had to pay on the tea they shipped to America. For the colonists, the tea imported from England, the finest in the world, was now far less expensive than tea imported from other nations, even with the tax. And the colonists, like their British counterparts, loved their tea. The question with which Warren, Samuel Adams, and the other radical leaders were faced was simple. How many Americans were willing to put their outrage at the British taxation policies aside in order to buy superior tea at cheaper prices? Fearing that the answer was "a great many," Warren and Adams came to the conclusion that the solution was to prevent the tea from landing. Otherwise, there would be buyers aplenty.

In late November 1773, the North End Caucus, a Boston political club, took the initial steps in preventing the landing of the tea. A committee, headed by Warren, confronted the American tea consignees and demanded that they pledge not to land or pay duties on the tea.

The agents refused. A series of confrontations with the agents who steadfastly refused to budge followed.

In one of these confrontations, Warren, along with fellow Patriot William Molineux, led a group of followers to the warehouse where the tea consignees' offices were located. Finding the door locked, Warren ordered that it be broken down. But even after he and his fellow Patriots entered and threatened the consignees with bodily harm, they remained steadfast. The tea, they insisted, would be unloaded.

On November 28, 1773, the first of the tea ships, the *Dartmouth*, arrived. It did not take long for the vessel's captain to realize that he had sailed into a hornet's nest. Unwilling to become involved in the dispute, he made it known that he intended to take his ship back to England with the tea still aboard. Governor Hutchinson responded by ordering a blockade of Boston Harbor to prevent the *Dartmouth* from sailing.

On December 16, eight thousand Bostonians gathered at the Old South Church, where they were informed of Hutchinson's determination to have the tea brought ashore. At an appointed moment, Samuel Adams stood up and exclaimed, "Gentlemen, this meeting can do nothing more to save the country." It was a signal. That evening a mob, thinly disguised as Indians, rowed over to the three ships that had now arrived, broke open more than 340 boxes of tea, and dumped it into the harbor. Informed of what had taken place, John Adams, who was out of town, declared,

> Last night three cargoes of Bohea Tea were emptied into the sea. This morning a man-of-war sails. This is the most magnificent moment of all. There is a dignity, a majesty, a sublimity, in this last effort of the Patriots that I greatly admire. . . . This destruction of the tea is so bold, so daring, so firm, intrepid and inflexible, and it must have so important consequences, and, so lasting, that I can't but consider it as an epoch of history.

It is not known whether Warren was among the tea-dumping "Indians." But given the events that were to quickly follow, it would be

Americans throwing the Cargoes of the Tea Ships into the River, at Boston

❖ This illustration of "Americans throwing the Cargoes of the Tea Ships into the River, at Boston" is from *The History of North America* by W. D. Rev. Mr. Cooper, published in London in 1789.

surprising if he were not. John Adams had been correct in his assessment of what became known as the Boston Tea Party. There would indeed be "important consequences," particularly for Warren. From that moment on, he became nothing less than the most important figure in the movement toward full-scale revolution.

The British government's reaction to the "tea party" was predictably severe. It came in the form of a series of measures variously called the Intolerable Acts, the Punitive Acts, or the Coercive Acts by the colonists. Included was a measure that abolished all elections for councilors, judges, and other colonial officers in Massachusetts, making all those positions subject to the appointment of the king and his ministers. At the heart of the acts, however, was another measure that was, by far, the most punitive of all. Called the Boston Port Act, it closed the port of Boston to all ships, no matter their business, until restitution was made for the tea that had been dumped into the harbor.

For many colonists, including many who had fervently hoped for a reconciliation with the mother county, it was the final straw. As historian D. W. Meinig wrote, "The British people of the Atlantic had become two peoples, separated by more than an ocean." In the fall of 1774, delegates chosen from the various colonies met in Philadelphia "to concert a general and uniform place for the defense and preservation of our common rights."

The delegates to the Continental Congress were leaders from twelve of the thirteen colonies, including cousins John and Samuel Adams from Massachusetts, John Jay from New York, John Dickinson from Pennsylvania, and Richard Henry Lee, Peyton Randolph, Patrick Henry, and George Washington from Virginia. Warren was not a delegate. He had even more important work to do, for what he was about to accomplish would have the most profound effect on what the Continental Congress would achieve and on the future of the American colonies.

On September 6, 1774, delegates from every town and district in Massachusetts's Suffolk County gathered in the town of Milton, where Warren read them a set of resolutions he had written. Thereafter known as the Suffolk Resolves, the document that the delegates adopted called for nothing less than preparation for war with the mother country and the establishment of a government outside the royal system. One cannot read Warren's preamble to his Resolves without seeing the roots of the Declaration of Independence, which was still some two years away:

> Whereas the power but not the justice, the vengeance but not the wisdom of Great Britain . . . now pursues us, their guiltless children, with unrelenting severity. . . . On the fortitude, on the wisdom and on the exertions of this important day, is suspended the fate of this new world, and of unborn millions. If a boundless extent of continent, swarming with millions, will tamely submit to live, move and have their being at the arbitrary will of a licentious minister,

they basely yield to voluntary slavery, and future generations shall load their memories with incessant execrations. On the other hand, if we arrest the hand which would ransack our pockets, if we disarm the parricide which points the dagger to our bosoms, if we nobly defeat that fatal edict which proclaims a power to frame laws for us in all cases whatsoever, thereby entailing the endless and numberless curses of slavery upon us, our heirs and their heirs forever; if we successfully resist that unparalleled usurpation of unconstitutional power, whereby our capital is robbed of the means of life; whereby the streets of Boston are thronged with military executioners; whereby our coasts are lined and harbours crowded with ships of war; whereby the charter of the colony, that sacred barrier against the encroachments of tyranny, is mutilated and, in effect, annihilated; . . . whereby the unalienable and inestimable inheritance, which we derived from nature, the constitution of Britain, and the privileges warranted to us in the charter of the province, is totally wrecked, annulled, and vacated. . . .

Warren's Resolves then called for the citizens of Massachusetts to ignore the Intolerable Acts, boycott British imports, curtail exports, refuse to use British products, support a colonial Massachusetts government free of British authority, and raise a militia of their own. It was nothing less than a call to prepare for war and to establish a government outside the royal system. Most important, it became the blueprint for the First Continental Congress.

Once the Suffolk Resolves were adopted, Revere, in one of the many rides he took long before the one that placed him in the history books, carried the Resolves to Philadelphia. There they were read aloud to the congress by the body's president, Peyton Randolph. When he finished, the entire congress erupted into cheering, surrounding the Massachusetts delegation with applause and congratulations. Every word of the Suffolk Resolves was then overwhelmingly adopted for all of the colonies. Because of Joseph Warren, a momentous step had been taken toward independence and the formation of a new nation.

In England, reaction to the Suffolk Resolves and their adoption was profound. In Parliament, longtime critics of the government's policies regarding the American colonies, such as the Whig statesmen William Pitt and Edmund Burke, were vocal in their praise for what Warren had accomplished. "For solidity of reasoning, force of sagacity, and wisdom of conclusion, under such complication of difficult circumstances, no nation or body of men can stand in preference to the General Congress at Philadelphia," Pitt stated in a

JOURNAL

OF THE

PROCEEDINGS

OF THE

CONGRESS,

Held at PHILADELPHIA,

September 5, 1774.

PHILADELPHIA:

Printed by WILLIAM and THOMAS BRADFORD,
at the London Coffee House.

M,DC C,LXXI V.

❖ THE COVER OF THE FIRST CONTINENTAL CONGRESS JOURNAL features the emblem of the Congress: a Liberty Column supported by hands and arms representing the states, and the Magna Carta at its base. Around the emblem in Latin is the inscription *HANC TUEMUR, HAC NITIMUR* (roughly translated as "This we defend, by this we are protected.").

parliamentary speech in January 1775. "[The American colonists], who prefer poverty with liberty to gilded chains and sordid affluence [will] die in defence of their rights as men," he continued. Pitt then urged the king and his ministers to act "with a dignity becoming your exalted situation, make the first advances to concord, to peace and happiness. . . . There is," Pitt concluded, "no time to be lost. . . . Nay, while I am now speaking," he stated, "the decisive blow may be struck." Two months later Burke echoed Pitt's sentiments by reminding British authorities that "an Englishman is the unfittest person on earth to argue another Englishman into slavery. . . . The question with me," he said, "is, not whether you have a right to render your people miserable, but whether it is not your interest to make them happy."

Their words fell on deaf ears. Hutchinson, now back in England, stated that Warren's Resolves were "undoubtedly treasonable" and "more alarming than anything that had yet been done." Lord Dartmouth, former secretary of state for the colonies, proclaimed Massachusetts as "plainly in a state of revolt or rebellion." King George III agreed. "Blows must decide whether they are to be subject to this country or independent," he wrote to his minister Lord North. In early February 1775, Parliament formally declared that Massachusetts was in a state of rebellion. With his Suffolk Resolves, Warren had created the spark to ignite a revolution.

It became further ignited with the delivery of the fifth annual Boston Massacre oration. This time there was no question as to who would be called upon to make the speech. It had to be Warren, a man now as esteemed by his fellow Patriots as he was detested by the British government. As the day of the oration approached, with British forces prominently stationed throughout Boston, tensions were extremely high. They became even higher on March 6, 1775, the day of the speech, when the hordes of citizens filing into Old South Church were greeted with the sight of some three hundred British officers and soldiers, there, according to some observers, to frighten Warren into silence.

They had chosen the wrong man to try to intimidate. Warren had prepared well for the event, not only in carefully crafting the speech he was about to deliver, but also in choosing his attire. He entered the hall dressed in a stark white free-flowing toga, the main garment of a freeborn Roman male, a garment as different in appearance from the stiff, tailored, bright red clothing of the British troops as could be imagined. It was an initial message that was not lost on a populace whose orators had so often reminded them of the virtues of ancient Rome.

According to some accounts, as soon as Warren approached the spot from which he was to speak, there were "a few hisses from some of the officers." One witness remembered that when one of the officers made a point of showing Warren his open palm, which contained several bullets, Warren silenced him by dropping a white handkerchief over the officer's hand.

Warren had heard reports that if his speech contained incendiary remarks concerning the events of March 5, 1770, his life would be in danger. From the beginning, his oration paid no heed to these threats. Speaking directly to the families of those slain in the "massacre," he explained in the style now familiar to those who so often had heard him speak, "Let me lead the tender mother to weep over her beloved son— come widowed mourner, here satiate thy grief; behold thy murdered husband gasping on the ground, and to complete the pompous show of wretchedness, bring in each hand thy infant children to bewail their father's fate."

As if this was not inflammatory enough, after stating that he never expected to see a British army in Boston after the massacre and declaring that Bostonians, knowing that "liberty is far dearer than life," would never be intimidated by this show of force, Warren went much further than even his greatest admirers in the audience believed he would dare go, surrounded by the huge British military presence.

> The interest and safety of Britain, as well as the colonies, require that the wise measures, recommended by the . . . continental congress, be steadily pursued. . . . But if these pacific measures are ineffectual, and it appears that the only way to safety is through fields of blood, I know you will not turn your faces from your foes, but will, undauntedly, press forward, until tyranny is trodden under foot.

Just as Warren finished his speech, the British 43rd Regiment appeared with their drums loudly beating outside the hall. At the same time, a number of the British officers and soldiers in the audience began derisively shouting "Fie, fie." Many in the crowd mistook the cries for "Fire, fire," and in the panic that followed, some, fearing that either the soldiers in the hall or those stationed outside were about to unload their weapons on them, jumped out the window. Others ran out into the street. Somehow, order was restored and no shots were fired. What easily could have been the beginning of the military aspect of the American Revolutionary War had been averted.

But not for long. Back in October 1774, the Massachusetts Provincial Congress had become the de facto government of Massachusetts, America's first autonomous ruling body. First with Hancock as its head, and then with Warren as its president, it had assumed all powers to rule the province, collected taxes, bought supplies, and raised a militia. By the first week of April 1775, the British government had had enough. Newspapers in England prominently printed the news that by the tenth of the month an army of more that thirteen thousand troops would arrive in Boston, commanded by three major generals.

On April 14, General Thomas Gage, the commander in chief of England's American forces, received a letter from the British authorities informing him that the home government considered Massachusetts to be in a state of rebellion and authorizing him to impose martial law. The main point of the letter was to inform Gage that a test should be made to determine if the colonials were really willing to fight a war. If there was to be a war, Gage was told, better that it be fought immediately rather than after the colonists had been given time to raise and equip a large army. It was the most critical time in Warren's life. Now fully recognized as the leader of the revolutionary movement, he knew that he had to take quick action. Concerned that Hancock and Samuel Adams—having returned from the Continental Congress—would be arrested, Warren persuaded them to move into the home of a patriotic clergyman in Lexington, some eleven miles from Boston. Extra stores of ammunition were transported to Lexington in case of a British attack on Boston. At the same time,

Warren set up a spy system, ordering a number of men, most notably Revere, to monitor British troop movements in and around the city.

Meantime, Warren's friends were deeply concerned about his own safety. Remarkably, throughout all of his political activities, writing, and speech giving, he had maintained his medical practice, even taking on students. When one of these students noticed a group of British soldiers standing watch over his mentor's house, he begged Warren not to visit his patients that evening. Warren put a pistol in each of his pockets, ignored the soldier's presence, and went off on his rounds.

IT WAS THE LAST TIME HE HAD THE LUXURY of tending his patients. On April 15, informed that ships preparing to carry British troops had appeared in the Charles River between Boston and Charlestown, Warren sent Revere off to Lexington to warn Adams and Hancock that it appeared that something imminent was about to happen. The next day some of the military stores were removed to Concord, some ten miles from Lexington.

Something indeed was about to happen. On April 18, Warren was informed by one of his spies that the British were about to march to Lexington, capture Adams and Hancock, and destroy the supplies stored there. By nine in the evening, when the British troops had formed, Warren had sent William Dawes off to Lexington to warn Adams and Hancock that the British were on their way. At ten in the evening Warren summoned Revere to his house and sent him too off to Lexington, instructing him also to warn the militia in the area of the advancing troops. As they rode toward Lexington, both Revere and Dawes accidentally met Samuel Prescott, who was returning home after spending an evening with his fiancée. Revere and Dawes asked Prescott to join them on their mission. It was a fortuitous recruitment. Once they warned Adams, Hancock, and the militia in Lexington, Revere and Dawes intended to ride on to Concord. But after leaving Lexington, they were stopped by British officers. Only Prescott got through to Concord, where he spread the alarm. By arousing the militia, Warren, counseled by Samuel Adams, had deliberately created the occasion for war, a war not declared by the Continental Congress or made in concert with other American colonies, but one that he felt was both inevitable and necessary.

The first British troops reached Lexington at dawn. As they approached the village green, they were shocked to find some seventy musket-bearing colonial militiamen lined up awaiting them. Immediately, the commanding officer ordered the colonials to thrown down their arms and disperse. The militiamen held on to their muskets but began to leave the green. It is not known who fired the shot that suddenly rang out, but it prompted a fusillade from the British troops. When the smoke cleared, eight colonials lay dead and ten were wounded.

Leaving the dead and injured behind, the British troops then marched on to Concord. After driving off a small group of militiamen, they searched for and found the remaining small store of supplies the

THE FIGHT AT LEXINGTON, APRIL 19, 1775.—FROM A PRINT OF THE TIME.

❖ A CA. 1776 PRINT of the Battle of Lexington.

colonists had stored there. They were ready to return to Boston. They were tired, they were hungry, and they knew that they had another twenty-one-mile march ahead of them, laden with heavy packs and muskets. What they did not know was that they were about to experience a nightmare.

All the way back to Boston, the British were forced to skirmish with companies totaling more than 3,500 militiamen who, after the warnings from Revere, Dawes, and Prescott and the events at Lexington and Concord, had assembled at strategic points along the road in less than twelve hours. Throughout their entire return march, the British were fired upon from houses and from behind trees and fences. Bloodied, exhausted, and humiliated, they finally reached Boston. What had been the first military engagement of what would become a war for independence had resulted in a British disaster.

As for Warren, as soon as dawn broke on the nineteenth, he left Boston and headed for Lexington. By ten in the morning, he had received news of the happenings on the green and rode as quickly as he could toward the town. Some five miles out he ran into the rear of a column of troops that had been sent out to reinforce the original British forces. He tried to pass around them but was stopped by bayonet-wielding soldiers.

Fortunately, neither they nor their officers recognized him, and after a long delay he was allowed to move on. His good fortune continued when, at a crossroads, he encountered William Heath, a Patriot with military experience. By this time, because of the delay, the events at Concord had taken place, the troops were on their way back to Boston, and colonial militiamen were scattered about the countryside. Immediately, Warren and Heath began to organize them and to place them in position along the British line of march. At Menotomy (now Arlington), Warren and Heath spurred the militiamen on to delivering the most intense gunfire the troops would encounter in their entire return trip. Warren was almost killed. As the British returned the colonials' fire, a musket ball came so close to striking his head that it knocked a pin out of the lock of hair that he wore near his ear.

The man who could not conceive of placing his countrymen in danger without sharing the risks had survived his brush with death, now knowing that he had more work to do than ever. Warren set about organizing and equipping a colonial military force, setting up a makeshift headquarters in Cambridge, and acting as both the president of the Provincial Congress and the head of the Committee of Safety that had been formed to maintain control of the local militias, among other things. On April 21, under his direction, the Committee of Safety voted to raise an army of eight thousand men. Warren wrote an appeal to every Massachusetts city and town:

> We conjure you . . . by all that is dear, by all that is sacred, that you give all assistance possible in forming an army. Our all is at stake, . . . Death and devastation are the certain consequences of delay, every moment is infinitely precious. An hour lost may deluge your country in blood, and entail perpetual slavery upon the few of your posterity, who may survive the carnage. We beg and entreat, as you will answer it to your country, to your consciences, and above all as you will answer to God himself, that you will hasten and encourage by all possible means, the enlistment of men to form the army.

It was an appeal answered not only in the recruitment of men, but in the acquisition of supplies as well. From throughout the colonies, food, gunpowder, and other supplies poured into Massachusetts. Virginia alone sent 8,600 bushels of wheat and corn. George Washington donated what today would amount to more than $10,000 to the cause.

On June 14, 1775, the Provincial Congress named Warren to serve as a major general in the army he was raising. According to the records of the Congress, "he was proposed as a physician-general; but, preferring a more active and hazardous employment, he accepted a major-general's commission." Just three days later Warren would become much more than a military commander in name only.

Immediately after the events at Lexington and Concord, New England militiamen had taken up positions in the hills surrounding

Major General Warren

❖ WARREN WAS NAMED major
general in June 1775.

Boston in an attempt to prevent the British troops garrisoned there from carrying out further raids on Massachusetts's communities. Cooped up within the city, Gage had asked for and received reinforcements from England, including generals John Burgoyne, Henry Clinton, and William Howe. Once they arrived, they decided that their first course of action would be to drive the colonial militia out of the hills. The British leaders' plan had been barely formulated when their intentions were discovered by spies from the network that Warren had originally established. Immediately, colonial militia dug themselves in on Breed's Hill on the Charlestown peninsula north of Boston.

At about nine o'clock on the morning of June 17, some 2,200 British troops were ferried across the Charles River and took up positions at the bottom of Breed's Hill. Hearing that the British had chosen to confront the militiamen on the hill, Warren rode to the site and presented himself as ready for duty. There he was met by General Israel Putnam, who offered Warren command of the militia forces. According to eyewitness Daniel Putnam, Warren replied, "I am here only as a volunteer. I know nothing of your dispositions; nor will I interfere with them. Tell me where I can be most useful." Putnam then pointed to a redoubt. Warren countered, "Don't think I come to seek a place of safety, but tell me where the onset will be most furious."

In the early afternoon, the British made their first assault on the militiamen entrenched at the top of the hill. Advancing in rigid European-style military formation, they paused only to fire at the colonials who were too far away to be hit. The militiamen, on the other hand, waited until the British were less than thirty yards away from them. Scores of soldiers were killed in the volleys of gunfire that followed. Most of the soldiers who made this first attack were members of the light infantry, the best troops in the British army. Later, their commander, General Howe, when asked to describe how he felt after being forced to retreat, replied by stating that he had "experienced a moment that I never felt before."

❖ A NINETEENTH-CENTURY PRINT depicts Joseph Warren (right) before the Battle of Bunker Hill, presenting himself for duty—"where the onset will be most furious"—to General Israel Putnam.

Once back at the bottom of the hill, the British regrouped and once again marched up the hill. Again they were beaten back; again they suffered devastating losses; again they were forced to retreat. But their commanders were determined that a victory be achieved. For the third time they marched up the hill, where their attack centered on the area in which Warren was situated. By this time the militiamen had only about 150 men left and their ammunition was all but gone. Still they fought on, using guns as clubs and throwing stones at their enemy. Finally, they were forced to retreat. Warren was among the last to leave the redoubt, and a short way down the back of the hill, he was struck in the head by a bullet and instantly killed.

THE COLONIALS HAD BEEN DRIVEN FROM BREED'S HILL. On paper it was a British victory. In reality, it was anything but that. The toll on the British forces was horrific—226 dead and more than 800 wounded out of the some 2,500 who taken part in a battle that would turn out to be one of the costliest encounters of the entire Revolutionary War. "It was a dear-bought victory," British general Henry Clinton later wrote; "another such would have ruined us." And the British had learned an important lesson. Speaking of the courage and discipline the militiamen had demonstrated throughout the bloody confrontation, Gage told Lord Dartmouth in his report that "the trials we have had show the rebels are not the despicable rabble too many thought them to be."

The Americans had suffered less than a third of the number of British casualties. But, at the most critical time in their march toward independence, they had lost their leader. Their anguish was intensified when, on June 23, a statement by British captain Walter Sloan Laurie, the officer in charge of the burial details after the Breed's Hill battle, was made public. "Doctor Warren, president of the Provincial Congress . . . I found among the slain; and stuffed the scoundrel with another rebel into one hole and there he and his seditious principles may remain."

It would be some ten months before the British were driven out of Boston and a search for Warren's body could be conducted, so that he could be given the dignified interment he deserved. In April 1776, two of Warren's brothers, aided by a group of friends, were able to scour Breed's Hill and find and exhume Warren's corpse. In what may well have been the first example of forensic dentistry in America, positive identification of the body was made by Paul Revere, who had created Warren's false teeth. Warren was first officially buried in Boston's Granary Burying Ground. In 1825 his remains were moved to a crypt at St. Paul's Cathedral before being reinterred in 1855 to the Warren family vault in Forest Hills Cemetery in Roxbury, his birthplace.

Warren's death occasioned an outpouring of tributes. In a letter to her husband, Abigail Adams stated that none of the actions of the British army distressed her as much as did Warren's death. "We mourn," she wrote, "for the citizen, the senator, the physician, and the warrior." John Adams, in a letter to Warren's brother James, stated, "Our dear Warren has fallen with laurels on his brow as ever graced an hero." One of the greatest tributes of all came from one of Warren's staunchest foes. After crediting Warren with extraordinary courage, Thomas Hutchinson stated that "if [Warren] had lived, he bid as fair as any man to advance himself to the summit of political as well as military affairs and to become the Cromwell of North America."

The acknowledgments of Warren's character and contributions continued in the early histories of the new nation that his actions had made possible. William Gordon, author of *History of the Rise, Progress, and Establishment of Independence of the United States of America* (1788), said of Warren, "Neither resentment . . . nor interested views, but a regard to the liberties of his country, induced him to oppose the measures of the Government. He stepped forward into public view, not that he might be noted and admired for a patriotic spirit, but because he *was* a patriot." *Eliot's Biographical Dictionary* (1809) stated simply, "As he lived an ornament to his country, his death reflected a luster upon himself, and the cause he so warmly espoused."

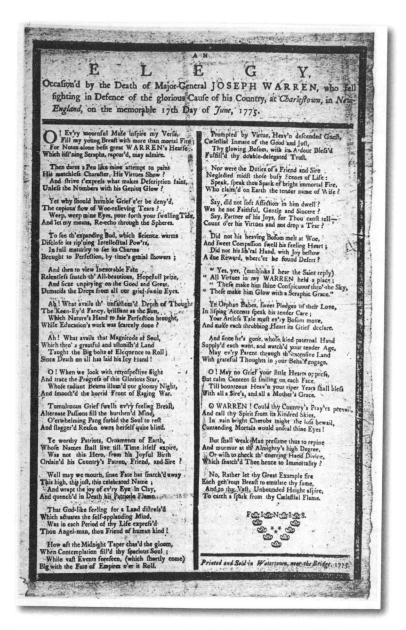

❖ THIS COMMEMORATIVE BROADSIDE was printed and sold in Watertown, Massachusetts, soon after Joseph Warren's death at the Battle of Bunker Hill. The text at the top reads "An elegy, occasion'd by the death of Major-General Joseph Warren, who fell fighting in defence of the glorious cause of his country, at Charlestown, in New England, on the memorable 17th day of June, 1775."

Why, then, did this man of such extraordinary accomplishments, a man recognized by his contemporaries on both sides of the Atlantic as so essential to the gaining of American independence, a man who gave his life to the cause in which he so fervently believed, fall into relative obscurity? Why does he remain so unrecognized today? The answer lies in the opening words of Hutchinson's assessment of his spirited foe: "If [Warren] had lived." Warren's role ended before the Declaration of Independence was written, before the United States Constitution was framed, and before a new, free nation was created. It is these events and those associated with them—Thomas Jefferson, John Adams, Benjamin Franklin—that have most captured the attention of those interested in the Revolutionary era. Yet it was Warren who made all these events and the achievements of these men possible. It was Warren who, in the words of historian William Tudor, written almost two hundred years ago, was regarded as "the personal representative of those brave citizens, who, with arms hastily collected, sprang from their peaceable homes to resist aggression, and, on the plains of Lexington and heights of Charlestown, cemented with their blood the foundation of American liberty." The full recognition that is owed Joseph Warren is long overdue.

FIVE

OUTDOING REVERE

History's Forgotten Riders (1777)

As Pulitzer Prize–winning author Virginius Dabney wrote, "If you mean to be a historical figure, it is a good idea to get in touch with a leading literary figure—a Longfellow, a Homer, or a Vergil." As Dabney points out, Paul Revere, Odysseus, and Aeneas "all took this precaution."

Dabney was right. As schoolchildren, we all learned of Paul Revere's ride through Henry Wadsworth Longfellow's famous poem "Paul Revere's Ride," first published in 1861. What we didn't learn was that Revere was not the only Patriot to embark upon a midnight ride to raise the alarm of an imminent British attack. What our history books didn't tell us was that there was not one, but two other of these rides, each more arduous and more dangerous than Revere's gallop. And what has also been lost to history is that each of those extraordinary endeavors had a greater impact on the American Revolution than the Boston silversmith's "immortal" achievement.

The first of these forgotten rides took place in the Long Island Sound region, an area where, from the outbreak of the war, towns in both Connecticut and New York lived in constant fear of an attack by British

❖ PAUL REVERE'S MIDNIGHT GALLOP, shown here in a ca. 1904 print, has long been regarded as the most vital alarm-spreading ride of the American Revolution. But lost to history has been the fact that two other riders undertook journeys that were longer, more dangerous, and far more important to the Patriot cause.

troops. However, it was not until April 1777 that the long-dreaded attack took place. The site of the assault was Danbury, Connecticut, a town that had become vital to the Patriot cause because of its use as a primary supply depot by the Continental Army. By the spring of 1777, a vast array of provisions was daily being brought into the town. Included in these supplies were clothing, medicine, ammunition, cooking utensils, tents, hospital cots, and foodstuff, including flour, beef, pork, sugar, molasses, coffee, rice, wine, and rum.

Alerted by his spies of the growing importance of Danbury to the colonial rebellion, General William Howe, commander-in-chief of the British Army in America, ordered Major General William Tryon, who also served as New York's royal governor, to attack Danbury and destroy the supplies located there. On April 24, 1777, twenty transport ships and six war vessels carrying some two thousand troops left New York Harbor and headed for Connecticut's Compo Beach. Arriving there the next day, the troops disembarked and, in what was to be the largest military engagement in Connecticut during the entire Revolutionary War, began the long march to Danbury.

James R. Case related how the British conducted their twenty-five-mile march to the unsuspecting and thinly guarded town as if on parade. Describing one of the soldiers, Case wrote: "Upon his head a metallic cap sword-proof, surmounted by a cone, from which a long, chestnut-colored plume fell to his shoulders. Upon the front of the cap was a death's head, under which was described the words: 'Or Glory.' A red coat faced with white, an epaulette on each shoulder, buckskin breeches of a bright yellow, black knee boots and spurs completing the costume. A long sword swung at his side, and a carbine was carried, muzzle down, in a socket at his stirrup. These were models of discipline and military splendor, and mounted on handsome chargers, sixteen hands high."

Arriving in Danbury shortly before three in the afternoon, the British found themselves engaged in a number of isolated incidents. In one, a mounted British soldier chased a taunting colonial horseman through the streets but failed to capture him after the townsman unrolled a bolt of cloth he was carrying and frightened the soldier's horse. In a much

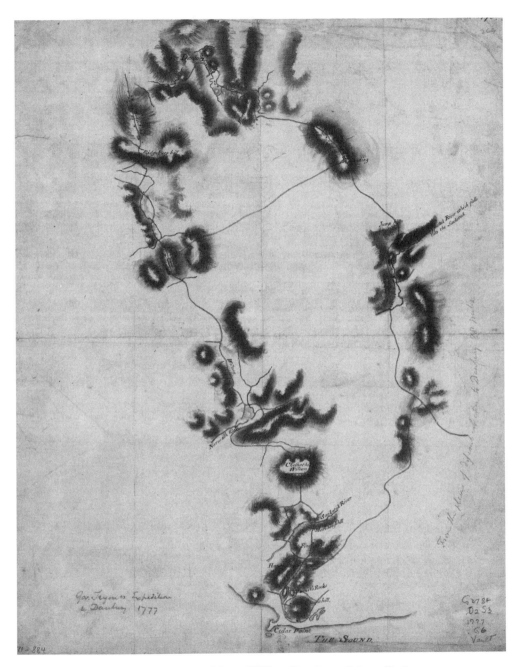

❖ THIS CA. 1777 MAP of the route of General William Tryon's expedition to Danbury was prepared by Captain John Montresor, a British military engineer.

more serious incident, four young Danbury men fired into a column of soldiers from the window of the home of one of the town's leading citizens. Troops then rushed into the house and burned it to the ground, trapping the four young men, who burned to death.

Determined to discourage any further resistance, the invaders then dragged out the cannon they had brought with them from New York. "As the British troops reached a point near the present location of the court-house," James Montgomery Bailey wrote, "their artillery was discharged and the heavy balls, six and twelve-pounders, flew screaming up the street, carrying terror to the hearts of the women and children and dismay to the heads of the homes thus endangered."

Tryon's troops then began a systematic house-by-house, building-by-building search for colonial supplies. Those provisions that were found in the homes of supporters of the king were dragged into the street to be burned. The houses of these loyalists, who convinced Tryon that they had been forced to store the supplies, were, however, spared. On the other hand, the homes owned by revolutionaries that were being used as storehouses were, along with their contents, burned to the ground.

The amount of supplies that were discovered and destroyed was enormous, its magnitude best seen in the official report of the raid sent by Howe to the British government back in England. "In the destruction of the stores at Danbury the village was unavoidably burnt," Howe reported.

The list of the material destroyed was as follows: A quantity of ordnance stores, with iron etc; 4000 barrels of beef and pork; 100 large tierces [containers] of biscuits; 89 barrels of rice; 120 puncheons of rum; several large stores of wheat, oats, and Indian corn, in bulk, the quantity hereof could not possibly be ascertained; 30 pipes of wine; 100 hogsheads of sugar; 50 ditto of molasses; 20 cases of coffee; 15 large casks filled with medicines of all kinds; 100 barrels of saltpeter; 1020 tents and marquees; a number of iron boilers; a large quantity of hospital bedding; engineers', pioneers' and carpenters' tools; a printing press complete; tar, tallow, etc; 5000 pairs shoes and stockings.

The destruction of so large a cache of supplies was a serious setback to the Continental Army, particularly the loss of the more than one thousand highly valued tents. Perhaps most interesting in the tally of the destruction was the listing of "120 puncheons of rum." If that was true, then there must have been more puncheons (a large cask containing between 72 and 120 gallons of liquor) than the British destroyed, for by nightfall, with Tyron having become emboldened by his easy success and lack of real opposition in Danbury, and harboring thoughts of moving beyond the town and carrying out destructive raids in other communities in both Connecticut and New York, he was confronted with a serious problem in his own ranks. The general discovered that with so much rum lying before them, hundreds of his men had become drunk and were becoming even more so with every passing hour. As James Case wrote, "The drunken men went up and down Main Street in squads, singing army songs, shouting coarse speeches, hugging each other, swearing, yelling, and otherwise conducting themselves as becomes an invader when he is very, very, drunk."

With so many of his men inebriated, Tryon abandoned any thoughts of carrying out further raids. He also began receiving reports from loyalist spies that, with the fires in Danbury burning so brightly, news of the raid was surely spreading and the local militia was bound to react. It became clear to Tryon that he had to get his troops, no matter how many of them were drunk, back to the ships at Compo as quickly as possible. As he was making this decision, a rider, bearing the news of what had happened at Danbury, galloped up to the home of Colonel Henry Ludington and his family in Fredericksburg, New York, less than twenty-five miles from the burning town.

LUDINGTON, ONE OF THE MOST RESPECTED men in his entire colony, had served his community and his country with distinction since 1756, when, at the age of seventeen, he had enlisted in the 2nd Regiment of Connecticut, troops in service to the king. He immediately fought in the French and Indian War, and took part in the Battle of Lake George, where he looked on in horror as both his uncle and cousin, who were fighting by his side, were slain. In 1759 he was assigned to escort a company of wounded soldiers from Canada to Boston, a march that was made in the dead of winter. He was forced, during the nights, to dig shelter in snowdrifts to keep from freezing. When his food ran out, he subsisted on bark, twigs, and berries. Still, he survived and returned home a hero.

In 1760, Ludington and his new bride, Abigail, moved to what soon became the Fredericksburg precinct of Dutchess County, New York (today the hamlet of Ludingtonville in Putnam County), where he not only carved a successful farm out of what had been wilderness but also quickly attained a position of influence and authority in the community. In 1761, Ludington was appointed subsheriff of the county, a position that required him to swear an oath to remain faithful to the king and "him to defend to the utmost of my power against all traitorous conspiracies and attempts whatsoever, which shall be made against his person, crown, and dignity."

In 1773, the captain-general and governor of the Royal Province of New York, none other than William Tryon, appointed Ludington captain of the Fifth Company of the Fredericksburg Regiment of Militia in Dutchess County. But shortly afterward, in a dramatic reversal, Ludington announced that he had decided that the king did not deserve his or any other colonist's loyalty and resigned his royal commission. Soon, both the Patriot's Provincial Congress of the Colony of New York and the Convention of the Representatives of the State of New York commissioned Ludington as colonel of the 7th Regiment of the Dutchess County militia and decreed that it should be officially known as Colonel Ludington's regiment.

The area of command to which Ludington had been assigned was a particularly difficult one, inhabited by a large number of Royalists and Tories, intent on providing whatever aid to the British troops they could. Dutchess County was also the operating grounds of bands of guerrillas known as "cowboys" and irregular British cavalry known as "skinners"

❧ THE SUCCESSFUL GUERRILLA-LIKE TACTICS employed by Colonel Henry Ludington's men and other Patriots at the Battle of Ridgefield, and later at other engagements such as the Battle of Saratoga (shown here in a 1975 painting by Hugh Charles McBarron Jr.), were vital to the winning of the War of Independence.

who supplied General Howe's forces with much of their cattle and grain by staging raids on colonial farms throughout the region. Within a short period of time, Ludington's regiment became so successful in curbing the activities of the cowboys and skinners that the British placed a price of three hundred guineas "dead or alive" on his head.

Now, on the night of April 26, 1777, Ludington was hastening to his door, anxious to discover who was pounding upon it so loudly. As soon as he opened it and heard the news of what had happened at Danbury from the exhausted messenger, he knew what had to be done. His regiment had to be assembled immediately and had to march to Danbury to confront Tryon and his troops before they could inflict more damage on the colonial cause. There was, however, a serious problem. Ludington's men had just gone home after a long period of duty. It was planting time in New England and New York, and Ludington had allowed them to get back to their farms in order to get their crops in on time. Now they had to be reassembled—and as quickly as possible.

The militiamen were scattered on their separate farms in what may well have been more than a one-hundred-square-mile area. Who was available to ride out and tell them that they had to return immediately? Certainly not the rider who had brought the news from Danbury. He was too tired to go any farther. Besides, he had no idea where the various militiamen lived or how best to get there. And Colonel Ludington could not go. He needed to begin making preparations for the march and had to be there as the members of his regiment returned.

Ludington realized, however, that there was one person who had perhaps the best chance of carrying out the vital mission. It was Sybil, the oldest of his twelve children—but still only just turned sixteen. But she was a marvel on horseback and knew the region extremely well. And she had taken on great responsibility by helping her mother care for her eleven brothers and sisters. Most important, for one so young she had already demonstrated genuine courage and ingenuity.

Knowing that there was a price on her father's head, Sybil had assumed a leading role in protecting him. As Louis Patrick wrote, "The Colonel's most vigilant and watchful companion was his sentinel daughter, Sibell [sic]. Her constant care and thoughtfulness, combined with fortuitous circumstances, prevented the fruition of many an intrigue against his life and capture." In his article, Patrick then described what had taken place when a group of reward seekers under the leadership of notorious Tory Ichabod Prosser surrounded the Ludington house and prepared to attack, only to be outsmarted by Sybil and her sister Rebecca. "These fearless girls, with guns in hand," Patrick wrote,

> were acting as sentinels, pacing the piazza to and fro in true military style and grit to guard their father against surprise and to give him

warning of any approaching danger. They discovered Prosser and his men and gave the alarm. In a flash, candles were lighted in every room of the house and the few occupants marched out and counter-marched before the windows and from this simple and clever ruse, Prosser was led to believe that the house was strongly guarded and did not dare to make an attack. He kept his men crouched behind the trees and fences until daybreak, when with yells they resumed their march toward New York City, ignorant of how they had been foiled by clever girls.

When the messenger arrived and began relaying the news from Danbury to Colonel Ludington, Sybil was busy putting the younger children to bed. Hearing the commotion downstairs, she joined her father and listened to the end of the man's report. As soon as he finished speaking and was given a place to rest, the Colonel turned to his daughter and told her that he had something terribly important to ask her. He had to go no further. Sybil knew what had to be done and knew that she was the one that had to do it.

Within minutes she was ready to go, fully aware of the difficulties, even the dangers, that lay ahead. It was a stormy night, and the heavy spring rain gave no indication of letting up. The narrow roads upon which she was about to ride were not really roads at all, but mere dirt tracks. They would be totally muddy, and washouts would be a constant danger. And even before her father reminded her, she was all too aware of the danger of being overtaken and captured by "cowboys" or "skinners" who might well be operating along the route she was about to take.

But she did not hesitate. At nine in the evening, dressed in a pair of her father's work pants, she mounted her horse Star. In her hand was a stick that she would use to prod Star on and to knock upon the militiamen's doors. Then, with the glow from the fires of a burning Danbury visible in the night sky, she was off from Fredericksburg to Carmel Village, into Mahopac and Mahopac Falls through Kent Cliffs, Farmers Mills, and Stormville, more than forty miles in all. Ignoring the driving rain and oblivious to the muddy rutted terrain beneath her, she charged on, banging on doors, crying out in a voice steadily growing hoarse, "The British are burning Danbury! Muster at once at Ludington's."

In some of the towns, a church bell was rung to warn the citizens that the British might well be on the way. In one of the communities, a man, astounded to see a young girl spreading the alarm and mustering the militia, offered to accompany her the rest of the way. Politely declining his offer, Sybil instead sent him off to the town of Brewster, which was not on her route, to warn the people there.

In his biography of Ludington, historian Willis Fletcher Johnson gave an early assessment of Sybil's accomplishment:

> One who even now rides from Carmel to Cold Spring will find rugged and dangerous roads, with lonely stretches. Imagination can only picture what it was a century and a quarter ago, on a dark night, with reckless bands of "Cowboys" and "Skinners" abroad in the land. But the child performed her task, clinging to a man's saddle, and guiding her steed with only a hempen halter, as she rode through the night, bearing the news of the sack of Danbury. There is no extravagance in comparing her ride with that of Paul Revere and its midnight message. Nor was her errand less efficient than his. By daybreak, thanks to her daring, nearly the whole regiment [of some four hundred men] was mustered before her father's house at Fredericksburgh, and an hour or two later was on the march for vengeance on the raiders.

They were not the only ones now on the march to keep Tryon from attacking other towns. Sybil's alarm had spread beyond Dutchess County. And colonial spies operating in the area had also spread the news about what had taken place at Danbury. In New Haven, Continental Army generals David Wooster and Benedict Arnold, along with a small group of Continental soldiers, began making their way toward Danbury. At the same time, General Gold Selleck Silliman, commander of the Fairfield County militia, was hastily calling his men to arms.

By two o'clock in the morning on Sunday, April 27, Wooster, Arnold, and Silliman had formed a plan. Aware that Tryon and his troops were following a route toward their ships at Compo Beach that would take them through Ridgefield, it was decided that Arnold and Silliman, with their combined forces of about four hundred men, would proceed to that town and prepare to attack the sure-to-be-weary British soldiers once they arrived. At the same time, Wooster, with his two hundred men and aware that Ludington and his regiment were soon to join them, was to catch up with the advancing British column and strike it from the rear.

Wooster's regiment was made up of men who knew the area between Danbury and Ridgefield well, and it did not take long for them to position themselves at a spot in the woods overlooking the trail they were certain the British would follow. Their instincts were perfect, and when the British arrived, Wooster's soldiers attacked Tryon's unsuspecting rear regiment and captured forty men. Later that morning, sensing the opportunity for an even bigger victory, Wooster ordered another attack. This time, however, the British were ready for them. Halting their march, they countered the American assault with artillery fire. According to historian Albert Van Dusen, as soon as the artillery fire began, Wooster turned in his saddle and cried out, "Come on my boys! Never mind such random shots." The words were hardly out of his mouth when a British musket ball struck the general in the back, killing him.

In the meantime, the British pushed on and reached the outskirts of Ridgefield, where Benedict Arnold and his men, although outnumbered four to one, were waiting for them. Less than three years later, Arnold's name would become a byword for treason in the United States, but at Ridgefield, as he had done earlier at the capture of Fort Ticonderoga and the Battle of Valcour Island, and as he would later do at the Battle of Saratoga, he was about to perform with extraordinary bravery in the Patriot cause.

Arnold had had his men erect a roadblock on the approach to Ridgefield, and as soon as Tryon and his troops reached it, the colonials greeted them with a barrage of musket fire. The British troops' superior numbers, however, soon enabled them to outflank the Americans. Arnold was the last of his troops to retreat, but as he did so, he was spotted by a British platoon who fired shot after shot at him, peppering his horse with bullets. As he tried to get his feet out of the stirrups, a bayonet-wielding soldier rushed at him, shouting, "Surrender! You are my prisoner!" Arnold, according to Van Dusen, calmly replied, "Not yet!" and shot the redcoat dead.

Then, after making his escape to a nearby swamp, Arnold returned to the outskirts of Ridgefield that night and rounded up his militia—who by this time had been joined by citizen-soldiers from other counties, including Ludington's regiment. The next day they forced the British to retreat back to their ship. Every step of the way to Compo, the British were set upon from all sides. Had it not been for a heavily armed, highly trained company of marines stationed aboard the English vessels who covered the last leg of the British retreat, Tryon's mission might well have ended in total disaster.

Tryon actually had accomplished what he had set out to do. The stores at Danbury had been destroyed—but at a cost of more than two hundred of Tryon's men, a loss that had come very close to being

❖ SYBIL RIDES STAR in the sculpture in Carmel, New York, by Anna Hyatt Huntington.

far worse. It was an experience that discouraged the British from any further attacks in the area. As a result, the American militia in the vital region gained precious time to organize and resist, in large part due to the efforts of sixteen-year-old Sybil Ludington, who was officially commended by General George Washington for her heroic ride. In 1961, American sculptor Anna Hyatt Huntington created a dramatic statue of Sybil riding Star and spreading the alarm. Versions of the statue were erected in Danbury, along Sybil's route near Carmel, and at the Daughters of the American Revolution headquarters in Washington, D.C. In perhaps the ultimate tribute, the name of her hometown was to be changed from Fredericksburg to Ludingtonville. Paul Revere traveled about twenty miles during his historic ride. Sybil Ludington made a much longer journey for the Patriot cause, and she did it over much more difficult terrain that did the Boston artisan and messenger. And, unlike Revere, Sybil Ludington completed her mission without being captured. Yet she remains largely unknown. As Virginius Dabney wrote, "Henry Wordsworth Longfellow, God rest his bones, put Revere on the map. Unfortunately for Sybil, no one with the talent or reputation of a Longfellow did that for her."

AND SHE IS NOT ALONE. There was another Patriot who had no Longfellow to immortalize him. Yet he made the longest, most hazardous ride of all, one that had even more important consequences than those of either Ludington or Revere. His story begins in the spring of 1781, a time when the fortunes of the rebelling American colonists, particularly those in Virginia, were far from promising. In that pivotal colony, the full force of the war was being felt as the traitorous Benedict Arnold, now a general on the British side, continued to raid and pillage colonial settlements all along the James River, from its mouth to Richmond. By May, Arnold's troops and those of Major General William Phillips had linked up with a much larger force led by British commander Charles Cornwallis that had moved into Virginia from the south.

In the face of these advancing troops, Governor Thomas Jefferson and the Virginia legislature had been forced to flee from the colonial capital in Williamsburg to Richmond. Then, on June 1, General Cornwallis learned from a captured dispatch that Jefferson and his fellow Patriots had fled again, this time to Charlottesville, the site of Jefferson's home at Monticello. It was, Cornwallis believed, a golden opportunity, a chance to deal the Americans what could be a near-fatal blow by capturing, in one fell swoop, a group of some of the most influential of all the rebellious colonial leaders. Included were Jefferson, author of the "seditious" Declaration of Independence; Patrick Henry, whose "Give me liberty, or give me death" motto had become the rallying cry of the Revolution; and Richard Henry Lee, whose resolutions presented to the Continental Congress had led to the adoption of the Declaration of Independence. Included also were Thomas Nelson Jr., who had been one of the first to cry out for armed resistance to Great Britain and had spent almost his entire fortune equipping soldiers for the Continental Army, and Benjamin Harrison, a signer of the Declaration of Independence and ancestor of two future presidents.

Cornwallis was aware that Washington and his Virginia troops were fully occupied in the northern area of the colony and that General Marquis de Lafayette, who had been so successful in harassing British troops, was too far away to provide protection for the legislators. On June 1, 1781, Cornwallis ordered one of his favorite officers, his "hunting leopard" Lieutenant Colonel Banastre Tarleton, to carry out a surprise attack on Charlottesville and to seize Thomas Jefferson and his fellow politicians. It was a plan that called for Tarleton, accompanied by 180 cavalrymen and 70 mounted infantrymen of the Royal Welsh Fusiliers, to march from Cornwallis's camp on the North Anna River to Charlottesville as quickly and as secretly as possible. By nine o'clock the night of June 3, Tarleton's troops had reached the Cuckoo Tavern in Louisa County, some forty miles from Charlottesville. Despite the size of the force, no one had detected its movements. And it is here that a twenty-seven-year-old, six-foot four-inch, 222-pound giant of a young man enters the story. His name was Jack Jouett Jr., and he

❖ This is the only known portrait from the life of Jack Jouett, a silhouette made by his son, Matthew Harris Jouett.

was a captain in the 6th Regiment of the Virginia militia. One of ten children, his family was extremely active in the Revolutionary cause. Both his father and he had boldly signed the Albemarle Declaration, a document that renounced King George III. Jack Jouett Sr. served as a "commissary," supplying the Continental Army with beef from his Louisa County farm. Jack Jr.'s older brother Matthew had been killed at the Battle of Brandywine. Two of his younger brothers were also Virginia militiamen.

When Tarleton and his 250 troops reached the Cuckoo Tavern, Captain Jack Jouett was there. Some accounts claim that he was asleep on the lawn and was awakened by the clattering of so many hoofs. Other reports state that upon spotting the British troops, he hid himself in nearby bushes so that he could discover what they were after. One newspaper of the day reported that he was inside the tavern showing himself off in a uniform he had taken from a British dragoon he had recently captured. Whatever the case, Jouett was definitely there. And, from conversations between the British officers and soldiers that he overheard, it became clear to him what their mission was.

The more he heard, the more he became alarmed. These troops meant to capture the government of Virginia, men upon whom the Revolution depended. Aware that the only colonial troops in the region were too far away to be of assistance, he realized that the only hope for Jefferson and his legislators was warning and escape. And he had an even more sobering personal revelation. Who but he was there to provide the warning? He and he alone had to save the General Assembly.

But how? He had read accounts of Paul Revere's ride. But Revere had ridden twenty miles at the most and over good roads. Warning Jefferson and his legislature required at least a forty-mile horseback ride in the dark over extremely rough terrain. It was a journey bound to be made even more difficult by the constant presence of British scouts all along the only barely passable road to Charlottesville. Jouett would have to make the entire long journey through the dense Virginia backwoods.

Yet he knew that it had to be done immediately. He had heard that some of the lawmakers were staying with Jefferson at Monticello, while the others had found quarters in the Swan Tavern two miles from Monticello in Charlottesville itself. He would have to go first to Monticello and then to Charlottesville in order to reach all those he needed to warn.

The clock was striking 10:00 p.m. when Jouett mounted his bay mare Sallie—a horse thought by many to be the fastest in the entire region—and took off on his improbable mission. The route he chose to follow was nothing more than an old Indian trail, grown over with thick brush and dense woods. As Virginius Dabney wrote,

> The unfrequented pathway over which this horseman set out on his all-night journey can only be imagined. His progress was greatly impeded by matted undergrowth, tangled bush, overhanging vines and gullies . . . his face was cruelly lashed by tree limbs as he rode forward and scars said to have remained the rest of his life were the result of lacerations sustained from those low hanging branches.

Still he kept on riding, always aware of the absolute necessity of beating the British to Monticello. At four in the morning, after having been in the saddle for six straight hours, he reached the village of Milton at the Rivanna River ford.

Jouett spurred Sallie on up the long, steep terrain between Milton and Monticello. Arriving at the mansion, he unceremoniously burst through the doors, awakened the governor of Virginia and future president of the United States, and the other members of the two houses of the General Assembly who were staying there. Once he heard what Jouett had to say, the ever-gracious Jefferson thanked the brave messenger profusely and then insisted on sharing a glass of his best Madeira with him. The young officer downed his drink quickly, telling Jefferson he had to get to Charlottesville immediately to warn the other members of the Assembly. Then he took off on the two-mile ride to the Swan Tavern.

Amazingly, neither Jefferson nor his houseguests were panic-stricken by Jouett's warning. Perhaps they didn't really believe that the British were on their way. In any event, as Jefferson later wrote, they all breakfasted at leisure before the assemblymen left for Swan Tavern to join their colleagues. In the meantime, Jefferson made arrangements to send his wife and children to a friend's estate some fourteen miles away. He then spent the better part of the next two hours gathering up his important papers and hiding them in secret places throughout the house.

If Tarleton had stuck to his determination to reach Monticello and Charlottesville without any delay, Jefferson's dallying could have been disastrous. But fortunately for the Patriot cause, the British officer, increasingly confident that he would catch the governor and the legislators unawares, deviated from his plan. First, about an hour after pausing at the Cuckoo Tavern, Tarleton halted his troops near a Louisa County courthouse, where he ordered a three-hour rest. Shortly after the march toward Charlottesville was resumed, the troops suddenly encountered and captured a train of eleven wagons loaded with guns, ammunitions, and clothing for General Nathaniel Greene's Continental Army troops in South Carolina. Now concerned with the fleeting time, Tarleton ordered that the wagon train and its valuable possessions be burned rather than hauled along with the troops. In the process, however, still more time was lost.

The result of the delays was that Tarleton and his troops reached the Swan Tavern just as the legislators were making their escape. The British were, in fact, so close on the trail of the legislators that even though Thomas Jefferson, Patrick Henry, Richard Henry Lee, Benjamin Harrison, Thomas Nelson Jr., and many others got away, seven Patriots were captured, among them a young Daniel Boone.

And it was here that Jack Jouett performed yet another act of heroism and ingenuity. One of the legislators attempting to make his escape was Brigadier General Edward Stevens, who was recovering from a wound he had received at the Battle of Guilford Courthouse on March 15 of that year. Stevens was plainly dressed and was riding a shabby horse. Jouett, who, according to historian Henry S. Randall, Jefferson's mid-nineteenth-century biographer, "had an eccentric custom of wearing such habiliments," was dressed in a fancy coat with a plumed military hat. Guessing correctly that the British would believe that the better-dressed man was the more important figure to be pursued, Jouett galloped off ahead of the British troops, leading them away from Stevens, who was then able to make his escape.

Frustrated by the escape of the legislators and aware that Jefferson had not been at the Swan Tavern, Tarleton ordered his chief officer, Captain McLeod, to leave immediately for Monticello in pursuit of the governor. One story, recounted by Randall, has it that when McLeod came into view on the approach to Monticello, Martin, one of Jefferson's slaves, was busily engaged in passing silver and other valuable articles to another slave named Caesar through a trap door in the floor. According to the story, when the British were first spotted, Martin quickly dropped the door, leaving Caesar in the cramped and dark place until the troops left some eighteen hours later.

In the meantime, Martin was not the only one to spot the British as they approached Monticello. Captain Christopher Hudson, en route to join Lafayette's forces, had also seen them and had immediately hastened to the mansion to warn Jefferson. Hearing the news, Jefferson finally left.

Jefferson sent his family off in their carriage and then departed himself. He was not convinced that British troops were on their way to take him prisoner, and after proceeding only a short distance he stopped and dismounted his horse. Jefferson trained his telescope on his home and saw no troops, but suddenly realized that, in leaving Monticello, he had dropped his "walking sword." As he headed back to retrieve it, he took another look through his telescope and was startled to see that British dragoons and mounted infantrymen had suddenly surrounded his house. Immediately, he mounted his horse and raced off into the woods.

Jefferson not only escaped, but also was able to make such good time through the woods that he was able to dine with his family that evening. However, he did not escape unscathed from Tarleton's raid. Political opponents inside and outside Virginia accused him of having behaved cowardly by fleeing and abandoning his post as Virginia's governor. For many years, his enemies continued to pursue these accusations, bolstered by statements from Tarleton, who reported that Jefferson "provided for his personal safety with a precipitate retreat."

Determined to clear his name, Jefferson appeared before the Virginia General Assembly in December 1781, stating that, as many of the legislators knew, at the time of his flight he believed that his term as governor had expired. Although legislators readily accepted Jefferson's explanation, his political opponents, particularly those in the Federalist Party, would for the rest of his life continue to charge him with incompetence, negligence, and even cowardice during the events of June 1781.

As for Jouett, his actions did not go unnoticed or unrewarded. On June 15, 1781, almost immediately after reconvening in Staunton, thirty-five miles west of Charlottesville, the Virginia General Assembly adopted a resolution that stated:

Resolved, That the Executive be desired to present to Captain John Jouett, an elegant sword and pair of pistols, as a memorial to the high sense which the General Assembly entertain of his activity and enterprise, in watching the motions of the enemy's cavalry on their late incursion to Charlottesville, and conveying to the Assembly timely information of their approach, whereby the designs of the enemy were frustrated, and many valuable stores preserved.

For whatever reasons, it was two years before Jouett received the pistols. And it took twenty years before he was presented with the sword. By that time, he had made a name for himself in what is now Kentucky. His move to there in 1782 had a most inauspicious start.

Jouett and some companions were traveling along Daniel Boone's Wilderness Road through the Cumberland Gap when, according to Virginius Dabney, they heard a woman's screams coming from an isolated cabin. Entering the small dwelling, Jouett discovered a man beating his wife. Ever gallant, he immediately went to the lady's rescue by knocking her husband down. The still young Jouett obviously had not learned how dangerous it could be to interfere in a marital dispute, for as soon as he struck her husband, the woman picked up a long-handled frying pan and struck such a heavy blow across his head that the bottom of the pan fell out and its rim became wedged around the would-be hero's neck. And there it remained until Jouett was at last able to find a blacksmith to remove it some thirty-five miles down the road.

Fortunately for Jouett, the years that followed were much more rewarding. He married his sweetheart, Sallie Robard; settled down in Mercer County, Kentucky; and entered politics. He was instrumental in helping Kentucky become a state and served four terms in its new legislature. He also began importing fine horses and cattle from England and is credited with having pioneered livestock breeding in the Bluegrass Region.

Jouett and his wife had twelve children, including the famous American painter Matthew Harris Jouett. After serving as a lieutenant in the War of 1812, Matthew, whose father wanted him to be a lawyer, went to Boston, where he studied with Gilbert Stuart. Even after his son had become highly acclaimed, particularly through his portraits of the Marquis de Lafayette and Thomas Jefferson, his father remained unimpressed. "I sent Matthew to college to make a gentleman of him, and he has turned out to be nothing but a damned sign painter."

It was through Matthew that the Jouett name was immortalized even further. Matthew's son, James Edward "Fighting Jim" Jouett, was a distinguished naval officer who, as Dabney commented, "shared his grandfather's fate in being forgotten by history." During the Civil War, James Edward Jouett was with Admiral David Farragut at Mobile Bay. It was there that Farragut became famous for having shouted the command, "Damn the torpedoes! Full steam ahead." But that has never been an accurate quote. What Farragut actually said was "Damn the torpedoes! Four bells! Captain Drayton go ahead! Jouett full speed!"

The exploits of Jack Jouett's son and grandson pale, however, in comparison to what the young militia captain accomplished on the long, dark night of June 3, 1871. Some early historians called his better than forty-mile horseback journey that night a ride that had been unequaled in history. Other historians agreed that had Jefferson and the other leaders whom Jouett saved that night been captured, it might well have meant the end of the Revolution. In 1926, Stuart G. Gibbony, president of the Thomas Jefferson Memorial Foundation, echoed the sentiment by stating, "But for Captain Jack Jouett's heroic ride, there would have been only unsuccessful rebels." Dabney provided the most detailed assessment of all:

> What would have been the fate of such men as Jefferson, Henry, Harrison, Nelson and Lee if they had fallen into British hands? They would almost certainly have been carried off into captivity by Tarleton . . . ; it is hardly conceivable that the men of the stature of Jefferson, Henry, and the rest would have been paroled. Their capture would have been a serious blow to the morale of the Continentals, especially at a time when things were going rather badly for their cause. Incalculable, even catastrophic results might have followed from such a coup.

So why, when he died in March 1822, was Jack Jouett buried in an unmarked grave? Why has he been lost to time and history? The answer seems clear. Like Sybil Ludington, he never had a Longfellow to immortalize what was undoubtedly a greater accomplishment than that of Paul Revere.

In June 1910, a bronze tablet was placed on the front wall of the Red Land Club, bearing the following inscription:

> *Site of Old Swan Tavern*
> *Where lived and died Jack Jouett,*
> *whose heroic ride saved*
> *Mr. Jefferson, the Governor,*
> *and the Virginia Assembly*
> *from capture by Tarleton*
> *June, 1781.*
> *Erected by the Monticello Branch*
> *of the Association for*
> *the Preservation of Virginia Antiquities,*
> *1910.*

But still no Longfellow has come to praise him. However, the tribe of poets has not died with Longfellow. There was one on the staff of the *Charlottesville Daily Progress* on October 26, 1909, at the time of the unveiling of the tablet to the memory of Jack Jouett. Unfortunately the name of the poet is unknown.

> *Hearken good people: awhile abide*
> *And hear of stout Jack Jouett's ride;*
> *How he rushed his steed, nor stopped nor stayed*
> *Till he warned the people of Tarleton's raid.*
> *The moment his warning note was rehearsed*
> *The State Assembly was quickly dispersed.*
> *In their haste to escape, they did not stop*
> *Until they had crossed the mountain top.*

And upon the other side came down
To resume their sessions in Staunton Town.
His parting steed he spurred
In haste to carry the warning
To that greatest statesman of any age,
The Immortal Monticello Sage.
Here goes to thee, Jack Jouett
Lord keep thy memory green;
You made the greatest ride, sir
That ever yet was seen.

It was hardly a poem for the ages, and definitely not a challenge to Longfellow's position as poet of the Revolution. What it does do, however, is remind us that, like Sybil Ludington, this man who has fallen through the cracks of history deserves a much better fate.

ELISHA KENT KANE
America's Greatest Hero (1847–57)

H e may be the most once-famous person you never heard of. During his all-too-brief lifetime, he became the United States' greatest hero. His death elicited the greatest outpouring of grief the nation had ever previously witnessed. His extraordinary adventures in the Arctic signaled the beginning of the scientific investigation of that still-mysterious region and led directly to the discovery of the North Pole. The two books he wrote describing his adventures inspired generations of adventurous souls to become explorers. Yet he has been all but forgotten.

His name was Elisha Kent Kane. Born on February 3, 1820, into one of Philadelphia's most elite and influential families, his father, John Kintzing Kane, had served as what today would be regarded as press secretary to Andrew Jackson before being appointed to the bench in eastern Pennsylvania. The elder Kane wanted his son to become the latest male member of the family to attend Yale. Elisha, however, wishing to avoid both Greek and Latin, chose instead to enroll at the University of Virginia, where he pursued his scientific interests and was able to join his professor William Barton Rogers on his mapping expeditions of the geological formations of the Blue Ridge Mountains. It was a happy time in the young student's life, one in which he seemed headed for a career in either geology or engineering. But when, in 1838 and 1839, his heart was

❖ Elisha Kent Kane, portrayed in an engraving from the mid-nineteenth century.

permanently damaged by a series of severe attacks of rheumatic fever, his dream of such rugged pursuits seemed closed to him forever.

Devastated by his illness and by his doctor's admonition that he could die "as suddenly as from a musket shot," Kane took to his bed for several weeks. The sight of him lying in such a pitiful state was even more devastating to his father, who, according to mid-nineteenth-century historian William Elder, ordered him out of bed, saying, "If you must die—die in the harness."

Taking his father's words to heart, Kane not only shook off his lethargy, but began the study of medicine at the University of Pennsylvania. He had no sooner graduated when the elder Kane's influence was exercised once again. Aware of his son's desire for both travel and adventure and the sad probability that his life would not be a long one, Judge Kane, without consulting his son, contacted the secretary of the navy and asked that Elisha be granted a commission as a naval surgeon. At the same time, knowing that the granting of naval commissions took considerable time, the judge arranged for Elisha to serve as a physician on a diplomatic mission to China that was about to depart. It was the turning point in Elisha Kane's life. From that time on until his death, Kane's life was characterized by travel and adventure. It was filled with something else as well: continual risk taking, motivated by what his friends were convinced was the result of his knowing that his days were numbered.

IN CHINA, KANE PRACTICED MEDICINE on a hospital ship in Whampoa (a district in present-day Guangzhou) for several months before returning home in 1845 through India, Egypt, Athens, and Paris. It was only the beginning. Now fully commissioned, he set off again, spending the next two years in the far corners of the world—the Mediterranean, Brazil, the African coast, the interiors of India and China. As historian Pierre Berton observed, he "explored the catacombs of Thebes, stood at the entrance to the pass at Thermopylae, walked across the Peloponnesus, and once hung suspended from a bamboo rope attached to a two-hundred-foot crag over a volcanic crater in the Philippines." During these travels he battled several serious illnesses, including cholera in China, typhoid in Egypt, and bacterial infection in Africa. Still, he kept going.

By the time Kane returned home again, his appetite for adventure had, if anything, intensified. The Mexican-American War was now fully under way and, in October 1847, he traveled to Washington, seeking "assignment to a duty more stimulating than ship's doctor." He got his wish—the dangerous task of carrying an important message to General Winfield Scott, the commander of all the American forces in Mexico, was assigned to him. In early January 1848, soon after his arrival in Mexico, Kane and a group of Mexican contra-guerrillas hired to accompany him headed for Scott's headquarters in Mexico City. Four days into their trek, near the tiny village of Nopaluca, the party suddenly encountered a company of Mexican soldiers commanded by Brigadier General Antonio Gaona.

In the battle that followed, one in which Gaona's troops were badly beaten, Kane received a lance wound. Even more seriously injured was General Gaona's son, a major in the Mexican army. In spite of his wound, Kane was able to keep the mercenaries from executing the general. Then he turned his attention to the younger Gaona. What happened next became the subject of newspaper reports that would soon be pouring into the United States. Typical was the article that appeared in the *Pennsylvanian* of October 24, 1847, which concluded by stating, "As soon as the old general was rescued, he sat down by the side of the major, his son, to comfort his last painful moments. When [Kane] observed that the individual was bleeding to death from an artery in the groin, he made an effort in his behalf. With the bent prong of a table-fork he took up the artery and tied it with a ravel of pack thread, and the rude surgical operation was perfectly successful." It was the public's introduction to Elisha Kane. What no one could have known was that far greater adventures and far greater fame lay ahead.

At the same time that Elisha Kane was performing his heroics in Mexico, a much different type of adventure was being played out in a very

❖ A PORTRAIT OF SIR JOHN FRANKLIN,
ca. 1830, fifteen years before he set out for
his fateful Arctic voyage.

different part of the world. Beginning in 1818, under the impassioned
leadership of Second Secretary to the Admiralty John Barrow, England
had begun a renewed effort to discover the fabled Northwest Passage
through the Arctic to the riches of the East. In 1845, after the British
had launched a series of unsuccessful expeditions to the frozen north,
Barrow sent out the world's most famous explorer, Sir John Franklin,
and some 280 men in the HMS *Erebus* and the HMS *Terror*—the two
most sophisticated and well-equipped ships of their day—in the hope of
at last securing the prize.

Franklin left with the expectations of all England sailing with him.
But when two years went by and not a word had been heard from him or
any member of the expedition, expectations turned first to fear and then
to dread. John Franklin's wife, Lady Jane Franklin, was a remarkable
woman, far ahead of her time. Her wealth and considerable influence
had played a major role in her husband's obtaining command of the 1845
expedition. Now she devoted all of her time to pleading with, cajoling,
and even threatening the admiralty and other British agencies to launch

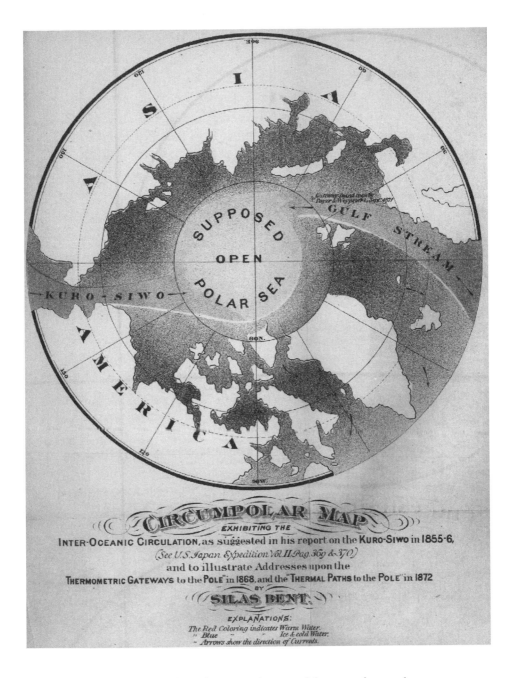

❖ A MAP FROM THE 1870s shows the circumpolar area and the supposed open polar sea, thought to contain the Northwest Passage.

searches for Sir John and his men. Eventually she would also use her considerable fortune to purchase and equip her own ships and send them out to seek her husband.

In April 1849, after the earliest of the British searches for Sir John failed to turn up even a trace of his expedition, Lady Franklin took her case beyond British shores. Writing to the new president of the United States, Zachary Taylor, she pleaded with him to launch an American search. "I am not without hope," she wrote, "that you will deem it not unworthy of a great and kindred nation to take up the cause of humanity . . . and thus make it generously your own." Humanitarianism aside, Lady Franklin pointed out, America's help in finding her husband might also lead to the United States, not England, finding the coveted Northwest Passage. "I should rejoice," she told President Taylor, "that it was to America we owe our restored happiness."

Eight months later, in December 1849, the relentless Lady Franklin wrote to the president again, once more urging him to launch a rescue effort. This second plea could not have come at a more opportune time. The noted American scientist Matthew Fontaine Maury, a man destined to become known as the father of modern oceanography, had recently captured attention by proclaiming that—based on studies of Arctic currents and the migration of whales in these waters—he was convinced of the existence of a Northwest Passage.

This time President Taylor acted, urging Congress to finance a rescue mission. But although most of the legislators were in favor of the endeavor, what promised to be lengthy debate broke out concerning how to appropriate the needed funds. At this point, New Bedford native Henry Grinnell, owner of a highly prosperous New York shipping firm, stepped in and offered to provide and provision two ships for the mission if Congress would place them under the control of the U.S. Navy. In May 1850, Congress accepted Grinnell's offer.

Two months earlier, having heard that Congress was seriously considering an Arctic mission, Elisha Kane had sent a letter to the secretary of the navy requesting a posting on the expedition. On May 12 he received a telegram telling him to report for duty at the New York

Naval Yard as soon as possible. He arrived at the facility on May 22, greeted by the sight of the two ships of the Grinnell expedition: the 144-ton *Advance* and the 82-ton *Rescue*. Also there to greet him was Lieutenant Edwin De Haven, who had been chosen commander of the expedition. It was an interesting pairing—the quiet, modest De Haven and the energetic, limelight-seeking Kane. Although no one could have foreseen it at the time, they were about to begin a voyage that would endow hero status not on the skillful, dedicated De Haven but on his thirty-year-old medical officer.

THE *ADVANCE* AND THE *RESCUE* sailed for the Arctic in July 1850. Although Kane had traveled much of the world, he was totally unprepared for what he encountered from the moment the expedition entered the still largely uncharted Arctic. The ice formations astounded him. Writing in a style that would eventually make him one of America's most widely read authors of his time, he proclaimed to his journal, "An iceberg is one of God's own buildings, preaching its lessons of humility to the miniature structures of man."

The ice formations were indeed magnificent, but he soon learned that they were terrifying as well. After having crossed Melville Bay, a body of water that earlier British explorers had felt was a key to finding both the Northwest Passage and traces of John Franklin, Kane described the area as a "mysterious region of terrors." He was referring to the ever-moving ice floes, some more than a mile across, furiously smashing against one another with extraordinary speed and effect. "Tables of white marble," he wrote, "were thrust into the air, as if by invisible machinery."

Less than a month into the search, he experienced his first Arctic mirage. In his journal, which became the basis for a best seller, he described what he experienced more vividly than any of his Arctic predecessors had been able to articulate. "There is a black globe floating in the air about three [degrees] north of the sun," he wrote. "Is it a bird or balloon? . . .

❖ THIS ENGRAVING WAS BASED ON A SKETCH Kane drew in 1853 while sailing past "God's own buildings." The engraving appeared in Kane's best-selling book *Arctic Explorations: The Second Grinnell Expedition in Search of Sir John Franklin, 1853, '54, '55* (1856).

On a sudden, it changes shape . . . It is a grand piano . . . *Presto*, it had made itself duplicate—a pair of colossal dumbbells. A moment! And it is the black globe again."

De Haven was steering a course for Smith Sound, another area where it was hoped traces of Franklin would be found, but when the two ships came upon it, it was completely frozen over. Undaunted, De Haven headed for Barrow Strait, hoping there would be channels open enough for passage. There were, and soon they reached a limestone projection of land that had been named Cape Riley.

They had come to discover, and it was here that they made their first find, albeit a secondhand one. As the lookouts aboard the *Advance* and the *Rescue* scanned the shoreline, they spotted two cairns, stone enclosures in which captains sailing in remote areas traditionally left messages describing where they had been on their voyage and where they were next headed. Immediately, a small party from each vessel was sent ashore. Inside one of the cairns, they found a note dated just two days before. Written by Captain Erasmus Ommanney, an officer aboard one of four British search vessels in an expedition commanded by Horatio Austin, the note revealed that here, at Cape Riley, the first discovery in the long and agonizing search for Franklin and his men had been made. "I had the satisfaction," Ommanney had written, "of meeting with the first trace of Sir John's expedition, consisting of fragments of stores and tagged clothing and the remains of an encampment."

Austin and his men were not the only other party searching in the area, and as the *Advance* and the *Rescue* made their way across from Cape Riley to Beechey Island, they were joined by two British vessels under the charge of a whaling captain named William Penny and three more commanded by famed naval hero and explorer John Ross. Shouting across the water at one another, De Haven, Penny, and Ross decided to meet on the island's shore to discuss how each of their vessels could best be deployed in the next stage of the rescue attempt. They had just begun conferring when one of Penny's sailors came racing down one of the island's hills, shouting, "Graves, Captain Penny, graves!"

Each of three captains had brought several of their men ashore with them, and now all of them, including Kane, rushed up the hill. Reaching the top, they encountered an agonizing sight. There before them were three mounds of earth, each topped by a weather-beaten grave marker. A quick reading of the markers revealed that underneath the mounds lay two of Franklin's sailors from the *Erebus* and one from the *Terror*.

Sobered by what they had discovered, De Haven, Penny, and Ross then ordered a search of the entire island. The crewmen soon found remains of a blacksmith's forge, charred areas where fires had been built, an enormous pile of some six hundred cans that had contained preserved meat, fragments of rope, scraps of paper, and other articles that had obviously belonged to the Franklin expedition.

It was the first indisputable evidence of where Sir John and his men had once been and what had happened to at least three of them.

But there was deep frustration as well. Early in the search, one of the groups scouring the island had come across what promised to be the most rewarding discovery of all. It was a large cairn, and surely it contained a message from Franklin informing anyone who found it where he was heading after leaving Beechey Island. But to the amazement of its discoverers, it was completely empty.

No one was more surprised than Elisha Kane. In his journal he wrote,

> The cairn was mounted on a high and conspicuous portion of the shore, and evidently intended to attract observation; but, though several parties examined it, digging around in it in every direction, not a single particle of information could be gleaned. This is remarkable; and for so able and practical an Arctic commander as Sir John Franklin, an incomprehensible omission.

It was both a mystery and a disappointment. A message left behind on Beechey Island would have been the most important indication in what had now become a six-year search of where the explorer and his

❖ THE GRAVES OF THREE FRANKLIN CREWMEN on Beechey Island; this engraving is based on a drawing by Kane, for his book *Arctic Explorations.*

men, if still alive, might be found. One clue, however, as to where the Franklin party may have gone after leaving the island *was* discovered. Again, taking to his journal, Kane wrote, "In a narrow interval between [Beechey Island's] hills . . . the searching parties of the *Rescue* and Mr. Murtaugh of the [*Advance*] found the tracks of a sledge clearly defined and unmistakable both to character and direction. They pointed to the eastern shores of Wellington Sound."

Acting on this clue, all of the ships anchored off Beechey Island—including all four of Austin's vessels, which had arrived while the search of the island was taking place—set sail for Wellington Sound. The British captains, experienced in Arctic travel, were aware that winter was fast setting in and they would undoubtedly, once again, have to spend long, dark months locked in the ice. De Haven and Kane, on the other hand, had no such intention. As the snow began to fall and as the ice began to build up at an alarming rate, they agreed that it was time to head for home. Suddenly, however, they became aware that the *Rescue* was no longer behind them; they had become separated in the storm. If they were to have any chance of escaping the Arctic, they and the others aboard the *Advance* would have to find their sister ship as quickly as possible.

They finally found her, but now they were spending most of their time trying to find open channels. "We are literally running for our lives," wrote Kane. "We are staggering along under all sail forcing our way where we can." Finally, they were compelled to give up. They could go no farther. They would have to spend the winter locked in the ice at the mouth of Wellington Channel, a prospect made even more dire by their awareness that the nearest British ship, in all probability, would be wintering at least fifty miles away. That distance "in these inhospitable deserts," Kane later wrote, "was as complete a separation as an entire continent."

He had faced death in battle, he had descended into the mouth of a volcano, and he had risked danger throughout the world, but never had Kane lived through what he and the rest of the men of the Grinnell expedition were forced to endure that winter. Even before the worst hardships began, it was determined that the *Rescue* had been so battered by the ice that it would have to be abandoned. All of the expedition's thirty-three men would have to winter it out aboard the *Advance*—a space, noted Kane, no bigger than his father's library back in Philadelphia.

It turned out to be one of the coldest winters in Arctic history. Burning hot coffee froze in the crews' mugs as soon as it was poured. If a man stuck out his tongue, it froze to his beard. Butter and lard had to be cut with an axe and a chisel. Then the Arctic winter darkness set in. Almost twenty-four hours a day it was pitch black. "I long for the sunlight," Kane wrote in his journal. "Dear, dear sun, no wonder you are worshipped."

Just when it appeared that conditions could get no worse, many of the men were stricken with scurvy, some so seriously that any activity caused them to faint. Fortunately, Elisha Kane was a physician far ahead of his time. Although in Kane's era there was a theory that citrus was claimed to cure or prevent scurvy (a discovery made by Scottish physician James Lind in 1747), citrus was still hotly debated as a scurvy panacea. Many still believed that scurvy could be kept at bay by exercise and hygiene, rather than diet, and scurvy continued to claim the lives of mariners throughout the world. The forward-thinking Kane, however, began forcing the crew to eat potatoes and sauerkraut and to drink lime juice, all rich in vitamin C, which we now know prevents scurvy. Later, De Haven and others credited Kane with having saved the expedition from total disaster.

By March 1851, the *Advance* was still frozen in, perched atop two huge mounds of ice. De Haven, in what turned out to be an inspired move, sent men across the ice to where the stricken *Rescue* lay. There they dug an eight-foot pit around the vessel's damaged hull and, despite the cold, repaired it. During the first week of April, open stretches of water began to appear, and the *Rescue's* crew returned to their ship. On June 5, the long-awaited breakup of the ice took place. The ordeal was over. The Grinnell expedition could, at last, sail for home.

ELISHA KENT KANE

THE *ADVANCE* ARRIVED IN NEW YORK on September 30, the *Rescue* on October 7. The first American expedition to the Arctic had survived. But, like their British counterparts, they had neither found John Franklin nor discovered whether he and his men were still alive. The Grinnell expedition had to report defeat. For Elisha Kane, however, it was a much different story. From the moment that the *Advance* and *Rescue* dropped their anchors in New York Harbor, both the public and the press demonstrated an intense curiosity about this first band of Americans who had braved the mysterious Arctic in search of the fabled Sir John Franklin. True to his nature, De Haven, who, as commander of the expedition, should have been its chief spokesperson, was not interested in publicity. After submitting his official report to the secretary of the navy, he faded out of view, leaving center stage to the limelight-loving Kane.

And Kane had a fascinating story to tell. He could relate a participant's view of what the Arctic was like, what being icebound for an entire winter was like, and what the search for Franklin was like. Moreover, he could give his own eyewitness account of the hottest news story thus far in a search that had captured the attention of the whole world: the discovery of the three graves at Beechey Island.

Kane had actually begun telling the story well before he set foot once again on American soil. As the *Advance* and *Rescue* sailed home, he began writing his account of the discovery of the three graves and of the other finds that were made on that desolate, frozen island. Days before he reached New York, and well before any of the British commanders who had been at Beechey Island could publish their accounts of what had taken place, the *New York Tribune* and the *New York Times* printed what Kane had written. The articles caused a sensation, creating a demand around the country for personal appearances by Kane.

He responded by undertaking a long and extensive lecture tour, drawing enormous and enthusiastic audiences wherever he spoke. As a scientist he enthralled those interested in the physical nature of the unknown Arctic. As an adventurer he thrilled the throngs interested in his story of survival. And as one who felt that his work in the Arctic was far from done, he used the speeches to lay the groundwork for what had become the greatest goal of his life—another expedition in search of Franklin, another journey to explore uncharted Arctic waters, this time with him completely in charge. As he explained to an overflow audience at a dinner given in honor of the Grinnell expedition:

> I must seize the present occasion earnestly to state that I hope the search is not yet ended. The drift by which the *Advance* and *Rescue* were borne so far, conclusively proves that the same influence might have carried us into the same sea in which Franklin and his companions are probably immured. . . . I trust for the sake of the United States, for the sake of the noble hearted woman, who has been the animating soul of all the Expeditions, for the sake of the flag, which has so triumphantly borne the battle and breeze, for the sake of the humanity which makes us all kin, I trust that [the] search is not yet ended and that the rescue of Sir John Franklin is yet reserved to his nation and the world.

It was a typically eloquent Kane oration, yet perhaps not an accurate reflection of how he truly felt. He knew that Franklin had been missing for more than six years and eight months, more than a year beyond the longest period for which his provisions could possibly hold out. But by now Kane had a much larger personal agenda. Like John Barrow, who had launched one English search after another, Kane had come to believe in the existence of an open polar sea, a vast open body of water beyond the Arctic ice cap that, once reached, would lead not only to the Northwest Passage, but to what to Kane had become the greatest prize of all: the discovery of the North Pole.

By the beginning of spring 1853, Kane was ready to apply to Congress for a return trip to the Arctic. Yet even with the sensation that his speaking tours and writings had caused, it became obvious that it would take months before the legislators granted him a ship, the men, and the necessary provisions for an expedition. Once again, however, Henry Grinnell stepped forth, offering the fully refurbished *Advance*. Various scientific organizations, eager to associate with Kane, provided many of the necessary navigational and scientific instruments.

On May 31, 1853, with an enormous crowd cheering him on, Kane with his company of seventeen officers and men sailed out of New York Harbor. "The object of my journey," Kane wrote to his brother, "is the search after Sir John Franklin. Neither science nor the vain glory of attaining an unreached North shall divert me from this one conscientious aim." However, it was almost certain that there was no longer a Franklin expedition to be found. Kane was determined to sail as far north as possible, to find an open polar sea and, Lord willing, even the North Pole.

On July 20, the *Advance* sailed to Greenland, where Kane recruited two other men for his crew, a nineteen-year-old Inuk named Hans Christian Hendrik and the Danish dog sledge driver Carl Petersen, who had sailed with William Penny in 1850–51. Kane was following a route previously traveled by the British Royal Navy officer Edward Inglefield, who was also convinced that there was an open polar sea. By the second week in August, Kane had made his way through the ice floes that had already formed in Baffin Bay, had sailed through Smith Sound, and had entered the great basin that would later be named for him. He had now gone farther north along this route than any other white man. But the ice was getting thicker and more treacherous, and winter was obviously setting in. The exhausted crew begged Kane to turn back. But he would have none of it. Later, Carl Petersen would write that it was obvious that Kane wanted to spend the winter farther north than any other English explorers had done because he felt deeply that "the Stars and Stripes ought to wave where no Union Jack had ever fluttered in the polar gale."

Finally, with ice beating against the sides of the *Advance*, Kane's officers convinced him that, for the safety of all those aboard, he had to find a safe haven for the winter. Fortunately, a sheltered bay was nearby, and, after naming it Rensselaer Harbor after his father's country estate, Kane dropped anchor there.

❖ THIS ENGRAVING WAS BASED ON Kane's grim, dark sketch titled "Life In The Brig: Second Winter." Kane placed himself in the center of the picture.

He had set the stage for extraordinary hardship. With the exception of a few non-Inuit inhabitants of the Norwegian island of Spitsbergen, no white man had ever spent the winter this far north. Even the Inuk Hans Hendrik was unprepared for it. "Never had I seen the dark season like this . . . ," he later wrote. "I was seized with fright and fell a-weeping." It was indeed a dark season—140 days of continuous darkness in which the crew "could not see to count their fingers."

By the end of February, the expedition's oil candles and coal had almost run out. Then a mysterious ailment struck, killing all but six of the fifty dogs. This, Kane knew, meant that once they resumed their journey north toward his longed-for open polar sea, the crew would have to haul the heavy sledges themselves.

Meantime, he was aware that for both their mental and physical health it was important to keep the men busy. This meant sending out a series of exploratory sledging expeditions, which often resulted in injury to one or more of the crew. On the positive side, on one of the forays, the ship's boatman, William Godfrey, and its surgeon, Dr. Isaac Hayes, were able to complete the first mapping of what became known as Kane Basin.

When spring arrived and the ice gave absolutely no sign of even beginning to break up, Kane mounted what he regarded as two vital investigations. As the *Advance* had made its way northward, he had sighted a massive glacier that he named for the famous German explorer and scientist Alexander von Humboldt. On April 25 he organized a party of eight men, including himself, to examine and perhaps climb the icy structure. Six of the men headed out that day. Kane and another crewmember left the ship the next day and quickly caught up with the others. As the men made their way, none of them had any idea that the newly named Humboldt was the largest glacier in the known world. What they did discover when they reached it was that it was impossible to climb. Three of them became temporarily snow blind, another suffered severe chest pains, and Kane himself both fainted in the effort and suffered a frozen foot.

The result of the second investigation that Kane had launched—sending William Morton and Hans Hendrik off to explore the rocky promontory that stood atop the basin—was, however, far different.

When they returned to the *Advance,* Morton reported that, after literally clawing his way up the promontory, he had looked out at an extraordinary sight—open water as far as he could see. Kane was beside himself. Both he and Morton were absolutely certain that what the steward had viewed was an open polar sea. In his journal an exuberant Kane wrote, "I can say that I have led an expedition whose results will be remembered for all time."

His expedition would indeed be remembered, but not for the discovery he believed had been made. For Morton had not seen an open polar sea. It did not exist. What he had experienced was yet another polar mirage caused by the intense Arctic light, the vast expanse of snow, and undoubtedly no small amount of wishful thinking.

❖ "Crossing the Ice Belt at Coffee Gorge." An engraving based on a sketch by Kane of a sledging party maneuvering across the ice in 1854.

But in mid-July 1854, Kane was blissfully unaware that Morton, like so many before him, had been deceived by the Arctic light and atmosphere. What *was,* however, painfully clear to him was that the ice was still thick, and that it was already mid-summer. There would be no escape for at least another year. He was also all too aware that his crew was becoming desperate and increasingly difficult to manage. He decided to undertake a desperate measure of his own. Kane knew that the *North Star,* the supply ship of a five-vessel British fleet still searching for John Franklin, was anchored off the same Beechey Island where he and others had encountered the now-famous three graves. He loaded five of his men along with himself in a whaleboat aptly named *Forlorn Hope* and set out, praying that he would find the *North Star* and acquire enough supplies to enable his expedition to survive yet another winter.

When they reached Baffin Bay, however, they found their progress completely blocked by ice. Trudging to a nearby iceberg, Kane climbed more than 120 feet to its pinnacle, where he saw nothing but ice stretching out for a radius of at least thirty miles. Disheartened, he led his men back to the *Advance*, knowing that he faced more long months of attempting to survive and attempting to buoy up the spirits of his crew. "It is *horrible*—yes that is the word—," he confided to his journal, "to look forward to another year of disease and darkness to be met without fresh food and without fuel."

He could have added that they would be looking forward as well to another year cut off from all knowledge of the world beyond the narrow area of their icy imprisonment. In August 1854, what Kane didn't know was that the British naval officer Robert McClure had actually discovered a Northwest Passage. Nor did he know that, almost a thousand miles away from where he and his men lay trapped, the Hudson's Bay Company explorer John Rae had found conclusive evidence of the fact that at least most of the members of Franklin's expedition were dead.

If he *had* known, it would have made no difference to him. All of his attention had to be turned to survival. Only 750 pounds of coal remained aboard the *Advance*. He would soon have to begin breaking up the ship for fuel. As it was, he and his crew were being kept alive only by the fact that he was occasionally able to trade for food with Etah Inuits, whose summer hunting grounds were nearby.

And then something for which Kane was totally unprepared took place. Morton informed him that several of the crew, having come to the conclusion that it was their only chance for survival, had decided to leave the ship and attempt to gain rescue by making their way to Upernavik. Kane could not believe what he was hearing. Upernavik was more than seven hundred miles south of where the *Advance* lay in ice, seven hundred miles of some of the most treacherous terrain in the world. And the season of ice and blizzards was upon them. It would be a disastrous journey.

After pleading with the crew members to reconsider, Kane asked them to put their decision to a vote. To his astonishment, nine of the crew, including Hayes, voted to leave. It was, Kane believed, a supreme violation. In his journal he wrote, "They are deserters, in act and in spirit. . . . They leave their ship, abandon their sick comrades, fail to adhere to their commander, and are false to the implied trust which tells every true man to abide by the Expedition into which he has entered."

The defectors left the *Advance* on August 28. Turning again to his journal, Kane wrote, "So they go. . . . I cannot but feel that some of them will return broken down and suffering to seek a refuge aboard. They shall find it to the halving of our last chip—but—but—but—if I ever live to get home—home! And I should meet *Dr. Hayes* or [the others]—let them look out for their skins."

He was angry; he felt betrayed, and yet he knew that he had no time to wallow in his feelings. He had to get the *Advance* ready for another winter. He began by having the remaining ten crewmen strip the planking off the vessel's upper deck to be used for firewood. Although he figured that this would supply him with more than a ton of fuel, he knew that it would last only through the end of January. To get through February and March, the worst of the winter months, the thick oak sheathing nailed to the *Advance*'s sides as a buffer against the ice would have to be removed, supplying him with at least two and a half more tons of firewood. Amazingly, he remained optimistic about the expedition's chances for survival. He would make certain that all of the planking that was removed was above the water line, ensuring that the *Advance*, stripped as it would be, would remain seaworthy. "God willing," he wrote, "I may get through this awful winter and save [the ship] besides."

Addressing the fuel problem was one thing; obtaining enough food to survive the winter was quite another thing. Half of his depleted crew were either too ill or too weak to be sent attempting to trade with the Eskimos for food. But, by December, Kane knew that it had to be done and that it would probably fall on his shoulders. Then, on December 7, yet another unexpected event took place. At about three o'clock in the morning, Kane was rudely awakened by one of the crew. Five sledges, he was told, pulled by six teams of dogs driven by totally unfamiliar Eskimos, were approaching the *Advance*. By the time Kane got himself dressed, a group of the natives had come aboard, and with them were two of the men who, fourteen weeks ago, had deserted the ship. Although both were in horrific physical condition, they managed to tell Kane that he had been correct in predicting that the defectors would not be able to reach Upernavik. As for the other deserters, they were huddled in a stone hut some 150 miles to the south, completely out of strength and close to starvation. The two men then pleaded with Kane to save their companions.

One can only imagine the emotions that Kane experienced as he heard this report. These were men who had betrayed him. Now he was being asked to save their lives. Moreover, truth be told, their defection in one way had been a blessing. He had estimated that without having to feed them he might actually, with careful rationing, make it through the winter. Their return would render that impossible. But he knew he had no choice. Despite what they had done, to turn his back on them would be unforgivable. After presenting the Eskimos with presents, he gave them food to bring to the stricken men and instructed them to bring the former crewmen back to the ship. When the deserters returned, having lost everything with which they had been supplied, Kane knew that he now had only one option. With nine more mouths to feed they would somehow have to make it through the winter, finding what meat they could while the deserters healed. They were iced in so severely, Kane realized, that as soon as the whole crew was fit, the *Advance* would have to be abandoned. Ironically, the only chance for survival was to attempt to reach Upernavik, the same plan that the defectors had tried to pursue.

They finally left on May 20, 1855. Over the next eighty-three days, in what would become one of the most extraordinary escapes in history, they dragged and sailed their small boats through blizzards, across ice floes, and around towering icebergs. It would never have been possible without Kane. Not only did he continually take the helm of one of the boats for as long as sixteen hours at a time, but he periodically backtracked, seeking food from Eskimo settlements, even returning to the *Advance* once during the early stages of the flight to bake life-sustaining bread.

Despite these efforts, which added almost one thousand miles to his own journey, by the time the men of the *Advance* reached and crossed Melville Bay, they were completely out of food. Only the serendipitous capture of a seal saved them from starving. But, spurred on by Kane, they kept on moving and, on August 1, entered the whaling grounds of Baffin Bay. Two days later a sail was spotted. It was the Danish oil boat *Fraülein Flairscher*, on its way to the tiny port of Kingatok to take on a load of blubber.

Kane and his men were immediately taken to Disko Island off the southernmost part of Greenland, where they were generously tended to and informed that back home in America they had not been forgotten. In fact, only a week before, a U.S. Navy steam vessel along with its tender had sailed through Baffin Bay searching for the expedition. On September 13, 1855, having been informed by telegraph that the men who had left the United States more than two years ago had been found, two American ships commanded by Captain Henry J. Hartstene arrived at Disko Island and took Kane and his men aboard. The long ordeal was over.

ELISHA KANE RETURNED HOME on October 11, 1855. During his two-year absence, his published journal of the first Grinnell expedition, filled with his poetic and haunting descriptions of icebergs and other Arctic phenomena and its accounts of the dangers he had faced at every turn, had made him a greater hero than ever before. When, the day after his arrival, the *New York Times* devoted its entire front page to a description of his second Arctic adventure and his extraordinary escape from death, his status rose even higher.

Now that he was home and very much alive, the praise rose to unprecedented heights. This time there was no need for the self-promotion

ELISHA KENT KANE

❖ KANE. AN ENGRAVING BY
T. Pillsbrown, after an 1850s
daguerreotype by Mathew
Brady.

that Kane had engaged in following his return from the first Grinnell
expedition. Everyone else, it seemed, was doing it for him. Members of
his crew wrote accounts extolling his virtues. Based on various stories
of the adventure Kane had told him, his brother wrote an account of
his heroic actions during the rescue journey. Everywhere he went and
everything he did was covered by the press. He was now more than a
hero; he had become an icon.

He was still only thirty-five years old. But the deliberately chosen
rigors of the life of this man with a rheumatic heart, a man who had
contracted cholera in China, typhoid fever in Egypt, bacterial infection
in West Africa, and scurvy during his Arctic endeavors, finally caught
up with him a year after his return. In October 1856, he traveled to
London to deliver, as he had promised, a report of the second Grinnell
expedition to Lady Jane Franklin. While there he became seriously ill
and sailed for Havana, hoping that its warm climate would facilitate a

quick recovery. En route to Cuba, however, he had a severe stroke. Early in February 1857, he was stricken again and died in Havana less than a week later.

What followed was unprecedented in America's history. Upon Kane's death, the governor of Cuba personally escorted his funeral cortege to New Orleans. From New Orleans the cortege made its way more than two thousand miles, traveling slowly to allow the public to pay respects to America's first Arctic hero. From New Orleans to Cincinnati, the banks of the Mississippi and Ohio Rivers were lined with thousands of mourners, as were both sides of the train tracks between Cincinnati and Philadelphia. It was the longest funeral train of the century, except for that of Abraham Lincoln eight years later.

The adulation did not end with the funeral. For the next six months, the nation's magazines and newspapers were filled with emotional eulogies and accounts of Kane's accomplishments. "Kane," the *New York Tribune* exclaimed in its eulogy, "was a man of whom the country became more proud with every new revelation of his character . . . Gallant, brave, heroic, smitten equally with a love of science and a passion for adventure, he possessed the mental forces to convert the dreams of imagination into reality." Several states and a number of scientific societies mounted campaigns to have memorials built in Kane's honor, many of them requesting that donation amounts to the funding be "fixed so low that even those of limited means might have the pleasure of contributing." At one point there were more poems written in praise of the "Archangel voyager" than any other individual.

Elisha Kent Kane sailed farther north than any other explorer of his time. He discovered the largest glacier in the world. The route through the Arctic that he blazed became the avenue followed by those whose efforts would lead to the discovery of the North Pole. Each of the books that he wrote about his Arctic expeditions not only became best sellers but, in the words of author Frank Rasky, "humanized the Arctic in terms that Americans could appreciate." Perhaps more important, at a time of mid-century turmoil in the United States, Kane's firsthand accounts of the adventures and sufferings of his expeditions reassured an entire nation that the indomitable American spirit was still alive. Not to be overlooked is the fact that generations of explorers who followed Kane—including Charles Francis Hall, Adolphus Greely, Roald Amundsen, and Robert Peary—publicly credited Kane's experiences and his writings with having directly inspired them to become explorers.

Yet in the twenty-first century he is nearly forgotten. Far more places in the Arctic are named for lesser explorers than the one basin that bears Kane's name. In almost all lists of American explorers his name is left out. It is a serious oversight, as mysterious as the land upon which he left his indelible mark.

SEVEN

THE *SULTANA*
Death on the Great River (1865)

The pages of history are filled with accounts of shipwrecks and other disasters at sea. Most schoolchildren on both sides of the Atlantic are familiar with the story of the *Titanic*. When, in 1912, that supposedly unsinkable ocean liner went down after striking an iceberg, it took with it the lives of an estimated 1,518 people. What has in great measure been lost to time is the fact that less than fifty years earlier another peacetime maritime disaster, this one involving a steamboat named the *Sultana*, resulted in the death of even more people than those who were lost in the sinking of the *Titanic*.

April 1865 was an extraordinarily eventful month, particularly as far as the American Civil War was concerned. On April 9, Confederate general Robert E. Lee surrendered his Army of Northern Virginia to General Ulysses S. Grant and his combined Union armies. Five days later, on April 14, Abraham Lincoln was assassinated. On April 26, the president's assassin, John Wilkes Booth, was caught and killed by Union troops. That same day, General Joseph Johnston surrendered the last remaining Confederate army. The long, tragic conflict was finally over.

❖ THE DOCKS AT VICKSBURG, MISSISSIPPI, 1864. In 1865, after the Civil War ended, thousands of Union and Confederate soldiers who had been prisoners of war were sent to the docks to begin their voyages homeward. For most of those who boarded the *Sultana*, it would be their last trip.

With the conflict ended, both the North and the South began releasing the tens of thousands of men they had held as prisoners of war. Thousands of Union soldiers and officers who had been held in Confederate prison camps were being taken by train to Vicksburg, Mississippi. There they were to be put upon steamboats and transported up the Mississippi River to Cairo, Illinois, where they would board trains that would take them home. The vast majority of the men who were scheduled to take this journey were in terrible physical shape, victims of the hunger, exposure, and disease that had plagued both the Confederate and Union prison camps. As Civil War historian Bruce Catton wrote,

> To become a prisoner in the Civil War, on either side, was no short cut to survival—Quite the opposite; and to understand how appallingly lethal were the prison camps, North or South, one need only reflect on this bit of simple arithmetic; about two and a half times as many soldiers were subjected to the hunger, pestilence, and soul-sickening of the prison camps as were exposed to the deadly fire and crossfire of the guns at Gettysburg—and the camps killed nearly ten times as many as died on the battlefield.

The Union soldiers who were about to board the steamboats had suffered more than most. Many had been held in Camp Sumter, Georgia's infamous Andersonville prison, where, during the course of the war, some 13,000 of the 45,000 prisoners held there had died. At one point the stockade, built to hold 10,000 men, contained over 32,000 prisoners. Conditions had been so bad at Andersonville that after the war Henry Wirz, the prison's superintendent, was tried on charges of war crimes, found guilty, and hanged—the only Civil War combatant executed for war crimes. Other released prisoners had spent long months in Alabama's Cahaba Prison, a facility built to hold 500 prisoners that, by 1865, was holding 5,000, many of whom had died from the unsanitary conditions there.

Physically weakened as many of them were, the soldiers who arrived at the Vicksburg docks were happier than they had been for a very long time. "Glad shouts of joy rent the air when news came to pull out of camp," Private George S. Schmutz of the 102nd Ohio Infantry later stated. "We were soldiers, prisoners of war, who had been shut up in prison pens, some for six months, some for twelve, some for eighteen months. One might think how glad all were to get home."

The U.S. government had hired the steamboats to take the soldiers up the Mississippi and was paying the vessels' owners $5 for each enlisted man and $10 for each officer transported. In 1865 these were relatively large sums of money (approximately $70 and $140 today), and the owners of the steamboats were eager to take as many men aboard their vessels as they could. They were so eager, in fact, that they were not above bribing

❖ IMAGES OF PRIVATION at Andersonville prison, drawn from memory by one of the inmates, Maine infantryman Private Thomas O'Dea.

the government and army officials whose job it was to assign the released prisoners to specific steamboats.

OF ALL THE STEAMBOATS waiting at the Vicksburg dock, none was more impressive than the 260-foot, 1,719-ton *Sultana*, a ship that the Cincinnati *Daily Commercial* had described as one of the best steam vessels ever constructed. Built in Cincinnati in 1863, the *Sultana* was designed to carry cotton along the Mississippi and Ohio Rivers from St. Louis to New Orleans, and it had been doing so for two years. Her owners were particularly proud of the latest safety features that had been installed on the vessel, including state-of-the-art safety gauges, designed to detect flaws in the operation of any of the boat's four boilers that supplied the steam to propel the vessel. No one, however, seemed concerned about the fact that the *Sultana* carried only one lifeboat and only seventy-six life belts, or that the army had not provided the ship with a single doctor to give medical help to the troops should the need arise.

The part owner and captain of the *Sultana* was thirty-four-year-old J. Cass Mason, one of the most experienced and skillful navigators of the often treacherous Mississippi. By 1865 he had owned and operated a number of steamboats and was regarded as the perfect mariner to captain so large a vessel as the *Sultana*. But in April 1865, Mason was also a man with a problem. Due to a series of setbacks, he was in dire financial straits. Perhaps more than any of the other owners of the steamboats waiting to make the voyage to Cairo, he was eager to pack his vessel with as many passengers as he could.

Acting with the cooperation of Union boarding officials, Mason managed to have soldier after soldier assigned to the *Sultana*. Soon, the ex-prisoners were jammed aboard both decks of the ship and were sandwiched into what seemed like every available space below. At the same time as this loading was taking place, some one hundred civilians asked Mason if they could book passage on his ship. Mason not only took them aboard, but as if his ever-growing human cargo was not enough, he arranged to make the voyage even more profitable by filling the *Sultana's* hold with 250 barrels of sugar and ninety-seven cases of wine, to be delivered to Memphis. Mason also loaded some one hundred mules and horses and an equal number of hogs onto the main deck at the very rear of the ship.

Later, William Butler, a cotton merchant standing on the *Pauline Carroll*, a steamboat docked next to the *Sultana*, described the scene aboard Mason's vessel:

> On every part of her the men seemed to be packed as thick as they could well stand. They were on the hurricane deck, on her wheel-house, forward deck . . . and a person could go from one part of the boat to another only with much difficulty. A gentleman who was standing by me . . . said it was a damned shame to crowd men on a boat in that way; that he did not believe the men would have as much room to lie down as was allowed to slaves on slave-ships.

The *Sultana* had been built to carry a maximum of 376 passengers, including its crew. It would never be known exactly how many men were finally packed upon the vessel. What *was* documented was a conversation held between the *Sultana's* first clerk, William Gambrel, and one of the dockside Union officials. Boasting that "if we arrive safe at Cairo, it will be the greatest trip ever made on the western waters," Gambrel told the official that there were more people aboard the *Sultana* than had ever been transported on any other single vessel on the Mississippi River. Asked just how many people he meant, Gambrel stated that, as it prepared to leave Vicksburg, the *Sultana* was carrying 2,400 soldiers, 100 civilians, and a crew of 80—a total of more than 2,500 people, this on a ship designed to carry 376.

Still, as the *Sultana* prepared to depart for Cairo, Captain Mason insisted that there was no cause for alarm as far as overloading was concerned. There was, however, another issue. The *Sultana* had docked at Vicksburg on April 23, having made its way up from New Orleans. During that journey, the vessel's middle boiler had ceased functioning.

Inspection at the Vicksburg dock revealed that a bulge had developed on one of the boiler's walls. Informed that a proper repair would take days, Captain Mason became disturbed. Fearful that such a delay would enable other steamboats to arrive from New Orleans and pick up soldiers that might otherwise be assigned to the *Sultana*, he ordered, rather than a full repair, that a simple patch be welded over the bulge. It would have to do, he told himself. He could not afford the delay.

At nine o'clock on the evening of April 24, the *Sultana* backed out of its Vicksburg berth and headed up the Mississippi. Despite being jammed together as they were, the released prisoners had only one thought. They were on their way home.

On April 25, the *Sultana* made a brief stop at Helena, Arkansas, where an incident took place that might well have abruptly, if not tragically, ended the voyage then and there. As the *Sultana* approached the dock, the sight of so many people crammed aboard one vessel attracted the attention of almost the entire population of the town. Among them was a photographer determined to capture an image of the spectacle. As he began to set up his tripod and camera, he was spotted by many of those aboard, who, eager to be included in the picture, hurried to the side of the boat facing the cameraman. Soon so many soldiers were crowding the railing that the *Sultana* began to list severely, in real danger of going over. Only the quick action of a Union officer who herded the men away from the railing prevented a calamity.

From Helena, the *Sultana* proceeded up the Mississippi. On April 26, it landed at Memphis, where Mason's cargo of sugar and wine was unloaded. While the steamboat was docked, William Michael and a group of fellow officers from the Union gunboat *Tyler* paid the vessel a visit. Michael later wrote of what he encountered:

> I . . . mingled with the living skeletons who had been rotting in southern prison-pens for months, but who were now happy at the prospect of soon meeting the dear ones at home. We cheered them with kindly words and rejoiced with them at the bright prospects before them. Some of the men were too weak to walk without being

❖ THE SEVERELY OVERCROWDED *Sultana* is shown here in a photograph taken a day or two before the explosion.

supported by more fortunate comrades. Others were compelled by sheer weakness to lie on cots or blankets spread upon the decks, while their wants were cheerfully provided for by devoted companions, who loved them because of the sufferings they had passed through together.

THE *SULTANA* REMAINED IN MEMPHIS only a few hours, and at eleven o'clock that evening it steamed across the Mississippi to Hopefield, Arkansas, where it took on over a thousand bushels of coal. By 1:00 a.m. on the twenty-seventh the *Sultana* was back on the river, headed for Cairo. As the vessel approached a bend in the river some seven miles out of Memphis, engineer Samuel Clemens, continually aware of the patch that had been placed on the faulty boiler, kept checking the safety gauges to make sure that they were operating properly. In the wheelhouse, pilot George Kayton prepared to steer the *Sultana* around the bend.

It was now 2:00 a.m. Suddenly, and without warning, three of the *Sultana*'s boilers exploded with indescribable force, filling the air with a sound that was heard as far away as Memphis. "The explosion came with a report exceeding any artillery I had ever heard," Private Benjamin Johnston of the Michigan cavalry later exclaimed, "and I had heard some that were very heavy at Gettysburg." Hundreds of passengers, many of them asleep, were killed immediately by the blast.

Just as immediately, thousands of hot coals scattered by the explosion turned the *Sultana* into an inferno, one that passenger Andrew T. Peery would never forget. "The fire shot up and I saw sights so terrible and heart-rending. I fail to have language to explain," Peery would later write. "Oh the awful sight! The lower deck for a considerable distance all around the boilers was covered with the dead and wounded. Some were scalded; some seemed to be blind, some of them would rise up partly

❖ A *HARPER'S WEEKLY* ILLUSTRATION depicts the gruesome scene of the burning *Sultana* surrounded by men struggling to stay afloat in the cold water.

and fall, and some were pinned down with timbers of the wreck. I saw hundreds in this frightful plight, crying, praying, screaming, begging, groaning and moaning."

With the *Sultana* now fully engulfed in flames, and with the fiery upper structures of the steamboat crashing down upon them, those who had survived the explosion realized that their only hope for survival was a slim and terrifying one. They had no choice but to jump into the freezing water. Soon there were hundreds of men leaping into the Mississippi from every part of the shattered vessel. The water around the wreckage became filled with the horrific sight of men struggling to stay afloat, most sinking beneath the waves, never to reemerge.

Throughout the long night that followed, there would be death upon death and, as in the case of most disasters, incidents of both bravery and far less admirable behavior. Among the additional passengers that the *Sultana* had taken aboard in Memphis were several women members of the Christian Commission, a Union organization formed to give aid and comfort to Northern soldiers. In his 1892 book *Loss of the Sultana and Reminiscences of Survivors,* Chester Berry described the heroic sacrifice made by one of the women:

> When the flames at last drove all the men from the boat, seeing them fighting like demons in the water in the mad endeavor to save their lives, actually destroying each other and themselves by their wild actions, [this woman] talked to them, urging them to be men, and finally succeeded in getting them quieted down, clinging to the ropes and chains that hung over the bow of the boat. The flames now began to lap around her with their fiery tongues. The men pleaded and urged her to jump into the water and thus save herself, but she refused saying: "I might lose my presence of mind and be the means of the death of some of you." And so rather than run the risk of becoming the cause of death of a single person, she folded her arms quietly over her bosom and burned, a voluntary martyr to the men she had so lately quieted.

As described a month after the tragedy by the Memphis *Argus*, some of the greatest heroics following the explosion were performed by the *Sultana*'s captain.

> Captain Mason rushed into the steam-filled main cabin from the broken hurricane deck and instantly began to help people there. While others ran about in fear, Mason began to hand out chairs, stateroom doors, pieces of wreckage—anything that would float—to the passengers and soldiers and tried to pull wounded and scalded people from the burning debris. His dream of the "greatest trip ever made" on Western waters was suddenly a nightmare. His efforts to get [as many people on board as he could] and the deals he had made were suddenly for naught. Now, during the last minutes of his beloved *Sultana*, as she burned around him, he worked to redeem his wrongs.

Unfortunately, others behaved much differently than the *Sultana*'s captain. As Private John Walker of the 50th Ohio Infantry later recollected: "I thought the sights on the battle-fields terrible, and they were, but they were not to be compared with the sights of that night when the animal nature of man came to the surface in the desperate struggle to save himself regardless of the life of others."

Survivors witnessed incident after incident in which men, desperate to survive, engaged in life-or-death struggles for possession of passing logs, mattresses, or anything that would keep them afloat. Many recalled how as many as 150 frantic souls fought for a place in the *Sultana*'s one lifeboat, once it had been tossed into the water. They remembered with horror how the small boat become so overcrowded with struggling passengers that it sank to the bottom, taking with it an untold number of them.

Perhaps nothing better illustrated the dark side of human nature than the experiences of a female passenger known only as Mrs. Perry. Shortly after the explosion, Mrs. Perry found herself in the river clinging tightly to a door along with six soldiers. Suddenly one of the soldiers, noting that the woman was wearing a life belt, attacked her and tried to tear the belt from her waist. Shoved underwater, Mrs. Perry resurfaced, managed to break away from her attacker, and once again grabbed hold of the door. But the soldier would not give up. Again he came at her, once again shoving her under the cold water.

Mrs. Perry was now close to drowning. But with the little breath that was left in her, she forced herself to the surface, where she spotted a second door floating not far away. Somehow she managed to swim to this door, only to find a soldier clinging to it and shouting for her to stay away. When Mrs. Perry grabbed hold of the door, this soldier also attacked her and for the third time she found herself thrust into the river. Even the amazing Mrs. Perry was ready to give up when miraculously the first door came floating by and she was able to grab hold of it. Fortunately for the courageous woman, this time her first attacker was nowhere to be seen among the others soldiers still clinging to the door.

Mrs. Perry was indeed fortunate. So too were James and Jesse Millsaps. When the explosion rocked the *Sultana,* the two brothers, who had fought side by side in the same unit during the war, became separated. Each found himself clinging to the end of a log, which he shared with another person at the opposite end. Because of the darkness, the other person could not be seen. It was not until they were rescued that the Millsaps brothers discovered that they had been clinging to the same log.

A number of those struggling to save their lives in the water had a special concern. Among the cargo that the *Sultana* had taken aboard was a live alligator transported in a large wooden crate. Not realizing that the animal had been killed so that the crate could be used to float upon, several of those struggling in the Mississippi were genuinely fearful that every splash they heard was the alligator ready to devour them. "Everyone that was on the *Sultana* knew something about the monstrous alligator that was on the boat," Benjamin Davis recalled. "While the boat was burning the alligator troubled me almost as much as the fire." Ira B. Horner had the same concern. "Although I felt that I would not drown," he wrote, "at the same time I did not feel comfortable from the fact that there was an alligator . . . keeping me company."

Unlike Horner, most of those who had somehow survived the explosion were hardly certain that they would not drown. Even those who managed to gain hold of some object to keep them from drowning had no idea if they would live to see another day.

J. Walter Elliott and another soldier had spent the night floating on a mattress that eventually carried them to a tree rising out of the waters that lapped the Arkansas shore. There, in the tree, they spent the longest night of their lives.

> Minutes seemed hours . . . There was no sound to break the oppressive silence save the splashing of the cruel waters and the gurgling moan of a poor fellow who had clasped his broken, scalded arms over a [branch] and drifted, with his mouth just above the water, and lodged near us, dying. An occasional feeble cry of distress near by on the other river side, was answered by voices up the bank. Oh, would morning never dawn on night so hideous?

DAWN FINALLY DID BREAK, and with it came the full realization of the enormity of what had taken place. The bodies of more than 1,700 soldiers were scattered up and down the river. The remains of the shattered and burned-out *Sultana* lay sunken in the riverbed off the tiny settlement of Mound City, Arkansas. As Ensign James H. Berry of the Union ironclad gunboat *Essex* sadly noted, "The cries of sufferers had ceased and all who had not been rescued had gone down."

Amazingly, there were hundreds who had survived, most of them clinging to trees and bushes on the riverbanks and on small, flooded Mississippi islands. Rescuers who came upon them had a strange story to tell. Many of those who they found in the trees or perched upon rocks on the Mississippi shore had spent the latter part of the long night cheering themselves and their fellow survivors on by singing familiar songs or by imitating the sounds of the birds and frogs whose voices rose above that of

❖ THE IRONCLAD USS *ESSEX* was enlisted in the search-and-rescue of survivors from the *Sultana* disaster.

the waves. All were grateful to be alive. As Ohio infantryman Alexander Brown later declared, "Now, when I hear persons talking about being hard up, I think of my condition at that time—up in a tree in the middle of the Mississippi River. A thousand miles from home, not one penny to my name, nor a pocket to put it in."

The coming of day also brought with it stories of heroic rescues that had taken place in the dark hours after the explosion. Survivors told of how, little more than an hour after the blast, the captain, crew, and passengers of the *Bostonia II*, a steamboat headed down the Mississippi to Memphis, had saved more than 150 lives by throwing the vessel's lines, along with planks, chairs, and anything else that would float, into the water, and how the *Bostonia II*'s lifeboats had made repeated trips to collect those who were still alive.

Throughout the night, small boats from the various U.S. military vessels that operated on the Mississippi, including the *Tyler* and the *Essex,* searched the disaster site, picking up survivors. They were joined by the Mississippi steamboats the *Jenny Lind* and the *Arkansas.* Each rescue had its own story.

"One poor boy clutched to the limb of a tree so tightly that we could not force him to let go his hold," reported an officer aboard the *Tyler.* "We took him and the limb aboard together."

Ironically, a number of the Union soldiers who were saved were rescued by former members of the Confederate troops. Among the former Confederates was eighteen-year-old DeWitt Clinton Spikes, who, along with his parents, three sisters, two brothers, and niece, had booked passage on the *Sultana* in New Orleans before the steamboat had made its way to Vicksburg. In the chaos following the explosion, Spikes had lost sight of his family. Saved by one of the rescue vessels, he was taken ashore at Mound City. Within minutes, however, he began helping in the rescue effort, all the while searching for his loved ones. He never found them, but before the night was over Spikes personally saved fourteen people and assisted in the rescue of twenty-five others. Another former Confederate soldier, J. G. Berry, along with his friend George Malone, played a key role in rescuing as many as one hundred people, almost all of them Union soldiers. Confederate officer Frank Barton was also credited with saving the lives of several soldiers, men who, not that long ago, had been his bitter enemies.

The last boat carrying survivors reached Memphis at about noon on April 28. Almost all of those rescued were taken to various Memphis hospitals or to the city's Soldiers' Home. Soon these facilities became filled with people searching for friends or relatives who had been aboard the ill-fated steamboat. Among them was Arthur Jones, who, in a letter to his brother, wrote:

> We are still in hopes that more of our boys will yet be found, but it is very doubtful. Those of us who are left can only mourn their loss, and deeply sympathize with their friends and relatives. It will

indeed be a great blow to those who were daily expecting their boys, fathers, and husbands home, many of them having been absent for years . . . . After all their suffering in Southern prisons, getting safely within our lines, on our route homeward . . . to have this terrible calamity, hurling so many into eternity, it makes me shudder as I write. No tongue can tell or pen describe the suffering that was on that boat on the morning of the 27th.

Just as the exact number of people who were loaded upon the *Sultana* will remain a mystery, the exact number of those who died in her sinking will never be known. One of the earliest official reports of the disaster placed the number of fatalities at 1,238. Later, the U.S. Customs Service placed the death toll at 1,547. Both figures are much too low. Given that there may have been as many as 2,500 people aboard the vessel, that bodies continued to be found for months—some as far away as Vicksburg—and that at least 300 of the 800 who were rescued later died in hospitals, the final death count, in all probability, was over 1,800: all but 100 of them Union soldiers.

Soon after the disaster, three separate military investigations into the tragedy were conducted. Hoping to save face, the army did not publicize the investigations and held them as secretly as they could. In the end, it was officially proclaimed that overloading was not the cause of the disaster. Nor was the temporary patch that had been placed on one of the boat's boilers found to be a contributing factor to the explosion. Instead, the army ruled that the cause of the disaster was mismanagement of the water levels in the *Sultana*'s four interconnected boilers, particularly when water shifted from one boiler to another whenever the vessel leaned sharply one way or another while rounding a bend in the river, leading to overheating.

Only one individual was charged with misconduct regarding the tragedy. He was Union officer Captain Frederic Speed, the assistant adjutant general at Vicksburg. Brought before a military court, Speed was accused with knowingly overloading the *Sultana* and with accepting bribes in the process. Found guilty, he was sentenced to be dishonorably

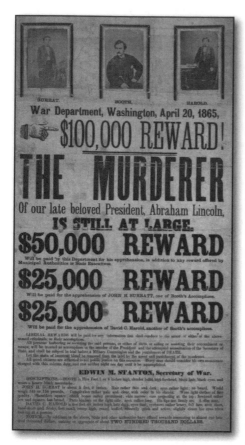

War Department, Washington, April 20, 1865,

$100,000 REWARD!

THE MURDERER

Of our late beloved President, Abraham Lincoln,

IS STILL AT LARGE.

$50,000 REWARD

$25,000 REWARD

$25,000 REWARD

EDWIN M. STANTON, Secretary of War.

❖ AN APRIL 20, 1865, War Department poster offered a $100,000 reward for the capture of Booth and his accomplices.

discharged from the army. Some six months later, however, a judge advocate general overturned the conviction, and Speed was honorably mustered out of the service. With the overturning of his conviction, all official inquiries into the *Sultana* tragedy came to an end. No one was ever held responsible for the calamity.

It is understandable why the army was determined not to publicize the violent death of such a staggering number of its soldiers, particularly men who had suffered so greatly in Confederate prison camps. But what about the nation's press? Certainly so enormous a tragedy should have filled the country's newspapers. Yet it didn't.

In part, the story was buried in the back pages for one of the same reasons that the army had conducted its investigations so quietly. After five years of civil war, the nation had grown accustomed to horrendous loss of life and was anxious to put such news behind it. As a reporter for the Memphis *Argus* wrote only eleven days after the disaster,

> We have, as a people, become so accustomed to suffering of horrors during the past few years that they soon seem to lose their appalling features, and are forgotten. Only a few days ago more than 1,500 lives

were sacrificed to fire and water, almost within sight of the city. Yet, even now, the disaster is scarcely mentioned—some new excitement has taken its place.

Another reason for the scant coverage had to do with other momentous events that were taking place at the time of the calamity. Details about Abraham Lincoln's assassination thirteen days before the *Sultana* explosion still filled the nation's newspapers. So too did coverage of the many funerals and memorial services honoring the fallen president. And readers demanded every detail the newspapers could provide about the capture and killing of Lincoln's assassin, John Wilkes Booth.

There were more subtle reasons as well for the lack of attention given to the *Sultana*. The tragedy had taken place in the West at a time when the nation's major and most influential newspapers were located in the East. Almost all the victims of the tragedy were from places far away from the East. As former Pennsylvania congressman John Covode wrote after looking into the disaster, "No troops belonging to States East of Ohio were lost." He might have added that almost none of the victims were either wealthy or well known. Had they been, their deaths would certainly have engendered greater newspaper coverage, even in the East.

So the nation's greatest maritime disaster slipped into obscurity. And there, for the most part, it has remained lost to time.

→ EIGHT ←

AMERICA'S FIRST SUBWAY
Secrets under Broadway (1870)

W hen the New York City Interborough Rapid Transit subway, commonly known as the IRT, was officially opened on October 27, 1904, it changed the nature of the nation's largest metropolis and was accompanied by one of the greatest celebrations the city had ever known. But few of those who engaged in that celebration were aware of the fact that the IRT was not the first subway built in New York, and most people today don't know about it. The amazing story of the construction of the city's first underground railway has been largely lost to history. At its heart is the tale of one man's determination to save the city he loved and to revolutionize the way people moved about within it. It is a story made even more remarkable by the fact that the subway he constructed was built almost entirely in secret.

By the time this secret subway was built, New York had become the envy of other metropolises around the world. As early as 1842, the editor of the daily *New York Aurora*, a twenty-two-year-old with a future named Walt Whitman, wrote, "Who does not know that our city is the great place of the Western Continent, the heart, the brain, the focus, the main spring, the pinnacle, the extremity, the no more beyond of the New World."

❖ An 1868 lithograph of a proposed rail arcade—an elevated railroad—was offered as one solution to the overcrowding in New York City's streets.

By the 1860s, New York had become a commercial, financial, and industrial giant, home to more than 800,000 people. Thousands of others poured into the city each year to take advantage of the growing metropolis's marvelous restaurants, department stores and shops, music halls, and theaters. Nowhere in the nation were there more libraries, museums, or other cultural institutions. It was, in many ways, indeed what young Walt Whitman claimed it to be.

But New York also had a tremendous problem. Its streets were so congested with traffic that the city was coming to a standstill. Every day, hundreds of horse-drawn, buslike vehicles called omnibuses clogged the streets, a situation made worse by the way their drivers raced recklessly from one side of the street to the other, competing for passengers. It was

❖ A chaotic New York City street ca. 1870.

not only a dangerous situation, but a frustrating one as well. "You cannot accomplish anything in the way of business without devoting a whole day to it," wrote author Mark Twain. "You cannot ride [to your destination] unless you are willing to go in a packed omnibus that labors, and plunges, and struggles along at the rate of three miles in four hours and a half."

Adding to the mayhem were hundreds of horse-drawn delivery wagons and private carriages. The health hazards caused by the traffic were not slight. Several New York doctors speculated that many of the nervous disorders suffered by the city's residents were caused by the constant clatter of horse hooves and wooden wagon wheels. What was not speculative was the very real danger caused by the tons of manure that the animals dropped on the streets every day. Obviously a solution was needed, a fact stated forcefully on October 8, 1864, by the *New York Herald*, when it described the experience of riding in city public transportation:

> The driver swears at the passengers and the passengers harangue the driver through the strap-hole—a position in which even Demosthenes could not be eloquent. Respectable clergymen in white chokers are obliged to listen to loud oaths. Ladies are disgusted, frightened and insulted. Children are alarmed and lift up their voices and weep. . . . Thus the omnibus rolls along, a perfect Bedlam on wheels. . . . The cars are quieter than the omnibuses, but much more crowded. People are packed into them like sardines in a box, with perspiration for oil. The seats being more than filled, the passengers are placed in rows down the middle, where they hang on by the straps, like smoked hams in a corner grocery. To enter or exit is exceedingly difficult. Silks and broadcloth are ruined in the attempt. As in the omnibuses pickpockets take advantage of the confusion to ply their vocation. . . . The foul, close, heated air is poisonous. A healthy person cannot ride a dozen blocks without a headache. . . . it must be evident to everybody that neither the cars nor the stages supply accommodations enough for the public, and that such accommodations as they do supply are not of the right sort. Both the cars and the omnibuses might

be very comfortable and convenient if they were better managed, but something more is needed to supply the popular and increasing demand for city conveyances.

It was a statement with which Alfred Ely Beach could not have agreed more. No one loved New York more than he, but every day as he looked down upon Broadway from his office he shook his head in dismay. Something had to be done to solve the city's horrific traffic problems. Someone had to come up with an idea for an efficient transit system. Beach was confident enough to believe that he might just be the person to do it.

BEACH WAS ONLY THIRTY-NINE IN OCTOBER 1864, but he had already led a remarkable life. In July 1846, thanks to money he received from his wealthy father, he and a former classmate, Orson D. Munn, purchased a small weekly journal called *Scientific American*.

Although he was only nineteen years old, Beach had ambitious plans for the publication. Aware that the nation was in the midst of an

❖ ALFRED ELY BEACH.

unprecedented technological and scientific revolution, he was determined to make the magazine the printed voice of the remarkable changes that were taking place. The fact that Beach increased the magazine's focus on descriptions of new inventions and newly applied-for patents ensured the success of the magazine and led to a whole new business avenue for the young entrepreneur. As the magazine became increasingly popular, inventors and tinkerers began appearing at *Scientific American*'s office, seeking advice about obtaining patents for their creations. Sensing a real opportunity, Beach and

Scientific American.

THE ADVOCATE OF INDUSTRY, AND JOURNAL OF SCIENTIFIC, MECHANICAL AND OTHER IMPROVEMENTS.

VOL. XIV.   NEW YORK, APRIL 16, 1859.   NO. 32.

THE
SCIENTIFIC AMERICAN,
PUBLISHED WEEKLY
At No. 37 Park-row (Park Building), New York,
BY MUNN & CO.

O. D. MUNN, S. H. WALES, A. E. BEACH.

Responsible Agents may also be found in all the
principal cities and towns of the United States.

Single copies of the paper are on sale at the office of
publication, and at all the periodical stores in this city,
Brooklyn and Jersey City.

Sampson Low, Son & Co., the American Booksellers,
47 Ludgate Hill, London, Eng., are the British Agents
to receive subscriptions for the SCIENTIFIC AMERICAN.

TERMS—Two Dollars per annum.—One Dollar in
advance, and the remainder in six months.

☞ See Prospectus on last page. No Traveling
Agents employed.

The Rise, Progress and Influence of the "Scientific American."

We spread before our readers, in this issue, several illustrations, accompanied by somewhat voluminous details of the rise and progress of the SCIENTIFIC AMERICAN, and also of the American & European Patent Agency Offices connected therewith. We think there are few of our readers, whatever may be their occupations or tastes, who will not find in these details something of interest and profit. There has been a question in the minds of some, as to the propriety of connecting these two departments of business in one establishment. This doubt will be dispelled at once, when it is considered that they very naturally unite themselves. In thus combining two professions, we were but imitating the practice of English and other European scientific journalists—for example, in England, Newton's London Journal of Arts and Sciences, the Repertory of Patents, the Mechanics' Magazine, the Artisan, &c.; and in Paris, L'Invention (by the late lamented M. Gardissal), Le Genie Industriel, &c., all of which are under the care of editors who are well known to be the ablest and most reliable patent-solicitors in Europe. If the scientific journalist is industrious, and at all competent to the discharge of his duties, his researches into the various fields of scientific literature and of mechanical art and invention are necessarily more extended than those of any other person; and hence his greater familiarity with "things new and old" in these branches.

In narrating the history of the SCIENTIFIC AMERICAN, we shall be compelled to refer more or less to ourselves, but we shall endeavor to do so in a manner not offensive to good taste. Our time, our talents, our energies, and our capital, for fourteen years past, have all been unceasingly devoted to the building-up of an establishment which has become almost, as it were, one of the fixed institutions of the country. We will not attempt to conceal the fact that we have an honest pride in contemplating the results of our labors—a pride which is equivalent to that which the patriot has towards his country, the father in the well-being of his children, and the right-minded ruler in the success of all good schemes for the prosperity and improvement of the people placed under his care.

Our reflections naturally revert to Volume I. of the SCIENTIFIC AMERICAN. On the 28th day of August, 1845, there issued from a little "7 by 9" office, No. 11 Spruce-street (within a stone's throw of where we are now sitting), the first number of what was destined to be an important feature in American literature, namely, a popular and enduring scientific journal. It was a folio sheet, 20 inches by 15, and in making its modest bow to the public,

its first column contained a scientific rhyme running thus:—

" *Attraction* is a curious power
That none can understand ;
Its influence is everywhere—
In water, air, and land.
It keeps the earth compact and tight,
As though strong bolts were through it.
And, what is more mysterious yet,
It binds us mortals to it !"

Rufus Porter was the founder and first

Volume I., No. 4, having the shape of a revoloidal spindle or, in other words, a winged Winan's steamer.

The engraving on the first page of Vol. I., illustrates an improved railroad-car which, although well executed for that time, now looks rather coarse by the side of those which now adorn our pages. A picture and description of the *Great Britain* steamship (the *Leviathan* of her day) and many interesting articles and items fill up the remainder of the paper. The editor, in his first public address, sets forth in plain terms the intention and purpose of the journal. He says:—"We have made arrangements to furnish the intelligent and liberal working men, and those who delight in those beauties of nature which consist in laws of mechanics, chemistry and other branches of Natural Philosophy, with a paper that will instruct while it diverts or amuses them, and which will retain its excellence and value when political and ordinary news-

editor of the SCIENTIFIC AMERICAN ; he was a man of eccentricity of genius, and by no means destitute of qualities of originality, as the contents of the first volume of this journal will abundantly testify. Most of the illustrations of *peculiarly unique* inventions, and the theological discussions that appeared weekly under the pictorial heading of "The Ark," prove

papers are thrown aside and forgotten. In conducting this publication we shall endeavor to avoid all expressions of sentiment, on any sectional, sectarian or political party subject ; but we shall exercise a full share of independence in the occasional exposure of ignorance and knavery." This was the standard the present editors were pledged to follow ; and we think that one grand element of our present success is owing to the fact that," throughout thirteen years and a half, we have earnestly striven to preserve that pledge inviolate. "Come good report or ill report," our course has been onward ; telling plainly our honest convictions and giving our reasons therefor ; none being more ready to confess their errors than ourselves whenever convinced that we were in the wrong. When the paper arrived at the age of forty-five weeks (the office having just previously been removed to No. 128 Fulton-street), it passed entirely under the control of its present editors ; and the

that he was not only a man of science but also a christian philosopher. But he was evidently designed for another epoch, and he retired long ago from the editorial chair ; and when last we heard from him, he was engaged in the great and laudable enterprise of getting up a joint-stock company to build an aerial chariot according to a plan illustrated in

name of "Munn & Company" first appeared in the imprint. At this time it had *less than three hundred* paying subscribers. Thus during the whole of the first year its progress had been very slow ; but at the close of the volume, the skies seemed to brighten somewhat, and we felt encouraged to enlarge the paper and to commence a new volume in its present "quarto" form. The illustrations improved in excellence ; and as we grew better acquainted with the tastes of our readers, we were better able to supply them with a scientific dish more palatable and digestible. Before the close of the second volume the inventive genius of the country began rather to concentrate its confidence in our humble office ; so much so that, on page 369 of that volume, we published a very modest announcement that we would undertake the preparation of specifications and drawings and otherwise attend to the prosecuting of applications for Letters Patent. This notice laid the foundation of

VIEW OF THE "SCIENTIFIC AMERICAN" OFFICE, NEW YORK.

❖ THE FRONT PAGE of volume 14 of *Scientific American*, April 16, 1859, depicts an illustration of the Scientific American Patent Agency building.

Munn established Munn and Co., also known as the Scientific American Patent Agency, a company devoted both to helping inventors compose their patent applications as effectively as possible and to monitoring the progress of each application once it was being processed by the U.S. Patent Office.

It was a unique business, and it became so successful that by the late 1850s more than three thousand patents were being filed by Beach's company each year. Ten years later, more than a third of all the patents awarded in the United States had been submitted by the Scientific American Patent Agency, which, by this time, had opened branches in other locations, including one in Washington, D.C., directly across from the U.S. Patent Office.

It is not surprising that Beach became an inventor himself, given that he was constantly surrounded by inventors, their creations, and their patent applications. Beach's agency filed patents for his own inventions, including a patent for the world's first cable railway system and another for a machine by which blind persons could create printed messages. Although Beach never followed up on these inventions, the cable systems later built in San Francisco and Chicago were based on his design, and his invention of a printing machine for the blind led directly to the development of the modern typewriter. And that was not all. He had become fascinated with the power of pneumatic tubes, particularly what he saw as their potential for transportation.

Still, with all that he had achieved, Beach was a dissatisfied man. There had to be a way, he believed, to solve New York's disastrous traffic problem. His first idea was to build elevated railways above the city, thus relieving the congested streets below. But as he thought through this idea more fully, he backed away from it. Elevated railways would make the streets below them dark and uninviting. They would be as noisy as the omnibuses that clogged the streets. Most important, they would not be able to carry enough people to provide a real solution.

No, he told himself, the answer lay elsewhere. It had to be something far more dramatic, far more effective. And increasingly he became convinced that he had the solution. It had to be a subway, an underground system that could move people away from all the congestion, noise, and health hazards. Subways weren't a completely new concept. The London subway, built in 1863, had already transported millions of people. But that system, based on locomotives pulling the cars, had proved terribly problematic. The locomotives gave off noxious fumes that had already made a number of people seriously ill. In addition, locomotives, which burned a low grade of coal, also gave off showers of sparks, and more than one passenger had had his clothing set afire. If a subway was the answer, then there had to be a much better way to propel the cars. And it had to be totally safe and totally clean.

He found his answer in work he had already done. In his fascination with pneumatics, Beach had spent considerable time reading about pneumatic railways that had been built in England to carry mail and small packages. He had been particularly impressed with the accomplishments of British engineer Thomas Rammell, who, in 1863, had constructed an underground pneumatic tube through which mail had been successfully transported. Sadly for Rammell, his system—which ran in Camden, London, between an arrivals parcel office and a district post office several miles away—proved too costly to be profitable and was eventually abandoned. But what impressed Beach the most about Rammell's primitive operation was not that it worked, but that several people had actually snuck aboard Rammell's cars and had safely made the journey, propelled by air through the underground tube.

He had become even more intrigued when he had read about how Rammell had built a small aboveground tube designed to carry passengers for about a quarter of a mile between two of the gates at London's great Crystal Palace Exhibition. Particularly interesting was a report on Rammell's tube that had appeared in *Mechanics Magazine* in 1864. "The entire distance [of the tunnel], six hundred yards," the publication proclaimed, "is transversed in about 50 seconds . . . The motion is of course easy and pleasant, and the ventilation ample, without being in any way excessive. . . . We feel tolerably certain that the day is not very distant when metropolitan railway traffic can be conducted on this principle with so much success, as far as popular likeing goes, that the locomotive will be unknown on the underground lines."

If there was anyone with whom that prediction would resonate, it was Beach. But he also knew that it was a prophecy that lacked details of how such a system could be made practical. First of all, there was the not so incidental challenge of building a tunnel, not under the open grounds of Crystal Palace Park, but under one of the busiest streets in the world. And Beach realized that another problem would have to be faced. How do you motivate city dwellers to descend into an ill-lit, spooky underground world to get on trains?

But the more he thought about it, the more he became convinced that a pneumatic subway was the only answer. One thing he knew for certain. Even in operating the first-stage experimental short line he was intending to build, he would need the biggest fan he could obtain to propel his cars with air and the largest steam engine available to most effectively power the fan.

After weeks of investigation, he discovered a company in Indiana that made a machine that was used in ventilating mines. In describing the machine (which he called an æolor after the Greek god of wind, Æolus), Beach later wrote, "[It] is by far the largest machine of the kind ever made. . . . [It] weighs fifty tons, or rather more than a common locomotive engine. The æolor is to the pneumatic railway what the locomotive is to the ordinary steam railroad. The locomotive supplies the power to draw the car; the æolor gives motive force to the air by which the pneumatic car is moved. The æolor is capable of discharging over one hundred thousand cubic feet of air per minute, a volume equal in bulk to the contents of three ordinary three story dwelling houses." No wonder that workers in the factory that made the machine gave it the nickname the "Western Tornado."

With his giant "blower," Beach now believed he had the machinery to power his unique subway. But he was well aware that in order to impress the New York legislature, the press, and the public, he would have to go a giant step further. He had to attract riders by making the subway as appealing and comfortable as possible. Beach began by designing a subway car equipped with one of the new marvels of the age, zircon lights, which burned clearer and far brighter than ordinary gaslights. His design called for the car to be fitted with the richest, most comfortable upholstery available and a sturdy pneumatically sealing airtight door. Then he was struck with a truly inspired idea.

Realizing that his subway needed a waiting room, and that the waiting room was where passengers would form their first vital impressions of the subway, Beach laid out plans for a 120-by-14-foot room that would be as elegant as the finest room in the most expensive New York hotel. Its features included a crystal chandelier, fine paintings, a grand piano, and a huge fountain filled with goldfish—all beneath the city. Nothing like it had even been imagined.

But would it all work? Beach was absolutely convinced that it would. In fact, now that he was convinced he had worked out the details, it was, to him, a most uncomplicated idea. What could be simpler, he later explained, than a system by which the blower propelled his car from one end of his tunnel to the other "like a sail-boat before the wind?" What could be more easily imagined than that the blower would then reverse the airflow, sucking the car back to where it had begun "like soda through a straw?" In what would become a phrase he would use over and over again, Beach would declare, "A tube, a car, a revolving fan. Little more is required."

It was an understatement, of course. Much more was, in fact, required. First he had to publicly demonstrate that his idea would work. Then he had to convince the New York legislature to give him a license to build an experimental line. And should all that be accomplished, there was the small matter of building a tunnel under New York's busiest street.

BEACH GOT HIS OPPORTUNITY TO demonstrate the pneumatic tube transport when he learned that the annual highly attended American Institute Fair was to be held on September 17, 1867, in New York. Here was his opportunity to introduce America to the wonders of pneumatic transportation, his opportunity to get the license he needed

❖ TOURISTS EXPERIENCE THE Pneumatic Passenger Railway at the American Institute Fair in New York, 1867.

to make his vision a reality. Over the weeks leading to the fair, he had workers build a 107-foot-long, 16-foot-wide tube. Then he built a car designed to carry ten passengers through this demonstration "tunnel." He provided pneumatic power for the cars by acquiring a fan powerful enough to serve his purposes. Finally, he had the tube hung by huge cables suspended from the armory's ceiling. For the next six weeks, more than 170,000 amazed and delighted men, women, and children rode in Beach's cars. By the time the fair ended, both the public and press

agreed that the "subway" was the event's most spectacular feature. Most important to Beach were the articles in the press that confirmed his belief that the subway was not a mere novelty but the answer to the city's transportation nightmare. The *New York Times* of September 16, 1871, extolled the invention:

> It is . . . estimated that passengers by a through city tube could be carried from City Hall to Madison Square in five minutes, to Harlem

and Manhattanville in fourteen minutes, and by sub-river to Jersey City or Hoboken in five minutes, and to the City Hall, Brooklyn in two minutes. . . .

Leaving to the imaginations of our accomplished readers the pleasant labor of converting, with all the material here afforded them, our confused and crowded city, with its no less crowded water boundaries, into a terrestrial paradise, where easy locomotion on land, on water, beneath them both, or in the air, can be enjoyed at will, we close this article, hoping, with them, that out of this great field of promise we may some day soon pluck flowers of comfort.

Many of the newspaper reports noted that Beach had not only built a tube for carrying passengers but had also, as part of his demonstration of the potential of pneumatic transportation, hung a smaller companion tube through which letters and packages were transported. When the fair finally ended, Alfred Beach's triumph was complete. Almost without hesitation the exposition's officials awarded him their two top prizes— one for his pneumatic passenger railway, the other for what he called his Postal Dispatch.

It was, of course, a great victory. But Beach knew all too well that many obstacles still lay ahead. He had to dig an enormous tunnel. And even before he could begin that daunting project, he had to obtain a charter from both city and state officials. And he was cognizant of the fact that in New York City, this meant getting approval from a man who not only controlled the city, but also may well have been the most corrupt public official that New York or any other American city had ever witnessed.

Standing six feet tall and weighing more than three hundred pounds, William Marcy "Boss" Tweed stood out in every crowd. A man of enormous appetites, his main desire was for money. Tweed entered New York politics as a city alderman in 1852. From that time on, this son of a Scotch-Irish chair maker pursued positions of increasing power as a means to wealth. At one time or another he was a U.S. congressman (1853–55), New York school commissioner (1856–57), member of the board of supervisors for New York County (1858), deputy street commissioner (1861–70), state senator (1867 and 1869), and commissioner of the Department of Public Works (1870). Every one of this staggering array of positions provided Tweed the opportunity to demand enormous bribes and to elicit huge payments for services he never performed. As head of a Democratic political machine in New York known as Tammany Hall, he was able to surround himself with men as dishonest as he was. Their crowning achievement was the way they managed to artificially inflate the cost of the construction of what was formally named the New York County Courthouse, but what came to be commonly called Tweed Courthouse. The building, which in 1858 was originally budgeted at $250,000, eventually cost taxpayers what has been estimated to be as much as $12 million—a good portion of which went into Tweed's pockets.

Some historians have estimated that, expressed in today's currency, Tweed stole between $1.5 billion and $8 billion, making it no surprise

that he was one of the wealthiest men in America. As Beach prepared to apply for his charter, Tweed's holdings included several homes, including a New York City mansion and a large Connecticut country estate, two steam yachts, a private railway car, one of the city's largest printing houses, and one of its most lavish hotels. Among the possessions for which he was best known was the enormous diamond pin without which he was never seen, an ornament that, according to one of his cronies, he wore "like a planet on his shirt front."

❖ AN UNDATED PHOTOGRAPH of William Marcy "Boss" Tweed.

Beach was well aware of both Tweed's power and his character. What troubled him most was the fact that the omnibus and horse-car companies were among the businesses that kicked back money to Tweed. Tweed, he realized, would never approve of a transportation system that might well put these companies out of business unless he was paid a record bribe, probably a large percentage of whatever profits the subway earned. This was something that Beach could not abide. He would have to come up with a plan every bit as creative as the one that had taken his dream of a subway this far.

He came up with a bold idea. Since Tweed was certain to block any plan to build a subway for carrying passengers, he would apply for a charter for the construction of an underground railway for the sole purpose of delivering mail and parcels. Once he secured his charter, he would build a passenger subway, an underground system so efficient, so safe, so comfortable, and so responsive to the city's greatest need that once it was revealed, even the mighty Boss Tweed would not be able to prevent the legislature from granting his ultimate goal: a charter to extend the subway throughout New York City.

His application to the legislature asking for permission to build two small mail delivery underground tubes was quickly approved. Even Tweed saw no threat to his interests in a mail delivery system. Once the license was granted, however, Beach put the second part of his plan in motion, asking permission to build a larger single tube to enclose the two smaller ones, which he claimed would make his mail delivery operation more efficient. This application was approved in May 1869, with Tweed seeing no reason to oppose it.

Now came the biggest challenge of all: not only building a subway that would be so impressive that officials would overlook his deception, but also building it without anyone finding out that it was really a passenger system until it was completed. The nation's first subway was about to be built in secret.

TESTING THE CORRECTNESS OF POSITION AT NIGHT.

❖ This illustration of engineers working at night on Beach's tunnel accompanied an article about the subway in the February 19, 1870, issue of *Frank Leslie's Illustrated Newspaper.*

LIKE EVERYTHING ELSE WITH WHICH he had been involved, Beach had planned well. His first step, back in December 1868, had been to rent one of the largest department stores on Broadway. The building had not one but two large basement levels. It fit Beach's scheme perfectly. His tunnel would be dug only at night, when there would be much less traffic overhead to detect what might be going on underneath. As they dug the tunnel, the workmen would pile the dirt in the basements. Then in the darkest hours of the morning, the dirt would be carted away in wagons with muffled wheels and dumped in New York's East River.

It was an inspired plan, but the greatest challenge of actually digging the tunnel remained. Long before he had applied for his charter, Beach had begun to address the problem. First, improving upon a design that had its origins in 1818 and one that was used by English engineer Marc

❖ A *FRANK LESLIE'S* ILLUSTRATION of workmen advancing the shield and bricking the tunnel walls.

Isambard Brumel in building the Thames tunnel in 1825, Beach built his own tunneling machine. He called it a hydraulic shield. Open at both ends and cylindrical in shape, it looked like an open-ended barrel. A hand pump within the machine exerted a pressure of some 126 tons, which kept the device stable while moving it forward, allowing the series of rams at the front to dig eight feet of the tunnel each night. Beach saw to it that as each portion of the tunnel was dug, workmen, following the shield, bricked the walls of the portion that had been completed.

For a man who had never seen a tunnel dug, let alone staked his dream on building one successfully, Beach proved masterful in overseeing many aspects of its construction. But he was also wise enough to realize that he needed expert help as well. Fortunately, he was able to hire the perfect person to serve as his chief engineer: Joseph Dixon, the Englishman who had overseen the building of the tunnel for the London subway.

Together, the two men, along with Beach's son Frederick, who served as foreman of the digging crews, made certain that progress was made each night. All three were certainly cognizant of how perilous the work was for all those involved. They were digging twenty-one feet below the surface, and even though traffic on Broadway at night was far lighter than during the daytime, Beach must have been constantly concerned that a portion of the street would be weakened by the digging and that a rider on horseback would fall through to the tunnel below, causing bodily harm and exposing the secret project to the outside world.

Amazingly, night after night the project moved on without incident, until it suddenly came to a standstill as workmen encountered a stone wall blocking their path. The vexing question for Beach was whether or not the wall could be removed without causing the street above to collapse, which would literally bring the project to a crashing and, in all probability, tragic halt. But, with Beach directing the removal stone by stone, the structure, which was later revealed to be the wall of an old Dutch fort, was successfully taken down.

By the end of the first week of January 1870, the subway was almost completed. But then the unexpected happened. Somehow, a reporter from the *New York Herald* found out what was really going on underneath Broadway, went through the department store, descended into the basement, and saw what was taking place. Beach was disappointed at having his secret uncovered so near to the end of the project, but he had to admit that it was remarkable that the project had not been discovered before then. When both the *Herald* and *New York Times* published stories describing what was being built below Broadway, he knew what he had to do next.

First, he needed to make sure that everything involving the tunnel, the cars, and the waiting room was as perfect as he could hurriedly make them. Then he needed to hold a lavish reception for city and state officials, showing off what had been accomplished. Then he would open the subway to the public. But before all that could be completed, he needed to buy himself some time, so he had Dixon write a letter to all the newspapers explaining the relatively brief delay. The letter was published in the January 8 edition, and stated in part:

> Our original intention was to construct the entire line of tunnel from Warren to Cedar-street, before opening it for inspection, but we have concluded to yield to the strong desire manifested by the Press for an earlier examination. We have, therefore stopped work on the tunnel, and are now fitting up the blowing machinery, engnes [sic], boilers, waiting rooms, &c, with a view of inviting public inspection. . . . Our tunnel commences at the southwest corner of Broadway and Warren-street, curving out to the centre of Broadway and continuing down a little below Murray-street. . . . The top of the tunnel comes within twelve feet of the pavement, so that the walls of adjoining buildings can in no way be affected. We should have preferred to keep silent until our work could speak for us; as it is we beg the Press and public to have a little patience, and in three or four weeks at furthest we will cheerfully afford them an opportunity of inspecting our premises and forming their own judgment as to its merits.

On February 26, Beach held his reception for the region's dignitaries and the press. It caused a sensation. Every newspaper featured the story on its front page. "PROPOSED UNDERGROUND RAILROAD—A FASHIONABLE RECEPTION HELD IN THE BOWELS OF THE EARTH—THE GREAT BORE EXPLORED," read the headline in the *Herald*. Other newspapers focused on what they viewed as an extraordinary accomplishment. "The problem of tunneling Broadway has been solved," exclaimed the *Evening Mail*. "There is no mistake about it . . . the work has been pushed vigorously on by competent workmen, under a thoroughly competent superintendent, whose name is Dixon. May his shadow increase for evermore." It was only the beginning of the praise heaped upon Beach and his subway. "Different papers [will] give different account of the enterprise," the *Sunday Mercury* wrote, "but the opening yesterday must have convinced them all of the power of human imagination." "This means the end of

❖ TRAVELING UNDERGROUND in comfort; from the *Frank Leslie's* article.

street dust of which uptown residents get not only their fill, but more than their fill, so that it runs over and collects on their hair, their beards, their eyebrows and floats in their dress like a vapor on a frosty morning," exclaimed *Scientific American*. "Such discomforts will never be found in the tunnel."

It was praise that exceeded Beach's hopes. Immediately he announced that on March 1 the subway would be open to the public and that for twenty-five cents, a passenger could experience the joy of being quietly and comfortably transported in a car propelled by air. By this time, each New York newspaper seemed to be trying to outdo its rivals in heaping praise on what had been revealed. "Such as expected to find a dismal cavernous retreat under Broadway," exclaimed the *New York Times*, "opened their eyes at the elegant reception room, the light, airy tunnel and the general appearance of taste and comfort in all the apartments, and those who expected to pick out some scientific flaw in the project, were silenced by the completeness of the machinery, the solidity of the work, and the safety of the running apparatus."

High praise indeed, topped only perhaps by accounts from those members of the public who were among the first to ride the pneumatic railway. "We took our seats in the pretty car, the gayest company of twenty that ever entered a vehicle," a passenger later wrote.

> The conductor touched a telegraph wire on the wall of the tunnel; and before we knew it, so gentle was the start, we were in motion, moving from Warren street down Broadway. In a few moments the conductor opened the door and called out "Murray street!" with a business-like air that made us all shout with laughter. The car came to rest in the gentlest possible style, and immediately began to move back again to Warren Street, where it had no sooner arrived, than in the same gentle and mysterious manner it moved back again to Murray street; and thus it continued to go back and forth for, I should think, twenty minutes, or until we had all ridden as long as we desired. No visible agency gave motion to the car, and the only way that we upon the inside could tell that we were being moved by atmospheric pressure was by holding our hands against the ventilators over the doors. When these were opened, strong currents of pure air came into the car. We could also feel the air-current pressing inward at the bottom of the door. I need hardly say that the ventilation of the pneumatic car is very perfect and agreeable, presenting a strong contrast to the foul atmosphere of [omnibuses and horsecars]. Our atmospheric ride was most delightful, and our party left the car satisfied by actual experience that the pneumatic system of traveling is one of the greatest improvements of the day.

Among the most glowing of the reports were those that hinted of things that even Beach would have declared to be impossible. "So the world goes on," stated Helen Weeks in the February 1871 issue of *Youth's*

Companion, "doing more and more wonderful things every day and who knows but that before you . . . readers are old men and women, you and I may go down [into the subway] and in a twinkling find ourselves in England? Who knows?"

Fanciful of course, but to Beach the reality of his overwhelming success meant that the time had come to push for a charter allowing him to extend his subway throughout New York. "We propose to operate a subway all the way to Central Park, about five miles in all," he stated. "When it's finished we should be able to carry 20,000 passengers a day at speeds up to a mile a minute." In her article, Weeks noted "The days of dusty horsecars and rumbling omnibuses are almost at an end. Snow and dust, heat and cold find no kingdom [in the pneumatic subway]. Warm in winter and cool in summer. . . . The weary man or woman who [now] spends hours daily getting to and from business may, when that joyful day of a completed underground comes, allow five minutes for going five miles."

Five minutes in five miles—what an incredible prospect, so much so that even the strictest legislators were ready to overlook the fact that by building a passenger system rather than a mail delivery system Beach had certainly deceived them. But there was one man who was not willing to either overlook or forgive. As acclaim for the subway mounted, so too did Boss Tweed's anger. His Tammany Hall cronies had never seen him so furious. The master of the art of deception had been hoodwinked. A passenger system, not a mail system, had been constructed under buildings across the street from City Hall, where Tweed spent so much of his time. Worst of all, as far as he was concerned, not a dime had passed into his pockets.

Despite Tweed's outrage, Beach was confident that the legislature would enthusiastically grant his charter. He was right. His application for the extension of the subway was overwhelmingly approved. But he had underestimated Boss Tweed's reach. Once the legislature had granted the charter, the only thing that could revoke it was a veto by New York's governor, John T. Hoffman. And, as Beach should have realized, Hoffman was controlled by Tweed. Not only did Hoffman veto the legislature's action, he gave his approval to another bill that had been submitted by none other than Tweed.

Known as the Viaduct Plan, Tweed's proposal called for the construction of several elevated railways at a cost of more than $80 million. Unlike the subway extension proposal, which Beach had promised to subsidize through money he would raise from private investors, Tweed's plan called for the elevated railway to be built at taxpayers' expense, which provided the Boss yet another way to steal millions of dollars.

Aware of what Tweed was attempting to do, the legislature met in special session in an attempt to override Hoffman's veto. But to Beach's shock and dismay, their vote fell short. After all the acclaim, after he had come so close to having his dream become a reality, Beach was being denied. Still he refused to give up. Mounting a direct appeal to the press and the public, he wrote, "It is only through an underground railway that rapid transit can be realized in New York. The elevated road is inevitably an obstruction, in whatever street it is built, for it is simply an immense bridge, which no one wants before his doors. On the other hand the underground railway is entirely out of sight and disturbs no one."

It was just one of scores of statements that Beach planted in the press. But as months wore on and as thousands of people continued to ride his short subway with joy, even he became discouraged. He could not get the legislature to make another attempt to override the governor's veto. Then yet another unexpected development took place.

In July 1871, an outraged and dissatisfied New York County bookkeeper appeared at the *New York Times* downtown offices. In his arms he carried a huge stack of county records. The documents, he claimed, provided the first concrete proof of the hundreds of bribes and kickbacks that Tweed had received over the years. Soon, other records that were produced provided proof of the millions of dollars that had been stolen during the construction of the new courthouse.

A GROUP OF VULTURES WAITING FOR THE STORM TO "BLOW OVER."—"LET US *PREY.*"

❖ TWEED AND HIS TAMMANY HALL CRONIES are depicted as a group of vultures waiting for the storm to "Blow Over" in this Thomas Nast cartoon from September 23, 1871.

The continuing series of *New York Times* articles that followed shocked even the most staid New Yorkers. Among them was a *Harper's Weekly* artist named Thomas Nast, who, when only twenty-four, had become the nation's leading cartoonist. Now Nast mounted his own anti-Tweed campaign, lambasting him in scores of widely viewed cartoons, calling for Tweed and his Tammany Hall villains to be brought to justice.

For his part, Tweed had been caught by surprise and taken aback by the *Times*'s revelations. But he was even more concerned with Nast's depictions. Arranging a meeting with *Harper's Weekly*'s editor, he reportedly shouted, "I don't care a straw for your newspaper articles; my constituents don't know how to read, but they can't help seeing them damned pictures!"

He was right, and soon the combination of the *Times* articles and Nast's cartoons had an effect that went beyond outraging the public. Other New York newspapers, which had for so long been afraid to challenge Tweed's influence, began printing their own exposés of his criminal acts. Ironically they were joined by a host of newly emboldened city and state officials, long angry with Tweed for not having included them in his payoffs.

Finally, on October 27, 1871, the hitherto indestructible Boss Tweed was arrested. So complex was the case against him that it took fifteen months before he was brought to trial. To the dismay of his prosecutors, the first attempt to convict him ended in a mistrial, but he was tried again in November 1873. This time he was found guilty of fraud and corruption and given a twelve-year sentence.

Tweed's lawyers, however, had another card to play. Filing an appeal to a higher court on the grounds that even though their client had been tried for multiple offenses he could only be legally sentenced for the punishment applicable to just one of the crimes, they succeeded in getting Tweed's sentence reduced to just one year.

The story was still far from over. Upon his release from prison, Tweed was arrested again on civil charges and placed back in prison until he could post bail of $3 million. When it originally appeared that he would be arrested, Tweed had responded to reports that, given his influence, he was bound to try to escape by stating: "Now is it likely I'm going to run away? Ain't my wife, my children's children, and everything and every interest I have in the world here? What would I gain by running away?"

But as he often did, Tweed had lied. During his second incarceration, in a prime example of the influence he still had, he had been allowed to pay a visit to his family. While there, on December 4, 1875, he simply walked out a back door and escaped. He fled to Cuba, then boarded a ship and headed for Spain. What he didn't know was that the government had discovered his eventual destination. When his ship put into a Spanish port, he was arrested, put on a U.S. naval vessel, brought back to America, and imprisoned once again.

Totally deflated and aware that, in exchange for lighter sentences, some of his closest Tammany Hall associates were about to testify against him, Tweed fell seriously ill. The end came on April 12, 1878, when the man who had spent most of his life surrounded by sycophants and curious onlookers died alone in a dingy prison cell.

For Beach, the demise of his greatest nemesis seemed to signal a complete reversal in his fortunes. In early 1873, the legislature, free of Tweed's influence, once again voted to give Beach his extension charter. And a new governor quickly signed the measure.

But the subway was not to be. In late 1873 the United States, as a result of overspeculation in the railroads and the financial markets, was experiencing the beginning of the worst economic depression it had ever experienced—one that would last six years. Many of those who had promised to invest in Beach's enterprise were among the hardest hit. Faced with financial disaster, the New York state and local governments found that supporting a subway system was far down on their list of priorities. Even Beach had to admit that his dream had vanished.

It would be more than a quarter century before New York City would get a subway—not through the vision of a man like Beach or the determination of a group of city officials, but, ironically, through an act of nature.

March 10, 1888, was one of the warmest and most beautiful early spring days that veteran New Yorkers could remember. But the next day was something else entirely. By the time most citizens arose, a howling blizzard was under way, threatening to bury the city in snow. Still, thousands of hardy New Yorkers went to work.

It was a gigantic mistake. By noon, as the snow continued to mount, thousands tried to make their way home. Fallen live electrical wires posed a deadly danger. Signs, tree limbs, and other objects flew uncontrollably through the air, striking and killing or severely injuring scores of others. In one of the most dramatic and dangerous events of the disaster, thousands of passengers attempting to get home via the elevated railroad found themselves terrifyingly trapped high above the city.

❖ A NEW YORK STREET is covered in snow during the blizzard of 1888.

More than four hundred people died in the storm, shocking city officials to the point that, at last, they realized the absolute necessity of constructing an underground transportation system. Mother Nature had accomplished what Beach and other subway proponents had been unable to do. It took two years for construction of the subway to begin. But Beach had been right. Within weeks of the subway's opening on October 27, 1904, New York City's traffic problem, at least for the foreseeable future, had been dramatically alleviated.

Within three years of its initial construction, the subway had become so popular that various extensions were being made, and Beach's vision of an underground system throughout New York and Brooklyn was being realized. Then, in 1912, a startling event took place. As workmen dug an extension of the Broadway line, they broke through a steel and brick wall and discovered Alfred Beach's pneumatic tunnel. There was the subway car, his tracks, his hydraulic shield, and even his fountain. Time, of course, had taken its toll, but they were all still there. Amazingly, rather than bringing these historic objects to the surface where they might be preserved and appreciated by generations to come, the workmen left them there and moved on. One cannot help but wonder what remains, a century later, of Beach's buried achievement. Devlin's Department Store has long been torn down and replaced by another structure, probably destroying the elegant waiting room in the process. Whatever other destruction of America's first subway has taken place, it's safe to say that it has been permanently buried from view.

So too has general knowledge about Beach's other extraordinary achievements. His printing machine for the blind led to the typewriter, the machine that transformed both business and the nature of the workforce. He was a pioneer in the development of pneumatics. The magazine he established remains the world's leading scientific journal. And his hydraulic shield revolutionized the way tunnels were dug. Yet, like his remarkable subway, his name and all that he did has been largely lost to history.

NINE

PESHTIGO

Great Fire in the Forest (1871)

Almost everyone has heard of the Great Chicago Fire of October 8–10, 1871. Although it didn't really start, as legend has it, with Mrs. O'Leary's cow kicking over a lantern in the barn, the Chicago Fire is the most famous of all American conflagrations, a blaze in which some three hundred people were killed and 100,000 were left homeless. Yet, on the very same day that the Chicago Fire started, a firestorm in the tiny lumbering community of Peshtigo, Wisconsin, and its surrounding forests destroyed the entire village and took the lives of more than 1,200 men, women, and children. It was the most devastating fire in U.S. history, but because of the attention historically given to the Chicago Fire, few have heard of it, history books have mostly ignored it, and it has been lost to time.

Located on both banks of a ninety-four-mile-long river that begins in the highest area of northern Wisconsin before descending more than one thousand feet into Green Bay (an arm of Lake Michigan), Peshtigo, like so many frontier settlements, was first inhabited by a succession of fur traders. The area, however, contained even richer resources—excellent farmland and, more important, some of the greatest forests of pine, spruce, and maple in America. By 1856, when Chicago millionaire entrepreneur William B. Ogden—who also served as Chicago's first mayor from 1837

❖ An 1885 illustration of loggers in northern Wisconsin.

❖ WILLIAM BUTLER OGDEN,
photographed in 1912.

to 1838—purchased 13,542 acres of land and a sawmill that had passed through several previous owners, the stage was set for the development of a vibrant, booming, often rowdy lumbering town. Wisconsin Historical Society records note that the name "Peshtigo" comes from a Native American term meaning "snapping turtle," or possibly "wild goose river" or "rapids." What is for certain is that by 1870 the town contained two hotels, a blacksmith shop and foundry, a machine shop, a grocery and butcher shop, a dry goods and clothing store, a barbershop, a jewelry store, an apothecary, and a number of saloons whose main customers were the bawdy lumberjacks who worked the forests surrounding the town. A bridge spanning the river and joining the east and west sides of Peshtigo had just been built, as had a Congregational church, a Presbyterian church, and a Catholic church whose pastor, Father Peter Pernin, was fast becoming one of the town's leading citizens. The pride of Peshtigo was its newly built schoolhouse, but the economic lifeblood of the town was the operations owned by William Ogden.

Ogden's Peshtigo Company was one of the largest sawmills in the nation, equipped with its own gaslight and waterworks systems. The Peshtigo Company had also established a barge line, which ran between Peshtigo Harbor and Chicago. The line allowed lumber manufactured at the sawmill to be transported to a Chicago lumberyard and warehouse, also owned by the company. By 1870, more than seven miles of railroad track running from the surrounding forests to the sawmill had been completed and Ogden had developed ambitious plans for expanding the line.

Closely allied to the Peshtigo Company was Ogden's Peshtigo woodenware factory, already the largest producer of tubs, pails, buckets, broom handles, barrel covers, clothespins, and other wooden household products in America. Ogden's holdings also included a boardinghouse, where many of his lumberjacks, mill workers, and their families lived, and a company dry goods store.

Although it was by far the largest and most fully developed town in the region, Peshtigo was surrounded by fast-growing communities. Six miles northeast was Marinette with its sawmills, the five largest of which produced 217 million board feet of lumber each year. Throughout the vast area known as the Sugar Bush (a popular term for areas of dense

❖ A BIRD'S-EYE-VIEW MAP of Peshtigo, Wisconsin, in September 1871, one month before the fire.

hardwood), divided into the Lower, Middle, and Upper Bushes, were scores of settlements inhabited by immigrants from Germany, Sweden, Norway, and other European and Scandinavian nations who had come to America to carve out farms on the frontier. One of the largest of these settlements was Brussels, established by Belgian Walloon immigrants, the first of whom had arrived in the area in 1853. By 1871 Brussels was a thriving community of sawmills, shingle mills, and flourishing farms. Schools, churches, and stores were being built, farms were being enlarged, and Brussels—like Peshtigo—was regarded as the very symbol of progress.

But there was also danger attached to this progress. It came in the form of deliberately set fires. As the lumberjacks felled hundreds of thousands of trees, they left in their wake enormous piles of tree limbs, pine needles, and sawdust. When they were done with an area, they set fire to the mounds and moved on to the next area of trees to be felled, leaving the wooden piles to burn down to ash.

The lumberjacks were not the only fire makers. Father Pernin wrote in an eyewitness account published in 1874 that

> Farmers had profited [by enlarging] their clearings, cutting down and burning the wood that stood in their way. Hundreds of laborers employed in the construction of a railroad had acted in like manner, availing themselves of both axe and fire to advance their work. Hunters and Indians scour these forests continually, especially in the autumn season, at which time they ascend the streams for trout-fishing, or disperse through the woods deer-stalking. At night they kindle a large fire wherever they may chance to halt, prepare their suppers, then wrapping themselves in their blankets, sleep peacefully, extended on the earth, knowing that the fire will keep at a distance any wild animals. . . . The ensuing morning they depart without taking the precaution of extinguishing the smoldering embers of the fire. . . . Farmers and others act in a similar manner. In this way the woods, particularly in the fall, are gleaming everywhere with fires lighted by man, and which, fed on every side by dry leaves and

branches, spread more or less. If fanned by a brisk gale of wind they are liable to assume most formidable proportions.

Father Pernin may have been concerned, but the lumbermen, the hunters, the farmers, and the railroad builders were not. Even if some fires failed to burn themselves out, they were usually extinguished by the constant rains that characterized the Sugar Bush.

But the fall and winter of 1870 had been particularly dry, and the spring and summer of 1871 were even drier. The many Native Americans

❖ An 1869 illustration of a literal log jam in a Wisconsin river.

who lived in and around Menominee were particularly feeling the effects of the drought. They had never seen the region so dry, with tall pines snapping in the wind and the grasses in the meadows turning brown earlier than ever before. Most alarmingly, by the summer of 1871 there was not enough water in the marshes to float the canoes that were used to gather the wild rice. The Native Americans were not the only ones affected. By the end of summer 1871, the men in the logging camps in both Peshtigo and Marinette found that the rivers were so low that logs could not be floated down them to the sawmills. They had been forced to pile the logs beside the rivers, waiting for rains to swell the rivers to normal size.

To aggravate matters, by the third week of September, the serious lack of rain had caused many of the fires in the woods that had not burned themselves out to spread. Still, most of the area's residents remained unconcerned. Father Pernin, on the other hand, learned firsthand that there indeed was much to fear.

> On September 22, I was summoned, in the exercise of my ministry to the Sugar Bush . . . where a number of farms lie adjacent to each other. Whilst waiting at one of these, isolated from the rest, I took a gun, and, accompanied by a lad of twelve years of age, who offered to guide me through the wood, started in pursuit of some of the pheasants which abounded in the environs. At the expiration of a few hours, seeing that the sun was sinking in the horizon, I bade the child reconduct me to the farmhouse. He endeavored to do so but without success. . . . In less than a half hour's wanderings we perceived that we were completely lost in the woods. . . . The only sounds audible were the crackling of a tiny tongue of fire that ran along the ground, in and out, among the trunks of the trees, leaving them unscathed but devouring the dry leaves that came in its way, and the swaying of the upper branches of the trees announcing that the wind was rising. We shouted loudly, but without evoking any reply. I then fired off my gun several times as tokens of distress. Finally a distant halloo reached our ears . . . when a new obstacle presented itself. Fanned

by the wind, the tiny flames previously mentioned had united and spread over a considerable surface. We thus found ourselves in the center of a circle of fire extending or narrowing, more or less, around us. We could not reach the men who had come to our assistance.... They were obliged to fray a passage for us by beating the fire with branches of trees at one particular point, thus momentarily staying its progress whilst we rapidly made our escape . . . I learned the following day, on my return to Peshtigo, that the town had been in great peril at the very time that I had lost myself in the woods. . . . Hogsheads of water were placed at intervals all round the town, ready for any emergency.

Father Pernin's narrow escape was a harbinger of things to come. So too was an unprecedented event that took place on the following evening. As the people of Peshtigo looked skyward toward the forests, they were amazed to see thousands of birds covered in white ash flying up out of the trees, many of them tall pines that had caught fire. Totally disoriented, the birds flew into one another before being pulled downward, sucked back into the branches of the burning trees. Peshtigo residents hardly had time to comprehend what they had just witnessed when the shrill whistle from the woodenware factory sounded. Sparks and cinders from the woodland fires had blown across the Peshtigo River and had set the sawdust and wood slabs next to the factory on fire. Hundreds of men instantly rushed to the river, formed a human chain, and passed buckets of water back to the factory, extinguishing the blaze before the factory itself could catch on fire.

SUNDAY, SEPTEMBER 24, DAWNED BRIGHT AND BEAUTIFUL, and many Peshtigo citizens, relieved that the town's main source of employment and income had been spared, went off to church. Services had hardly begun when once again the Peshtigo Company's fire whistle sounded. Sawdust and piles of slabs had been set afire again. Again, the men of the river formed a human chain, this time Father Pernin among them. By this time, the priest had become truly alarmed at what fate might be in store for his town and its people. "I have," he wrote, "seen fires sweep over the prairies with the speed of a locomotive and the prairie fire is grand and terrific, but beside a timber fire it sinks into insignificance. In the timber it may move almost as rapidly, but the fire does not go out. . . . It is as though you attempted to resist the approach of an avalanche of fire hurled against you."

Again, the fires beside the woodenware factory were extinguished. Again, most of the Peshtigo residents were left with the belief that the town was in no real danger, a conviction made stronger by a sudden shift in the wind. "Monday, the wind veered to the south and cleared away the smoke," Father Pernin wrote. "Strange to say not a building was burned—the town was saved. Monday the factory was closed to give the men rest, and today, September 27, all is quiet and going on as usual."

It would not last. In the first week of October the fires in the forest intensified. During the day, the sky glowed an eerie shade of yellow. At night it turned bright red. Then the wind changed direction, blowing directly toward Peshtigo. If modern meteorologists were describing what was about to happen, they would label it the "perfect storm." More accurately, it would be described as the "perfect firestorm." On October 7, a huge cyclonic storm swept in from the west, with winds up to as high as one hundred miles per hour. Natural gases, resulting from the burning trees and the peat that was part of much of the woodland soil, rose into the air. Burning coals began falling from the atmosphere like snowflakes.

On October 8, the firestorm struck Peshtigo. A contemporary north Wisconsin journal reported that on

> Sunday evening, after church, for about half an hour a death-like stillness hung over the doomed town. The smoke from the fires in the region around was so thick as to be stifling, and hung like a funeral pall over everything, and all was enveloped in Egyptian darkness. Soon

light puffs of air were felt; the horizon at the south-east, south, and south-west began to be faintly illuminated; a perceptible trembling of the earth was felt, and a distant roar broke the awful silence. People began to fear that some awful calamity was impending, but as yet no one even dreamed of the danger. The illumination soon became intensified into a lurid glare; the roar deepened into a howl, as if all the demons of the infernal pit had been let loose, when the advance gusts of wind from the main body of the tornado struck. Chimneys were blown down, houses were unroofed, and, amid the confusion, terror, and terrible apprehensions of the moment, the fiery element, in tremendous inrolling billows and masses of sheeted flame, enveloped the devoted village.

As soon as the fires appeared on the edge of the town, Father Pernin set his horse free in the street and began digging a trench around his house, spurred on by a "fear, growing more strongly each moment into a certainty." As he dug, he became aware not only of a growing crimson reflection in the western part of the sky, but also of a noise unlike any he had ever heard. "This sound," he later wrote in his diary, "resembled the confused noise of a number of cars and locomotives approaching a railroad station, or the rumbling of thunder, with the difference that it never ceased, but deepened in intensity each moment more and more." There was only one thing to do, he told himself. He had to seek safety in the river. Everyone else in Peshtigo, it seemed, had the same thought.

To reach the river . . . was more than many succeeded in doing . . . How I arrived at it is even to this day a mystery to myself. The air was no longer fit to breathe, full as it was of sand, dust, ashes, cinders, sparks, smoke, and fire. It was almost impossible to keep one's eyes unclosed, to distinguish the road, or to recognize people, though the way was crowded with pedestrians, as well as vehicles crossing and crashing against each other in the general flight. Some were hastening towards the river, others from it, whilst all were struggling

alike in the grasp of the hurricane. A thousand discordant deafening noises rose on the air together. The neighing of horses, falling of chimneys, crashing of uprooted trees, roaring and whistling of the wind, crackling of fire as it ran with lightning-like rapidity from house to house—all sounds were there save that of the human voice.

It was not just the residents of Peshtigo who rushed to the river. From throughout the outlying areas, hundreds also headed for what they believed to be their only chance of survival. Among them was Jane Phillips, who later wrote one of the most vivid accounts of the frantic flight:

> Horses' manes and tails blowin' to the right, on fire. Rigs comin' out on the road ever'where. Could hardly get through. Some was wrecked, and the people started to run on foot. . . . Little crick, wood bridge burnin'. People diggin' themselves into the mud of the crick bed. Wind about to tip our wagon over. Passed a buggy, upset, woman and children runnin'. . . . Open well by the road. Man shovin' women and children down it. Teams, cows, people runnin' for the river. Goin' down hill. Rose, hold onto the babies! Hogs in the road! Hogs in the road! Wagon bounced right through a blazin' herd of hogs. Horses and oxen jammed into trees on the riverbank. Bridge on fire. Wind, people, horses, screamin'. . . . My shirt was on fire, ripped it off. I jumped out and turned to get Rose and the little ones down to the water. Wagon . . . was empty. Nothin' in the box . . . empty.

Phillips was far from alone in her tragic discovery. Later the true story was told of the man who was carrying his wife to the safety of the river when he tripped over some obstruction and dropped her. Struggling to his feet, he looked frantically about him and finally found her. Picking her up, he made it to the river only to find that it was not his wife he was carrying, but a total stranger. He never saw his wife again.

❖ PREVIOUS SPREAD: A contemporary illustration of the rush to the river during the Peshtigo fire, by G. J. Tisdale.

It had only been a matter of minutes, but Peshtigo was now enveloped in unbridled disaster. As publisher and editor Frank Tilton of the *Green Bay Advocate* later reported, "Scores failed to reach the river at all. Strangled by the smoke, or foul gases, or both, they fell, and their charred and shriveled bodies lying on the streets presented a ghastly and horrible sight next morning. . . . some were burned to death within a few feet of the river, some in their houses, some in the woods, and some on the roads attempting to escape."

Father Pernin did make it to the bridge at the river, but was greeted by sights and sounds he never could have imagined.

The bridge was thoroughly encumbered with cattle, vehicles, women, children, and men, all pushing and crushing against each other so as to find an issue from it. . . . I was thus obliged to ascend the river on the left bank, above the dam, where the water gradually attained a great depth. After placing a certain distance between myself and the bridge, the fall of which I momentarily expected, I pushed [myself] . . . as far into the water as possible. It was all that I could do. . . . The banks of the river as far as the eye could reach were covered with people standing there, motionless as statues, some with eyes staring, upturned towards heaven, and tongues protruded. The greater number seemed to have no idea of taking any steps to procure their safety, imagining, as many afterwards acknowledged to me, that the end of the world had arrived and that here was nothing for them but silent submission to their fate. . . . I pushed the persons standing on each side of me into the water. One of these sprang back again with a half smothered cry murmuring: "I am wet;" but immersion in water was better than immersion in fire. I caught him again and dragged him out with me into the river as far as possible. At the same moment I heard a splash of the water along the river's brink. All had followed my example. It was time; the air was no longer fit for inhalation, whilst the intensity of the heat was increasing. A few minutes more and no living thing could have resisted its fiery breath.

They had sought the waters of the Peshtigo for salvation, but if anything, the conditions in the river were even more disastrous than those that most had already experienced. The river was a struggling sea of humanity, filled with men, women, and children trying desperately to stay alive. As always, the Peshtigo was filled with logs, waiting to be floated to the sawmill. Set afire by the heat and flames, the logs became flaming missiles, crashing into the terrified hordes. The bridge above the river had itself become a weapon of death. As hundreds, attempting to flee across the bridge from the west side of town, bumped into those trying to cross from the opposite direction, the bridge collapsed under the weight, hurling all of them into the water.

> Standing in the cold water of the river, or clinging to logs— sometimes the logs on fire, were men, women, and children, grasping for breath, their eyes blinded by smoke, and saving themselves from burning even in the water only by covering their heads with blankets which they kept wet, or wetting their heads continually. The roar of the tornado and of the fire was mingled with shrieks of anguish from the suffering, and groans and lamentations from those bereaved of relatives and friends. Cattle, too, rushed into the river and swam about bewildered, sometimes rolling over the logs to which wretched human beings were clinging, and sending them to a watery grave.

Phillips had her own recollections:

> Ever'thin' was driftin' up against us, cows, water-logged sheep, dead fish. . . . Flashes of fire kept sweepin' over the water. Ever'thin' had to duck or be burnt to the waterline. . . . Ox swam by with a woman hangin' to its burnt stub of a tail. I caught her and dragged her to the lee of the bank. Woman was in labor. . . . Baby was born in the water, never saw it. Old folks dyin' couldn't stand breathin' that terrible stove heat. Old lady, not burnt, but dead, bumped up against us, had to push her off.

Amazingly, in the midst of the horror, there would be what some survivors would describe as "miraculous incidents." "Not far from me," Father Pernin described, "[a cow] overturned in its passage the log to which [a] woman was clinging and she disappeared into the water. I thought her lost; but soon saw her emerge from it holding on with one hand to the horns of the cow, and throwing water on her head with the other. . . . what threatened to bring destruction to the woman had proved the means of her salvation."

Sadly, the "miraculous incidents" were all too few. "At the moment I was entering the river," Father Pernin also wrote, "another woman, terrified and breathless, reached its bank. She was leading one child by the hand and held pressed to her breast what appeared to be another, enveloped in a roll of disordered linen, evidently caught up in the haste. Oh horror! On opening these wraps to look on the face of her child—it was not there."

Father Pernin and the others who were fortunate enough to survive spent almost five and a half hours in the river before the firestorm abated enough for them to feel it was safe to leave the water. Emerging from the river, youngster Fred Shepherd encountered a sight that would remain with him for the rest of his life:

> I looked up the street at the top of the bluff toward the north. Coming toward us down the road, silhouetted against the sky, I saw a long file of men, women and children who wended their way down to where we were [huddled around a pile of burning coal in an attempt to warm ourselves]. They had passed the night clinging to the booms and logs of the deep water above the dam. They were all of the remaining survivors of the village. Some were fairly well clothed, others only partially so, some with nightdresses only. All gathered in a circle around the pile of burning coal. Distress and agony were in their faces. They were asking each other, "Have you seen my Willie, my Mary; have you seen my wife, my husband?" So pathetic was this scene that even I, a boy of eight years, could not endure it and withdrew to a distance.

One of the most horrendous stories of all was that of church construction worker C. W. Towsley and his family, who found themselves trapped inside their house encircled by a wall of flame with no means of escape. Pernin wrote how, after watching flames engulf and kill his wife and one of his youngsters, Towsley grabbed a kitchen knife and slit the throats of his two other children and then himself.

Gradually, those who had managed to survive the hours in the river began to hear other accounts of fellow townspeople who had not been able to make it to the water. "My father saved his orphaned children in the mud of Bundy Creek," one young girl reported, "but our neighbors died in their root cellar." "My oldest brother got us children to the river," a youngster explained, "but our mother fell behind with the baby in her arms. We found them in the potato field." Another tale was that of William Curtiss. As fire engulfed his home, he, as did a good number of others, sought refuge in his well. But because of the prolonged drought, there was not enough water to immerse himself. As flames entered the well, Curtiss looped the bucket chain around his neck and hanged himself.

A particularly tragic story was later recounted by Frank Tilton in the *Green Bay Advocate*.

> At the boarding house, a strange hallucination seemed to prevail that it could be saved, and a large number of people took refuge there. On the opposite side of the street was the fire-engine house, and the engine was taken out, the hose stretched across the street, and water thrown on the boarding house. The number who gathered inside the boarding house is variously estimated at from thirty to seventy-five persons. When the flames struck the building, the whole front was on fire in an instant. It was in fact completely surrounded with whirling, writhing coils of flame. The hapless inmates had their choice between an atmosphere of fire without and hell of fire within, and it mattered little which they chose, as few of them could have succeeded in crossing the street to the river. A heap of indistinguishable . . . bones and charred flesh in the ruins of the building, giving no clue to sex or number, was all that remained.

Tilton was horrified by what had happened at the boardinghouse, but he was even more devastated by his walk through the streets of Peshtigo, after the fire had finally abated.

> Here lay a group of father, mother, and children, their clothes all gone and their bodies shriveled up to two-thirds their natural size; . . . the child of Mr. Tanner [was] found in a kneeling posture, as if in the attitude of prayer, his head bent down upon his hands and his body completely roasted; and there were groups lying all around the site of the village, some of the bodies with their limbs burned off, all of them naked, and, with one exception, all lying on their faces. . . . We leave our readers to picture, if they can, the grief of parents that morning on recognizing the bodies of their idolized children; and of a husband when he distinguished the blackened, unsightly remains of his beloved wife; and the agony, mingled with faint hope, of those whose dear ones were among the missing.

The survivors' desperate search for missing loved ones was heartrending. "Whilst wandering among the ruins I met several persons, with some of whom I entered into conversation," recalled Father Pernin. "One was a bereaved father seeking his missing children of whom he had as yet learned nothing. 'If, at least,' he said to me, with a look of indescribable anguish, 'I could find their bones, but the wind has swept away whatever the fire spared.'"

Like Frank Tilton, owner and editor Luther Noyes of the *Marinette and Peshtigo Eagle* had made his way into Peshtigo almost as soon as the fires abated. Like Tilton, he was totally unprepared for what he encountered. Gigantic boulders lay split in half. All that remained of the seven-hundred-pound bell that had adorned the firehouse was a pile of melted metal. Amazing also were the stories Noyes heard. He found one account particularly incomprehensible. Eyewitnesses reported that at the height of the conflagration several Peshtigo residents, well away from the fire, had suddenly burst into flames.

Noyes also heard stories of heroic, but most often futile, efforts by some of the townspeople to save their families and neighbors. But Father Pernin had another type of tale to tell.

> Alas that I should have to record an incident such as should never have happened in the midst of that woeful scene! . . . Enslaved by the wretched vice of avarice, [a man] had just been taken in the act of despoiling the bodies of the dead of whatever objects the fire had spared. A jury was formed, his punishment put to the vote, and he was unanimously condemned to be hanged on the spot. But where was a rope to be found? The fire had spared nothing. Somebody proposed substituting for the former an iron chain which had been employed for drawing logs, and one was accordingly brought and placed around the criminal's neck. Execution was difficult under the circumstances; and whilst the preparations dragged slowly on, the miserable man loudly implored mercy. The pity inspired by the mournful surroundings softened at length the hearts of the judges, and, after having made him crave pardon on his knees for the sacrilegious thefts of which he had been guilty, they allowed him to go free. It may have been that they merely intended frightening him.

THE CONFLAGRATION BECAME KNOWN as the Peshtigo Fire, because it was in this ill-fated village and the farming area immediately surrounding it that both industry and population were most concentrated and where the majority of fatalities occurred. But the fire was of far greater magnitude than the destruction of Peshtigo. Before the last fires had been put out, 2,400 square miles (1.5 million acres) had been ravaged, numerous settlements and isolated farms had been destroyed, and hundreds of lives beyond Peshtigo had been lost.

One of the earliest accounts of the disaster that had taken place beyond Peshtigo came from Frank Tilton. "After daylight, stragglers

❖ A LOCAL NEWSPAPER FRONT PAGE from October 14, 1871. The Peshtigo story was far overshadowed by the Chicago Fire.

began to pour in from the Sugar Bush farming settlements. . . . They told of square miles of flourishing farming settlements utterly depopulated; of houses and barns swept away, and of scores and hundred of dead bodies in the roads and fields. . . . In the entire extent of the three Sugar Bush settlements, but eight houses were left standing, and the loss of life was horrible in the extreme."

As described in the *State Gazette Extra* of October 10, 1871, none of the outlying settlements was hit harder than Brussels. The fire, the newspaper reported, "raged with terrific violence, destroying about one hundred eighty houses, and leaving nothing of a large and flourishing settlements but five houses. . . . On Monday morning two hundred people breakfasted on four loaves of bread. Hopeless and homeless, they camp out on their land, and seem struck dumb with their great losses."

As reports from the outlying area filtered in, stories as horrific as those that had emerged from Peshtigo began to be heard. One was that of the Karl Lamp family. Lamp and his wife were German immigrants who had cleared the land and carved out a farm in the Lower Sugar Bush. When the fire approached, Lamp hitched his team of horses to a wagon, put his wife and their five children inside it, and headed for Peshtigo. At one point, he heard his family screaming as their clothes had caught fire; however, Lamp knew he could not stop with the conflagration so close behind. They reached the main road when suddenly one of the horses fell. Lamp got off his seat and tried unsuccessfully to help the horse back on its feet. Turning then to speak to his wife, he discovered that in the brief time that he had gone to the horse's assistance his wife and all five children had been enveloped in flames and were now dead.

There were inspirational tales as well. Journalist and author Elias Colbert later described how the one house in the Upper Bush country that survived the inferno was saved. "In the entire Upper Bush country there is only one house left, the home of 'old man' Place," Colbert wrote. "Many years ago this man settled here soon afterward marrying a squaw, by whom he has had many children. He has always engaged in trading with the Indians, who have had his house as their headquarters. When the fire came, about twenty Indians covered his house with their blankets, which they kept wet down, thus saving the house. One great big fellow stood at the pump for nine hours, showing an endurance possessed by very few white men."

The most common story that was told throughout the entire region, from Peshtigo to Green Bay and beyond, was what was later regarded as the most extraordinary phenomenon of the entire disaster. Typical was the account given by Lower Sugar Bush resident Alfred Griffin. "When I heard the roar of the approaching tornado," Griffin stated, "I ran out of my house and saw a great, black, balloon-shaped object whirling though the air over the tops of the distant trees, approaching my house. When it reached the house, it seemed to explode, with a loud noise, belching out fire on every side, and in an instant my house was on fire in every part."

In the days following the Wisconsin fire, newspaper headlines screamed out the news of what had happened in Chicago. News of what had taken place in tiny, remote Peshtigo—a tragedy far greater in scope, far more horrific in loss of life—received far less attention. Fortunately, a telegram sent from Peshtigo on October 9 reading, "We are burning up; send us help quick," did get through to the office of Wisconsin's governor, Lucius Fairchild. And a real heroine emerged. When the telegram arrived, the governor was in Chicago, attempting to aid that city. The clerk who received the message, not knowing what to do with it, brought it to the governor's house and gave it to Mrs. Fairchild.

Frances Fairchild, the governor's wife, was only twenty-four years old, but immediately after reading the telegram, she hurried to the state capitol. As her daughter later stated, once there "she took charge of everything and everybody, and they all obeyed her." Appalled by the preliminary reports of what had happened in the lumbering districts, Fairchild redirected a train loaded with relief supplies for Chicago and had it sent instead to Peshtigo. She then sent telegrams to every major American city, pleading with them to send aid to the stricken area.

The response was overwhelming. From throughout the nation, and even from some foreign countries, money and supplies poured into Peshtigo. A new village began to rise, in great part because of the contributions and efforts of one man, William Ogden.

Ogden, who had lost over $1 million in property in the Chicago Fire, arrived in Peshtigo late in October and immediately announced, "We will rebuild this village—the mills, the shops,—and do a larger winter's logging than ever before." True to his word, Ogden worked timelessly drawing up plans, hiring work crews, and personally leading the rebuilding efforts. The fire had destroyed the construction of Ogden's pet project, the building of a railroad connecting Peshtigo with the outlying districts, and he devoted additional efforts to restoring this construction, offering a $75,000 bonus to the railroad's builder if he completed laying the rails to Menominee by the end of 1871.

❖ THE CHICAGO FIRE WAS still front-page news at the end of October, as shown on the front page of *Frank Leslie's Illustrated Newspaper* of October 28, 1871.

Spurred on by Ogden, tracks reached Marinette on December 22 and Menominee on December 27, 1871.

On February 24, 1872, in a tribute to what Ogden had accomplished, the *Eagle* exclaimed, "The action of [Ogden] since the great disaster, has been of more real advantage to the village of Peshtigo and her people, than all the ample and generous relief forwarded by a sympathizing and noble hearted public." For the residents of Peshtigo, however, there was one major disappointment.

It had been fully expected that Ogden would rebuild his woodenware factory, the soul of Peshtigo's economic activity. But even before the fire, he had become more interested both in accelerating his railroad interests and in expanding his more profitable sawmill operations at Peshtigo Harbor. The woodenware factory would not be rebuilt. Peshtigo had made a remarkable recovery. But without the woodenware factory and its many allied operations, it never regained the vibrancy that had distinguished it from so many other small towns.

WHAT WOULD ALWAYS SET PESHTIGO APART, however, was the unfortunate distinction of having been the center of the single deadliest fire in the United States, one that took more lives than the next two worst conflagrations combined. It has been estimated by several sources that 1,200 people died in Peshtigo and its environs. That number is probably far too low by half. As Father Pernin wrote,

> The true total will never be known, since whole farmsteads were erased, leaving no trace, and no one knows how many itinerant workers died in Peshtigo's company boardinghouse or in its two churches to which many fled in panic, or in isolated logging camps deep in the surrounding woods. People simply became piles of ashes or calcinated bones, identifiable only if a buckle, a ring, a shawl pin, or some other familiar object survived the incredible heat.

What *is* known is that for years after the fire, the remains of people who were killed in the firestorm were still being found in the woods and in Peshtigo itself. And there was another type of casualty. In a report to the Wisconsin state legislature, Captain A. J. Langworthy, chairman of the Peshtigo Relief Committee, stated that "many who escaped the fiery visitation . . . were paralyzed with fear, from the effects of which they will probably never recover." Sadly, his prediction was correct. In Marinette alone there was a building in which sixty-five physically and emotionally traumatized orphans of the fire were housed.

The Peshtigo Fire was not only catastrophic, but inevitable. As wildfire expert Stephen J. Payne explains, "A prolonged drought, a rural

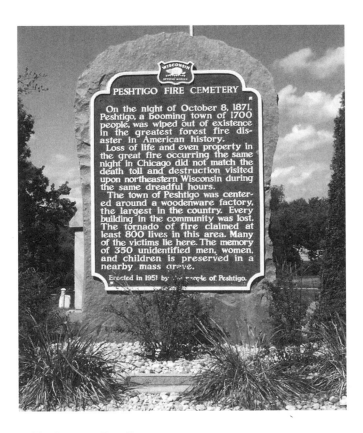

❖ THE PESHTIGO FIRE CEMETERY MEMORIAL.

agriculture based on burning, railroads that cast sparks to all sides, a landscape stuffed with slash and debris from logging, a city built largely of forest materials, the catalytic passing of a dry cold front—all ensured that fires would break out, that some would become monumental, that flames would swallow wooden villages."

That is exactly what happened. What is extraordinary is that the "monumental" fire took place on the very same day that one of the nation's largest cities grabbed the headlines by suffering its own conflagration, and that the greatest American fire was, in great measure, forgotten.

Gustav Weisskopf

GUSTAVE WHITEHEAD
The First to Fly? (1901)

A lmost every schoolchild knows the story. On December 17, 1903, two bicycle makers from Ohio, Wilbur and Orville Wright, achieved immortality by performing the world's first successful controlled, powered, and sustained heavier-than-air human flight. What has been lost to history is the fact that this historic breakthrough may well have been accomplished two years, four months, and three days earlier by a German immigrant named Gustave Whitehead. And there is a great deal of evidence to support that claim.

Christened Gustav Albin Weisskopf, he was born in Leutershausen, Germany, on January 1, 1874, a time when aviation pioneers were absorbed with experimenting with kites and gliders in a determined effort to unlock the secrets of aerodynamics that would lead to manned powered flight. While still a youngster, he became obsessed with the mystery of how birds flew, and he spent hours experimenting with paper kites. What had been a carefree family life came to an abrupt end in 1886, when he was orphaned.

Only twelve years old, he made his way to Hamburg, where he was taken aboard a ship as a cabin boy. He emigrated to Brazil in 1889 and then spent four years at sea, years that gave him the opportunity

❖ AN EARLY PHOTO of Gustav Albin Weisskopf, who anglicized his name to Gustave Whitehead in the United States.
Copyright by William J. O'Dwyer and Flughistorische Forschungsgemeinschaft Gustav Weisskopf.

to study the flight of sea and land birds around the world. He also survived four shipwrecks, the last of which, in 1894, put him ashore off the coast of Florida.

Taking on whatever jobs he could find, Weisskopf (who by this time had changed his name to Whitehead) worked his way northward, ending up in Boston in 1897. There he got a job with the Boston Aeronautical Society, for whom he built several gliders. His travels next took him to New York City, where he met his future wife, and then to Buffalo, where the couple was married (on the marriage certificate Whitehead listed his occupation as "aeronaut"). From Buffalo, the restless couple moved to Baltimore, where, according to the January 1988 edition of the journal *Air Enthusiast*, "There can be little doubt that Weisskopf was experimenting not only with aircraft design but also with engines." In 1899, the couple moved yet again, this time to Pittsburgh. And it was there that Whitehead began his efforts at achieving powered flight.

By the time he arrived in Pittsburgh, Whitehead was seriously short of funds. He was forced to find employment in a coal mine, but he devoted every spare moment to building a two-man aircraft powered by a steam engine with the help of a newly acquired friend, a blacksmith

named Louis Darvarich. In an affidavit signed by Darvarich dated July 19, 1934, we are informed of what, if true, is a remarkable event in aviation history.

❖ Louisa Tuba, a German-Hungarian living in Buffalo, married Gustave Whitehead in 1897.

Copyright by William J. O'Dwyer and Flughistorische Forschungsgemeinschaft Gustav Weisskopf.

In approximately April or May 1899, I was present and flew with Mr. Whitehead on the occasion when he succeeded in flying his machine, propelled by steam motor, on a flight of approximately a half mile distance, at a height of about 20 to 25 feet from the ground. This flight occurred in Pittsburgh, and the type of machine used by Mr. Whitehead was a monoplane. We were unable to rise high enough to avoid a three story building in our path, and when the machine fell, I was scalded severely by steam, for I had been firing the boiler. I was obliged to spend several weeks in hospital, and I recall the incident of the flight very clearly. Mr. Whitehead was not injured, as he had been in the front part of the machine steering it.

Along with Darvarich's testimony, there are also the sworn statements of Pittsburgh fireman Martin Devance, who was called to the scene of the crash. "I believe I arrived immediately after the [flying machine] crashed into a brick building, a newly constructed apartment house on the O'Neal Estate," Devance affirmed. "I recall that someone was hurt and taken to the hospital. I am able to identify the inventor Gustave Whitehead from a picture shown to me."

If Darvarich is to be believed, this 1899 flight can only be regarded as historic. But it cannot officially be claimed as the first manned, powered flight, because there is no evidence that Whitehead made any attempt to record the event, and no measurements—speed, altitude, and exact distance flown—were taken. It also cannot be credited as a controlled flight since it resulted in a crash. And Darvarich's testimony is the only eyewitness account of the flight itself that has ever been found. Still, it seems to have been an unprecedented achievement—one that would be a prelude to even more significant accomplishments when Whitehead moved to Bridgeport, Connecticut, in 1900.

While the evidence of Whitehead's 1899 flight might be limited, his growing reputation as a builder of aircraft and engines, if not news of the flight itself, obviously preceded him to Bridgeport. Shortly after he arrived, a total stranger approached him and presented him with a gift of $300 to be used in building a small workshop where he could carry

on his aeronautical experiments, particularly in the development of engines. As soon as the workshop was constructed, Whitehead set about repairing and modifying the steam engine that had been damaged in the 1899 flight.

By the spring of 1901, Whitehead had not only repaired and improved the engine, he had, with the help of a young machinist named Anton Pruckner, begun building a new flying machine, which he named *Airplane No. 21*.

By June, *Airplane No. 21* not only had been completed, it also had captured attention well beyond Bridgeport. On June 8, 1901, in an article that most certainty must have piqued the interest of all those interested in pioneering aeronautical progress, *Scientific American* reported:

A novel flying machine has just been completed by Mr. Gustave Whitehead of Bridgeport, Conn., and is now ready for the preliminary trials. Several experiments have been made, but as yet no free flights have been attempted. The machine is built after the model of a bird or bat. The body is 16 feet long and measures 2½ feet at its greatest width and is 3 feet deep. It is well stayed with wooden ribs and braced with steel wires and covered with canvas which is tightly stretched over the frame. Four wheels, each one foot in diameter, support it while it stands on the ground. The front wheels are connected to a 10 horse power engine to get up speed on the ground, and the rear wheels are mounted like casters so that they can be steered by the aeronaut. On either side of the body are

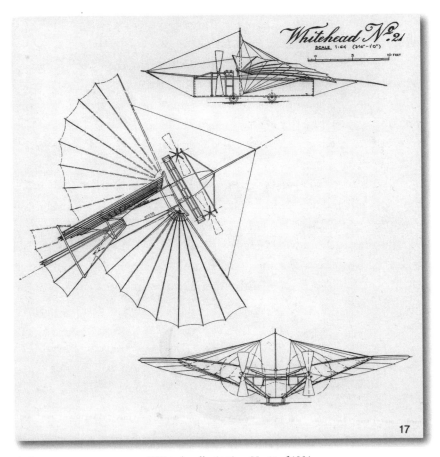

❖ A THREE-VIEW DRAWING of Whitehead's *Airplane No. 21* of 1901.
Copyright by William J. O'Dwyer and Flughistorische Forschungsgemeinschaft Gustav Weisskopf.

large aeroplanes, covered with silk and concave on the underside, which give the machine the appearance of a bird in flight. The ribs are bamboo poles, and are braced with steel wires. The wires are so arranged that they can be folded up. The 10-foot rudder, which corresponds to the tail of a bird, can also be folded up and can be moved up and down, so as to steer the machine on its horizontal course. A mast and bowsprit serve to hold all the parts in their proper relation.

Throughout the months of June, July, and August 1901, Whitehead, with the aid of several boys from his neighborhood, hauled *Airplane No. 21* out to a field near Fairfield, Connecticut, where the wheels, engines, wings, and propellers of the craft were tested. By August 14, he was ready to give his flying machine the supreme test. What took place on that day was observed by reporter Richard Howell of the *Bridgeport Herald*, who recorded the events in a long, detailed article that appeared in the *Herald* four days later.

According to Howell's account, Whitehead began his momentous day even before dawn broke by placing two bags of sand, each weighing about 110 pounds, in *Airplane No. 21* for ballast. He then set the controls so that the machine would make one unmanned revolution in the air before the power would automatically shut off and the plane would land. If this final trial was successful, Whitehead would be ready to fly the machine itself. Howell reported the dramatic events:

> When the power was shut, the air ship settled as lightly on the ground and not a stitch was broken or a rod bent. . . . An early morning milkman stopped in the road to see what was going on. His horse nearly ran away when the big white wings [were] flapped to see if they were all right.
>
> The nervous tension was growing at every clock tick and no one showed it more than Whitehead. . . . He stationed his two assistants behind the machine with instructions to hold on to the ropes and not let the machine get away. Then he took up his position in the great bird.
>
> He opened the throttle of the ground propeller and shot along the green at a rapid rate. "I'm going to start the wings!" he yelled. "Hold her now." The two assistants held on the best they could but the ship shot up in the air almost like a kite. It was an exciting moment.
>
> "We can't hold her!" shrieked one of the rope men. "Let go then!" shouted Whitehead back. They let go and as they did so the machine darted up through the air like a bird released from a cage.

Whitehead was greatly excited and his hands flew from one part of the machine to another. The newspaperman and the two assistants stood still for a moment watching the air ship in amazement. Then they rushed down the sloping grade after the air ship. She was flying now about fifty feet above the ground and made a noise very much like the "chug, chug, chug," of an elevator going down the shaft.

Whitehead was calmer now and seemed to be enjoying the exhilaration of the novelty. He was headed straight for a clump of chestnut [trees] that grew on a high knoll. He was now about forty feet in the air and would have been high enough to escape the [trees] had they not been on a high ridge. He saw the danger ahead and when within two hundred yards of the [trees] made several attempts to manipulate the machinery so he could steer around, but the ship kept steadily on her course, heading for the trees. To strike them meant wrecking the air ship and very likely death or broken bones for the daring aeronaut.

Here it was that Whitehead showed how to utilize a common sense principle which he had noticed the birds make use of thousands of times. . . . He simply shifted his weight more to one side than the other. This careened the ship to one side. She turned her nose away from the [trees] within fifty yards of them and took her course around them as prettily as a yacht on sea avoids a bar. The ability to control the air ship in this manner appeared to give Whitehead confidence, for he was seen to take time to look at the landscape about him. He looked back and waved his hand exclaiming, "I've got it at last."

He had now soared through the air for fully half a mile and as the field ended a short distance ahead the aeronaut shut off the power and prepared to light. He appeared to be fearful that the machine would dip ahead or dip back when the power was shut off but there was no sign of any such move on the part of the big bird. She settled down from a height of about fifty feet in two minutes after the propellers stopped. And she lighted on the ground on her four wooden wheels so lightly that Whitehead was not jarred in the least.

Two days after the *Bridgeport Herald* article was published, two other news accounts, each brief and almost exactly alike in content, appeared in the *New York Herald* and the *Boston Transcript*. "Mr. Whitehead," these articles stated in part, "last Tuesday night with two assistants, took his machine to a long field back of Fairfield and the inventor, for the first time, flew in his machine for half a mile. It worked perfectly, and the operator found no difficulty in handling it. Mr. Whitehead's machine is equipped with two engines, one to propel it on the ground, on wheels, and the other to make the wings or propellers work."

Gustave Whitehead's 1899 flight had not, as far as is known, been reported by any newspaper. But here were three newspaper accounts including one in the *New York Herald,* one of the nation's most prestigious publications. And, unlike the 1899 flight, there was also in the *Bridgeport Herald* article a firsthand recorded reaction from Whitehead himself.

It's a funny sensation to fly. I never felt such a strange sensation as when the machine first left the ground and started on her flight. I heard nothing but the rumbling of the engine and the flapping of the big wings. I don't think I saw anything during the first two minutes of the flight, for I was so excited by the sensations I experienced. When the ship had reached a height of about forty or fifty feet I began to wonder how much higher it would go. But just about that time I observed that she was sailing along easily and not raising any higher. I felt easier, for I still had a feeling of doubt about what was waiting for me further on. I began now to feel that I was safe and all that it would be necessary for me to do to keep from falling was to keep my head and not make any mistakes with the machinery. I never felt such a spirit of freedom as I did during the ten minutes I was soaring up above my fellow beings in a thing that my own brain had evolved. It was a sweet experience. It made me feel that I was far ahead of my brothers for I could fly like a bird, and they must walk.

After recounting how Whitehead personally described how he had maneuvered around the clump of trees, Howell quoted Whitehead as stating:

> Not far ahead the long field ended with a piece of woods. When within a hundred yards of the woods, I shut off the power and then began to feel a little nervous about how the machine would act in settling to the ground, for so many flying machines have shown a tendency to fall either on the front or hind end and such a fall means broken bones for the operator. My machine began to settle evenly and I alighted on the ground with scarcely a jar. And not a thing was broken. That was the happiest moment of my life for I had demonstrated that the machine I have worked on for so many years would do what I claimed for it. It was a grand sensation to be flying through the air. There is nothing like it.

If the *Bridgeport Herald, New York Herald,* and *Boston Transcript* articles are to be believed, then for more than one hundred years the world should have been celebrating Gustave Whitehead, not the Wright brothers. Yet skeptics have long challenged these articles, particularly the *Bridgeport Herald* account, upon which the other two shorter articles were obviously based. A good deal of the skepticism has to do with Richard Howell's description of how Whitehead—before flying *Airplane No. 21* on August 14, 1901—had placed sandbags in the machine and conducted a brief, unpiloted test flight. Those who doubt the veracity of the article state that such an unpiloted flight, no matter how brief, would have been impossible in such a primitive aircraft.

Yet why would a respected newspaper such as the *Bridgeport Herald* report such a momentous successful flight if it didn't really take place? Those who refuse to believe the article point out that although it has long since disappeared from the newspaper business, the practice of "hoax journalism" was widespread. Howell, the critics claim, looking for a sensational story, simply could have made the whole thing up.

❖ GUSTAVE WHITEHEAD POSES in 1901 with *Airplane No. 21* and his four-cylinder gasoline engine, which turned *Airplane No. 21*'s propellers.
Copyright by William J. O'Dwyer and Flughistorische Forschungsgemeinschaft Gustav Weisskopf.

But Howell's account of the events on August 14, 1901, is not the only eyewitness testimony. According to several individuals, Whitehead made three other flights on that day aside from the one Howell detailed, and each of these individuals swore they witnessed at least one of these flights. One of them was Whitehead's chief assistant, Anton Pruckner. "I did witness and was present at the time of the 14 August 1901 flight," swore Pruckner. "The flight was about a half mile in distance and about 50 feet or so in the air. The plane circled a little to one side and landed easily with no damage to it or the engine or the occupant who was Gustave Whitehead."

Junius Harworth was one of the boys who had helped Whitehead haul his flying machine from his workshop to the test field. In an affidavit dated August 21, 1934, Harworth swore, "On August 14, 1901, I was present and assisted on the occasion when Mr. Whitehead succeeded in flying his machine, propelled by a motor, to a height of 200 feet off the ground. . . . The distance flown was approximately one mile and a half and lasted to the best of my knowledge for four minutes." According to the January 1988 issue of *Air Enthusiast,* the discrepancies in the Pruckner and Harworth affidavits arise from the fact that they describe two different flights of the four that Whitehead made on August 14, 1901.

Like Junius Harworth, Alexander Gluck was also a schoolboy at the time of Whitehead's achievement. In an affidavit dated July 19, 1934, Gluck swore that "approximately 1901 or 1902. . . . I was present on an occasion when Mr. Whitehead succeeded in flying his machine, propelled by a motor on a flight of some distance. . . . The machine used by Mr. Whitehead was a monoplane with folded wings. I recall its having been pushed from the backyard of the residence where the Whitehead family then lived, 241 Pine Street, Bridgeport, Connecticut, which was opposite my residence at the time."

One of the most interesting accounts in support of the veracity of Whitehead's flights came from a respected Bridgeport citizen and navy veteran, Frank Layne. When, in 1968, he was asked if he would agree to be interviewed, Layne, then ninety-two years old, responded to the reporter, "I do not understand why you would want to interview me. I think you are wasting much of your valuable time. Look, I never knew Mr. Whitehead personally or anything about his aircraft. All I did was watch him fly." What Layne was most certain about, he told the reporter, was the date on which he saw Whitehead successfully take to the air. It was, he stated, August 14, 1901, the anniversary of his discharge from service in the Spanish-American War.

Of all those who swore that Whitehead's 1901 flights were genuine, the most respected authority was Stanley Yale Beach, aeronautical editor of *Scientific American.* In four separate issues of the magazine in the year 1906, Beach referred to Whitehead's "1901 powered flights." In one of these articles, Beach actually made the statement that "Whitehead in 1901 and Wright Brothers in 1903 have already flown for short distances with motor powered airplanes." If nothing else, such a statement from so respected a person as Beach certainly seems to verify the magnitude of Whitehead's 1901 achievement.

According to both his neighbors and his various assistants, Whitehead spent the year following his 1901 flights constructing a new flying machine that he named *Airplane No. 22*. It was a craft very similar to its predecessor with the notable exception that it was powered by a kerosene-fueled, rather than steam-fueled, motor. And, according to several of Whitehead's neighbors and assistants, on January 17, 1902, Whitehead again took to the skies. Although no eyewitness accounts of what took place on that day exist, what is certain is that the editor of the highly respected publication *American Inventor* obviously received news that Whitehead had again gone aloft. The editor then wrote to the aeronaut, asking him to verify what had taken place.

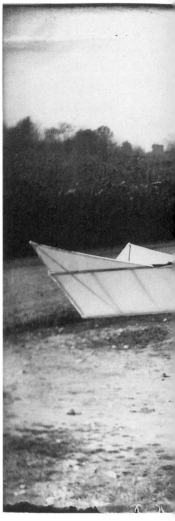

"This new machine has been tried twice, on January 17, 1902," Whitehead replied to the editor.

It was intended to fly only short distances, but the machine behaved so well that at the first trial it covered nearly two miles over the water of Long Island Sound, and settled in the water without mishap to either machine or operator. . . . On the second trial it started from the same place and sailed with myself aboard across Long Island Sound. The machine kept on steadily in crossing the wind at a height of about 200 feet, where it came into my mind to try steering around in a circle. As soon as I turned the rudder and drove one propeller faster than the other the machine turned a bend and flew north with the wind at a frightful speed, but turned steadily around until I saw the starting place in the distance. I continued to turn but when near the land again, I slowed up the propellers and sank greatly down on an even keel into the water, she readily floating like a boat. . . .

❖ An undated photo of one of the assistants transporting one of Whitehead's gliders, designed with foldable wings for easier transport.
Copyright by William J. O'Dwyer and Flughistorische Forschungsgemeinschaft Gustav Weisskopf.

The length of flight on the first was about two miles, and on the second about seven miles. The last trial was a circling flight, and as I successfully returned to my starting place with a machine hitherto untried and heavier than air, I consider the trip quite a success. To my knowledge it is the first of its kind. This matter has so far never been published.

I have no photographs taken yet of No. 22 but send you some of No. 21 as these machines are exactly alike, except the details mentioned. No. 21 has made four trips, the longest one and a half miles on August 14, 1901. The wings of both machines measure 36 feet from tip to tip and the length of the entire machine is 32 feet. It will run on the ground 50 miles an hour, and in the air travel about 70 miles. I believe that if wanted, it would fly 100 miles an hour. The power carried is considerably more than necessary.

Believing . . . that the future of the air machine lies in an apparatus made without the gasbag, I have taken up the aeroplane and will stick to it until I have succeeded completely or expire in the attempt of doing so. As soon as I get my machine out this spring, I will let you know. To describe the feeling of flying is almost impossible, for, in fact, a man is more frightened than anything else.

Trusting that this will interest your readers, I remain,

Very truly yours,
Gustave Whitehead.

After receiving Whitehead's letter, the editor of *American Inventor*, realizing the importance of what Whitehead was claiming, immediately wrote back, asking Whitehead to confirm what he had written, to which Whitehead replied:

Dear Sir:

Yours of [January] 26th received. Yes, it a full-sized flying machine and I, myself, flew seven miles and returned to the starting point. In both the flights described in my previous letter, I flew in the machine myself. This, of course, is new to the world at large, but I do not care much in being advertised except by a good paper like yours. Such accounts may help others along who are working in the same line, as soon as I can I shall try again. This coming spring I will have photographs made of Machine No. 22 in the air and let you have pictures taken during its flight. If you can come up and [take the pictures] yourself, so much the better. I attempted this before, but in the first trial the weather was bad . . . and the snapshots that were taken did not come out right. I cannot take any time exposures of the machine when in flight on account of its high speed. . . .

Yours truly,

Gustave Whitehead.

Whitehead's two published letters in *American Inventor* are important in several regards. His statement that in operating a powered flying machine "a man is more frightened than anything else" offers a rare personal glimpse into a man who set down so little of his feelings in writing. So too does his declaration "I . . . will stick to it until I have succeeded completely or expire in the attempt of doing so."

Even more significant is Whitehead's statement that his accomplishments in successfully flying both *Airplane No. 21* and *Airplane No. 22* were "new to the world at large." Did he really believe that he had achieved the enormous distinction of being the first to accomplish manned, powered flight? And does his statement "I do not care much in being advertised" help explain why he did not push more for being credited for that achievement?

It seems that the editor of *American Inventor* was ready to believe. In publishing Whitehead's letters, he responded to Whitehead's promise of photographs of future flights by ending his column with: "Newspaper readers will remember several accounts of Mr. Whitehead's performances last summer [August 1901]. Probably most people put them down as fakes, but it seems as though the long-sought answer to the most difficult problem Nature ever put to man is gradually coming into sight. The editor and the readers of the columns await with interest the promised photographs of the machine in the air."

Unfortunately there would be no photographs. Nor would there be any other Whitehead flights. Throughout his life, Whitehead had struggled financially, and the years following the events of January 1902 were more difficult than ever. Forced to take a job in a Bridgeport factory, he was blinded in one eye when he was hit by a steel fragment and then suffered another serious physical setback when struck in the chest by a piece of factory equipment, an injury that led to a series of angina attacks. Throughout it all, according to a March 1996 article in *Aviation History,* Whitehead kept inventing. Competing for a prize offered by a railroad company, he invented a braking safety device but failed to win the prize. According to *Aviation History,* he also invented an "automatic" concrete-laying machine, which was used to help build a road near Bridgeport. But as *Aviation History* also stated, "He profited no more from these inventions that he did from his airplanes and engines."

On October 10, 1927, Gustave Whitehead died of a heart attack, leaving his family only the home he had built himself, a small amount of land, and eight dollars. The man who may well have made one of history's greatest accomplishments was buried in a pauper's grave. He was only fifty-three years old.

In the 1930s, more than thirty people signed affidavits swearing that they witnessed Whitehead flights well before the Wright brothers' Kitty Hawk achievement in 1903. In October 1964, Anton Pruckner, the man closest to Whitehead, gave sworn testimony that prior to 1903, Orville and Wilbur Wright actually visited Whitehead in his Bridgeport workshop and "left here with a great deal of information" regarding the secrets of manned, powered flight. Stanley Beach of *Scientific American* almost matter-of-factly stated that Whitehead had flown more than two years before the Wrights. And, as exemplified by his published letters in *American Inventor,* Whitehead himself, whose truthfulness was never questioned by those who knew him, gave detailed descriptions of his 1901 and 1902 flights. So why then has Gustave Whitehead not been given the credit for one of the most momentous firsts in history?

One of the reasons undoubtedly has to do with the fact that Whitehead was so absorbed with constructing flying machines and engines and piloting his creations that he paid no attention to keeping records, business or technical. A contributing factor to this may have been his extreme poverty. He was continually forced to take on jobs in factories and other establishments that left little time for record keeping even if he had been so inclined, and he may well not have had the money needed to patent his inventions even if he had desired to do so.

Aside from disorganization and a shortage of time and funds, Whitehead's lack of self-promotion stemmed also from the fact that, according to his assistants, he never believed that he had achieved what he personally regarded as the most important aeronautical goal. As officials at Germany's Gustav Weisskopf Museum proclaimed, Whitehead was convinced that manned, powered flight would be meaningful only when an operator could fly a considerable distance to a specific destination. "To a large extent," the museum stated, "it was Whitehead's own dissatisfaction with what he had achieved, that he fell into oblivion." As proof of this opinion, the museum offers Whitehead's documented statements to Anton Pruckner in which he stated, "All [my] flights are not much good because they don't last long enough. We just cannot fly to any old place. Flight will only then become of importance, when we can fly at any given time to any given place."

There are other reasons as well. Throughout the mid-1950s several Connecticut newspapers claimed that it was because of intense anti-German feeling brought about by the events of World War I that Whitehead, a German immigrant, did not receive the acclaim that he deserved. Perhaps most important of all, there is no question that Whitehead suffered from being so far ahead of his time. The public, the majority of whom ascribed to the long-held belief that "if man was intended to fly, God would have given him wings," was highly skeptical of any claims of manned, powered flight. It was a fact discovered by the Wrights, whose patent for their flying machine was not granted until late May 1906, more than three years after it was filed, and whose claim to have conquered the air was not genuinely accepted until after many flights following Kitty Hawk in both the United States and Europe.

All of these are viable reasons why Gustave Whitehead's accomplishments have been lost to history. Perhaps the greatest reason is what those few modern-day champions of Whitehead's achievements regard as nothing less than a conspiracy. If true, it is a conspiracy that involves one of America's most prestigious institutions. In modern times, the most active Whitehead supporter was Major William O'Dwyer. O'Dwyer was a World War II air force flight instructor and later a ferry pilot with the Air Transport Command. For more than thirty years beginning in 1963, O'Dwyer—with the aid of archivist Harvey Lippencott of the New England Air Museum and Harold Dolan, a Sikorsky Aircraft engineer and vice president of the Connecticut Aeronautical Historical Association—conducted intense research into every scrap of evidence that could be uncovered pertaining to Whitehead's flights. After spending what he said was "a small fortune" in this endeavor, O'Dwyer's conclusion was that history had been "tampered with." Speaking of those historians who dismissed Whitehead's claims almost out of hand, O'Dwyer stated, "It's strange that [their] opinions evolved without extensive research, official inquiry, or probe."

At the heart of William O'Dwyer's conviction that Gustave Whitehead was denied his just rewards was his uncovering of a remarkable contract that existed between the Smithsonian Institution and the Wright brothers' estate. The contract was the result of challenges to the Wright brothers' application for a patent for the first flying machine. It was motivated also by the fact that first Orville Wright and later he and his brother's heirs had taken exception to the fact that the Smithsonian had proclaimed that Samuel Langley's 1896 flying machine was the first machine capable of manned flight. The Wright brothers' heirs were, in fact, so upset with that statement that it was not until 1948 that the family allowed the Smithsonian to exhibit the *Flyer*—and only, as O'Dwyer discovered, after an agreement signed by the secretary of the Smithsonian Institution, which read:

> Neither the Smithsonian Institution or its successors, nor any museum or other agency, bureau, or facilities administered for the United States of America by the Smithsonian Institution or its successors shall publish or permit to the displayed a statement or label in connection with or in respect of any aircraft model or design

of earlier date than the Wright Airplane of 1903, claiming in effect that such an aircraft was capable of carrying a man under its own power in controlled flight.

William O'Dwyer and his fellow Whitehead supporters were not the only ones distressed by the Smithsonian/Wright brothers' estate agreement. As evidenced by an article in its January 1988 issue, the publication *Air Enthusiast* also viewed the agreement as a serious miscarriage of justice. The journal stated,

> Weisskopf's excommunication from the halls of aviation history was an unmerited sentence imposed not by history, but by contract. The evidence amassed in his favor strongly indicates that, beyond a reasonable doubt, the first fully controlled, powered flight that was more than a test "hop" . . . took place on 14 August 1901 near Bridgeport, Connecticut. For this assertion to be conclusively disproved, the Smithsonian must do much more than pronounce him a hoax while willfully turning a blind eye to all the affidavits, letters, tape recorded interviews and newspaper clippings which attest to Weisskopf's genius. Though the Wrights finally succeeded in setting their names firmly in all the books, we should remember that the history written by the victor is only a half-truth, after all.

The Smithsonian connection to the Whitehead saga did not end with the unique agreement. In the January 27, 1906, issue of *Scientific American,* Stanley Beach had described the first annual exhibit of the Aero Club of America, held at New York's 69th Regimental Armory. In his article he reported that a "single blurred photograph of a large bird-like machine constructed by Whitehead in 1901 was the only photo of a motor driven aeroplane in flight." Some seventy years later, one of the members of the research committee assembled by William O'Dwyer discovered a book titled *A Dream of Wings,* in which the same photograph was shown. In what can only be regarded as supreme irony, the author of the book was Thomas D. Crouch, the Smithsonian

❖ Gustave Whitehead sits with his assistants under *Airplane No. 21*, daughter Rose on his lap.

Copyright by William J. O'Dwyer and Flughistorische Forschungsgemeinschaft Gustav Weisskopf.

Institution's curator of early aircraft, and the photograph was credited to the Smithsonian.

Despite O'Dwyer's efforts to have the photograph blown up by using computer technology, he had to admit that it was impossible to positively identify it as clearly showing Whitehead in flight. But the fact that such an authority as the aeronautical editor of *Scientific American* was convinced that it depicted Whitehead in flight was to O'Dwyer and his committee significant additional evidence that Whitehead had been the first to fly.

There is no question that, although relegated to obscurity, Gustave

Whitehead was one of the most important pioneers of aviation. As O'Dwyer wrote in his book *History by Contract: The Beginning of Motorized Aviation*, Whitehead was the first to cover the wings of a flying machine with silk and the first to build a concrete runway, and, according to O'Dwyer and others, Whitehead introduced rubber tires for takeoff and landings. Most of these accomplishments were achieved before December 17, 1903. But did he beat the Wright brothers into the sky? Perhaps someday someone will come forward with a photograph unequivocally revealing Whitehead in the midst of one of his 1901 or 1902 flights. Perhaps some other type of proof even more conclusive than the considerable amount of compelling evidence that already exists will be discovered. If not, it is a question that will never be satisfactorily answered. "Meantime," as modern-day aviation journalist Frank Delear has written, "the long-suffering ghost of Gustave Whitehead still stands in the wings awaiting its summons on stage."

ELEVEN

EXERCISE TIGER
A Rehearsal for D-Day (1944)

Most of us know the significance of June 6, 1944. We have been taught, have read about, and have seen movie and television depictions of how, on that date during World War II, Allied forces crossed the English Channel and stormed the beaches of Normandy, France, in the largest amphibious attack in history. What is little known, however, is the devastating sacrifice of a convoy of ships and men as they staged a rehearsal for the attack on Normandy's Utah Beach, a sacrifice that resulted in a greater death toll than was later exacted during the actual invasion of Utah Beach.

Plans for the Normandy invasion had been launched in Morocco during the Casablanca Conference, where U.S. president Franklin D. Roosevelt and British prime minister Winston Churchill met with their top military advisors from January 14 to 24, 1943. The plan was code-named Operation Overlord, and its architects were well aware that they were setting in motion one of the greatest military invasions ever launched, one that would include an Allied force of some three million men, including one and a half million Americans. Transportation for this enormous force was to be provided by a fleet of more than 1,200 warships that would protect 4,126 landing craft and 1,600 merchant

❖ U.S. TROOPS REHEARSE LANDINGS on April 25, 1944, on a beach in England in preparation for D-Day on June 6.

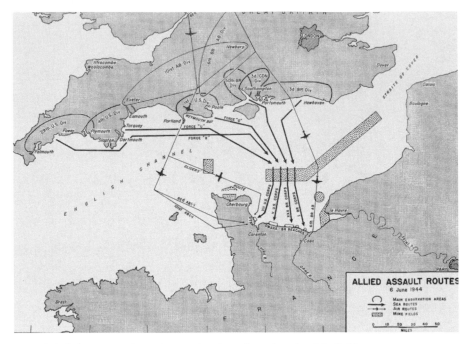

❖ A U.S. ARMY MAP shows the complex plans of assault outlined for D-Day.

ships and other vessels. Support was also to be provided by some 11,590 airplanes and 3,500 gliders.

It was, to say the least, to be a monumental undertaking, and there were many Allied officers who were less than confident that their troops were ready for it. As Harry C. Butcher, an aide to Supreme Commander Dwight D. Eisenhower, wrote in his memoirs,

> I am concerned over the absence of toughness and alertness of young American officers . . . they seem to regard the war as one grand maneuver in which they are having a happy time. Many seem as green as growing corn. How will they act in battle . . . ? A good many of the full colonels also give me a pain. They are fat, grey, and oldish. Most of them wear the Rainbow Ribbon of the last war and are still fighting it. . . . On the Navy's side, our crews are also green, but they seem to know how to handle their boats,

yet . . . I recall that in plain daylight, with a smooth sea with our [ship] standing still, she nearly had her stern carried away by a landing craft . . . fitted out as an anti-aircraft ship. We were missed only by inches—in clear daylight.

Butcher's concerns about the readiness of the Allied forces were far from his alone, and it was decided that in the months preceding the actual assault a series of mock invasions fully simulating the real landings would be staged. Numerous invasion exercises were held in various places in southern England, with several of them being staged at Woolacomb.

During these rehearsals, landing craft would attempt to land "invading" troops on coastlines similar to Normandy while artillery and land forces would try to beat them back. The first of these mock invasions, to be held in three phases in January and February 1944, was code-named Exercise Duck. The second, Exercise Beaver, would take

❖ USS *LST-325* IN OPERATION during Exercise Duck at Slapton Sands, England, January 1944.

place in late March, and the largest—and most controversial—rehearsal would be launched in April. It was code-named Exercise Tiger.

The military had deemed simulated invasions necessary not only because of concern over the readiness of the troops and the magnitude of the actual assault but also because the real landings would be unlike anything that had ever been attempted. The landings would not only be larger and more complex, but they would also involve a whole new military tactic. Earlier World War II invasions had been carried out by first sending in infantry and combat engineers, who established a beachhead by clearing away mines and any other human or man-made obstacles to a successful assault. Once the beachhead was established, the armored equipment was sent in. At both Utah Beach and Omaha Beach, which were to be invaded by American forces, the procedure was to be markedly different. The initial assault wave would be made up of engineers and demolition teams. Then a relatively new military weapon—amphibious tanks known as LSTs (landing ship, tank)—would be floated in. LSTs would carry the troops, the battle tanks, and all the other armored equipment. First developed after the British disaster at Dunkirk demonstrated a vital need for that type of ship, LSTs were constantly improved during World War II. They had proved to be key to the successful invasions of Algeria and various Japanese-held Pacific islands.

The site for Exercise Tiger was carefully chosen, the criterion being a place that closely resembled Utah Beach. And the beach bordering the village of Slapton, Devon, on Lyme Bay, east of Plymouth, fit the bill perfectly. Like the Utah Beach area where the actual invasion would take place, the locale known as Slapton Sands featured a broad gravel beach that fronted a wide expanse of land, which in turn fronted a lake. Like the Utah Beach environs, the area around Slapton Sands was characterized by hedgerows and narrow lanes.

In November 1943, the villagers of Slapton along with those in neighboring Torcross, Strete, East Allington, Blackawton, Sherford, Stokenham, Blackpool Sands, and Chillington received astounding news. Under authority of the 1939 Compensation (Defence) Act, the

❖ A RECENT PHOTOGRAPH of the broad beach at Slapton Sands.

British government ordered that 3,000 people, 750 families, 180 farms, and numerous village shops be totally evacuated within six weeks. All household goods, animals, farm machinery and other agricultural implements, and as many crops as could be quickly harvested were to be removed. In return, the British government promised to pay all costs connected with the evacuation, pledged that it would do everything it could to find and pay for accommodations for the evacuees, and would pay for any damages to the villagers' property incurred during Exercise Tiger operations.

The residents of the area were shocked. After repeated explanations from government and military officials, most came to understand the need for rehearsals for the upcoming vital invasion. But why Slapton and the surrounding villages? Why such a rich agricultural area when the need for homegrown food was greater than ever? But there was no room for argument. The government made it clear that the residents had no choice. The stage was set for Exercise Tiger.

This notice was posted several weeks before the evacuation:

NOTICE

The public are reminded that requisition took effect from 16th November, from which date compensation is calculated. They will not, except for special reason, be disturbed in their possession until December 21st, but from that date the Admiralty may at any time, and without prior notice, enforce their right to immediate possession. It is therefore essential that EVERY PERSON SHOULD LEAVE THE AREA BY DECEMBER 20TH.

On December 21st the supply of electricity in the area will cease. The present measures for supplying food will not be continued, but will be replaced by arrangements of a purely emergency character. The police stations will be closing during the present week.

The giant series of rehearsals for Exercise Tiger commenced on April 22, 1944, with the first assault landings scheduled the morning of the twenty-seventh. According to English author Ken Small, who devoted more than twenty years to attempting to unlock the secrets of Exercise Tiger, and others, the initial rehearsal was characterized by the same type of tragic blunders that would mark the entire operation. According to Small, because of concerns over the battle readiness of the officers and troops and in order to simulate real battle conditions, Eisenhower had ordered that live ammunition be fired over the heads and in front of the "invading" troops. But vital errors were made in conveying the radio frequency numbers to be used in establishing communications between the ships that were shelling the beach with live ammunition and the troops that were being landed. The situation was made even more disastrous when the troops hit the Slapton Sands beach a full hour after their scheduled arrival. The result was that dozens of soldiers were killed when the shellings and the landings took place at the same time. And even more men lost their lives when, again because of a lack of communications caused by the radio frequency errors, some fired at one another in mock combat without realizing that their ammunition was live. For years the U.S. Department of Defense denied that these "friendly fire" incidents ever took place. And they were but a prelude to a much greater disaster that lay ahead.

The stage for that tragedy was set in the beginning of the last week of April 1944, when a convoy of eight huge LSTs carrying thousands of troops in the 4th Infantry Division and the 1st Amphibian Division made their way toward Slapton Sands. Also packed from stem to stern on each LST were tons of heavy equipment, including tanks, amphibious vehicles, trucks, and other military vehicles to be used in the actual invasion. They began plowing their way toward Lyme Bay and Slapton Sands. The eight ships (in order numbered 515, 496, 511, 58, 499, 289, 507, and 531) proceeded in a single line with each vessel some four or five hundred yards behind the ship in front of it. Among the orders that commanders aboard the LSTs had been given was "Attack by enemy aircraft, submarines and E-boats [fast-moving surface vessels carrying either two or four torpedoes, "E" standing for "enemy" in the parlance of British and American sailors] may be expected en route to and in the exercise area." Even though the probability of such an assault seemed slim, several general alarm drills had been held on April 26 and 27. But although the troops and the sailors had been sent scrambling to their assigned positions, they had received absolutely no instructions about procedures for abandoning ship or what was expected of them in the event of an attack.

Protection for the convoy was the responsibility of the Royal Navy. Two British destroyers, three motor torpedo boats, and two motor gun boats were assigned to patrol the entrance to Lyme Bay, and several motor torpedo boats were sent to monitor the Cherbourg area, where German E-boats were based. Leading the convoy itself was HMS *Azalea*, a 205-foot Royal Navy corvette, armed with one four-inch cannon and several anti-aircraft guns. A second British vessel, the World War I destroyer HMS *Scimitar*, was assigned the task of flanking the flotilla of eight LSTs for added protection.

❖ A FULLY LOADED USS *LST-507* was photographed in Brixham Harbor, England, late in the afternoon of April 27, 1944. Less than twelve hours later, she was torpedoed and sunk in the English channel by German E-boats off Slapton Sands, England.

Shortly after midnight on the twenty-eighth, just as the convoy was entering Lyme Bay, HMS *Onslow*, one of the destroyers patrolling the area, spotted an E-boat racing across the bay. The German vessel was moving too rapidly to be pursued, but the *Onslow* reported the sighting to British headquarters at Plymouth. Minutes later, the *Onslow*'s radar detected three groups of E-boats some ten miles outside the Lyme Bay entrance. This news was also immediately conveyed to headquarters, which relayed the information via radio to the *Azalea* and the eight LSTs.

The *Azalea* got the message, but those aboard the LSTs heard nothing. Once again, errors had been made in conveying radio frequencies, and the radiomen aboard each of the LSTs were tuned to the wrong wavelength. For the same reason, the LSTs did not receive another bit of news: the *Scimitar* had experienced mechanical problems and had put into Plymouth for repairs. Only one destroyer, and a slow one at that, was now protecting the convoy.

By about 1:30 a.m. on the twenty-eighth, the convoy was well inside Lyme Bay. Aboard the LSTs, preparations were being made for the most efficient landing of troops and the hundreds of vehicles once the beach at Slapton Sands was reached. Suddenly, out of the darkness, nine E-boats appeared. On routine patrol out of Cherbourg, their commanders were startled to see a long line of Allied ships.

Called *Schnellboots* (literally, "fast boats") by the Germans, the E-boats were a special kind of war vessel. Because of restrictions imposed by the 1919 Treaty of Versailles that limited the size of military ships built by Germany, the E-boats were thirty-eight yards long and were powered by three Daimler-Benz engines totaling 6,150 horsepower. This made them extremely fast—ideal vessels for hit-and-run raids. In addition to torpedoes, most E-boats were equipped with two or three twenty-millimeter cannons. Some were armed with either a thirty-seven-millimeter or a forty-millimeter gun.

The E-boats that came upon the LST convoy had left Cherbourg at about 10 p.m. on the twenty-seventh and had been undetected by the British destroyers and smaller vessels responsible for monitoring

❖ TORPEDOES BEING LOADED onto a German E-boat, ca. 1944.

the area. Later, one of the E-boat commanders, a German lieutenant named Günther Rabe, described what happened in Lyme Bay some three and a half hours later. "We crossed the convoy route without any sign of ships," Rabe recalled, "and cruised easterly in the inner bay. Shortly before [2:30 a.m.] on the twenty-eighth we saw in the southeast, indistinct shadows of a long line of ships that we did not immediately identify as LSTs. . . . We thought at first they were tankers, or possibly destroyers."

As the Germans came within firing range of the LSTs, each E-boat slowed down to ten knots and launched two torpedoes. Manny Reuben, a petty officer aboard USS *LST-496*, the second LST in line, was on the bridge of the vessel when, as he later recalled, someone shouted, "I can see a bow wave." Then, as he remembered,

> We all saw it. A speedy craft, low and slender, was indistinctly seen, about 1,000 yards off our port bow, slipping through the silky smooth water. We fired many rounds at it with our standard 40-mm battery but observed no results, although it was clearly outlined by our tracers. The captain zigzagged, trying to keep our stern directed toward flares and a searchlight that flashed off after a few seconds. Our lookout reported a torpedo passing forward of our bow. An excited soldier in a half-track on our deck fired its 50-mm machine gun to the port quarter at what he imagined was an E-boat. It was too dark to tell. His slugs struck *LST-511* behind us, causing—I later learned—many severe wounds. We also had several holes slanting upwards, from the low-slung E-boats shooting high at us with their 20-mm and 40-mm cannon. One of these shells hit our galley and another creased my head, knocking me out.

The cannon fire from the E-boats was doing damage, but aboard his vessel Rabe was surprised that the two torpedoes he had launched had not struck home. For the first time he began to suspect that perhaps the Allied ships were shallow-draft LSTs and that the torpedoes had passed harmlessly underneath them. Aiming higher, he launched two more torpedoes at the last ship in the convoy. "[At 2:30 a.m.]," he later reported, "We saw that we had hit the target. Fire was spreading from bow to stern rapidly, and a dense cloud of smoke rose from the ship."

The ship that Rabe had hit was USS *LST-507*, and the result was something that Eugene Eckstam, a young doctor aboard the vessel, would never forget.

> General Quarters rudely aroused us. . . . I remember hearing gunfire and saying they had better watch where they were shooting or someone would get hurt. . . . I was stupidly trying to go topside to see what was going on and suddenly "BOOM!" There was a horrendous noise accompanied by the sound of crunching metal and dust everywhere. The lights went out and I was thrust violently in the air to land on the steel deck on my knees, which became very sore immediately thereafter. Now I knew how getting torpedoed felt. But I was lucky. The torpedo hit amidships starboard in the auxiliary engine room, knocking out all electric and water power. . . . I checked below decks aft to be sure no one required medical attention there. All men in accessible areas had gone topside.
>
> The tank deck was a different matter. As I opened the hatch, I found myself looking into a raging inferno which pushed me back. It was impossible to enter. The screams and cries of those many American troops in there still haunt me. Navy regulations call for [closing and locking] the hatches to preserve the integrity of the ship, and that's what I did. [It was] one of the most difficult decisions I have ever made, and one that gave me nightmares for years—and still does . . . but knowing that there was absolutely no way anyone could help [those below in the tank deck], and knowing that smoke inhalation would end their miseries soon, I closed the hatches. . . .
>
> We were forced to leave the ship. . . . Gas cans and ammunition exploding and the enormous fire blazing only a few yards away are sights forever etched in my memory.

LST-507's nineteen-year-old motor mechanic's mate, Angelo Crapanzano, had his own vivid memories. When he heard his ship's guns firing, Crapanzano approached an officer to ask him what was happening. The officer replied, "I guess they're trying to make it as real as possible." The officer's words were hardly out of his mouth when, as Crapanzano later recalled,

> There was a deafening roar, and everything went black. I felt myself going up and down, hitting my head on something. I must have blacked out for a few seconds, but then I felt cold water around my legs. I scrambled up the ladder. The six guys in the auxiliary engine room, just forward of where I was, never knew what hit them. . . .
>
> When I got topside, I couldn't believe what I saw: The ship was split in half and burning, fire went from the bow all the way back to the wheelhouse. . . . And the water all around the ship was burning, because the fuel tanks ruptured. And the oil went into the water. . . . We had fifteen Army ducks [amphibious vehicles] and every Army duck had cans of gasoline on them, and all that was going into the water, so it was like an inferno.

Four ships ahead of *LST-507* on USS *LST-511*, medical officer Clifford Graves looked on in horror as *LST-507* erupted into flames. "Suddenly," he later wrote, "there was [another] explosion. It had a dull sound, as though a great heavy mass had fallen onto a heavily carpeted floor. The *LST* behind us [*531*] burst into flames all at once. She seemed to have disintegrated with that one burst."

Gazing in horror at USS *LST-531*, seaman Thomas Holcombe, aboard one of the other LSTs, saw "trucks, men, and jeeps flying through the air."

Less than ten minutes after being torpedoed, *LST-531* sank to the bottom.

In the explosions that had destroyed both *LST-507* and *LST-531*, almost every lifeboat had been obliterated. Faced with only one choice, those aboard these ships who had survived the blasts were forced to jump into the waters of Lyme Bay. "Now we've got to go into the water," Crapanzano remembered.

> There were a lot of guys on the front end of the ship, and the tank deck was burning right under them. . . . A lot of guys didn't want to jump into the water right away. I didn't want to either. It got so hot on the deck that [our] shoes started smoking, because the tank deck was burning fiercely, and that's all metal. It's just like a gas jet stove, and all the heat's going up to the top deck. . . .
>
> I run to the railing and I look down and I see all those guys in the water already. Now I say, "what am I gonna do? I'm gonna jump and I'm gonna hit somebody." Then I'm saying—this is all in a split second—"when I jump in the water how deep down do I go before I come up? Or do I come up right away?"
>
> [What I know] because in the engine room you had to take readings of a bunch of gauges . . . . was that the reading on the salt water coming in was 43 degrees. What I didn't know was what 43 degrees felt like. So when I hit the water, it took my breath away, that's how cold it was.

Hundreds of the soldiers and sailors from *LST-507* and *LST-531* died from hypothermia in the frigid water. And there was another terrible problem. Not only had there been no abandon-ship drills conducted on the LSTs as they made their way to Lyme Bay, there had been absolutely no instructions given to the soldiers on the proper way to put on their inflatable life belts. Already loaded down with backpacks and rifles, the soldiers found it easier to put their life belts around their waists instead of under their armpits as they should have done. The horrible result was that their high center of gravity pitched scores of men face down into the frigid water, where they drowned. "The worst memory I have," crew member Dale Rodman of *LST-507* later exclaimed, "[was] setting off in the lifeboat away from the sinking ship and watching bodies float by." *LST-507* and *LST-531* were not the only unfortunate vessels in the bay. As torpedo wakes surged past both sides of USS *LST-289*, its captain,

❖ The remains of USS *LST-289* in port, after being struck by a German torpedo.

Lieutenant Harry Mettler, began zigzagging his vessel furiously. Just when it looked like the evasive action would be successful, another torpedo was sighted heading for *LST-289*'s stern. Immediately Mettler ordered full right rudder, but it was too late. As petty officer Martin MacMahon, stationed on *LST-289*'s deck, later reported, the torpedo struck his ship "like an earthquake." When MacMahon looked behind him he saw that the entire rear section of the ship was "smashed and curled over the navigation bridge." Everyone on the bridge had been blown off onto the deck, many of them terribly injured. Miraculously, Mettler was not badly hurt. Observing that the forward end of his ship was free of damage, he came up with what proved to be a brilliant plan. Immediately he ordered that the two small landing craft aboard the LST be lowered and that towlines be attached to them. Although it took hours, *LST-289* was eventually towed to shore.

As Graves later wrote, *LST-511* was even more fortunate.

> The convoy was now broken up. . . . It was every ship for itself. We headed for the nearest land which was 20 miles away; . . . I found out later that the captain of our ship had no chart, and no idea of the minefields that had been laid down by the British. Even if he had been able to call for help, it could never have got to us in time. The corvette that was supposed to be our protection, we never saw.
>
> We sat and waited for the torpedo we knew would come. Our work was done. There was nothing to do but wait. But the torpedo never came. The only way we would figure it was that they had run out of torpedoes. Nothing else was there to stop them. At about six o'clock in the morning, in the grey mist, we were able to make out land. An hour later we were at anchor in the little harbor of Weymouth. Columbus himself wouldn't have been happier at the sight of land than we were that morning.

Graves had been right about the corvette assigned to protect the convoy. Throughout the entire disaster, from the time the surface firing began, through the torpedo strikes and the sinkings, the LSTs received no help from the *Azalea*. Remarkably, the corvette's captain later reported that he saw no E-boats and received no calls for help from the LSTs (that, at least, was understandable given the tragic wavelength errors). And Graves was also correct in assuming that his ship and shipmates had been spared because the E-boats had run out of torpedoes—that, and the fact that the whole operational policy of the German raiders was to hit and run as quickly as possible.

As they sped back to Cherbourg, the commanders of several of the E-boats were still uncertain as to what type of Allied ships they had torpedoed. But they could not help but be aware that they had made a major strike. What they could not know was that theirs was to be the most successful E-boat raid of the entire war. The carnage they left behind was horrific. Hundreds of soldiers and sailors had been killed in the explosions. Hundreds of others had drowned. Scores of frightened men remained in the sea, waiting to be saved.

Although the *Azalea* was still nowhere to be seen, two sister ships of the *Onslow* did arrive to help in a rescue effort. "We arrived in the area at daybreak, and the sight was appalling," a warranty officer aboard one of the British vessels later wrote. "There were hundreds of bodies . . . in the sea. Many had their limbs and even their heads blown off, but some were still alive. We took aboard all those we could find living and applied first aid and resuscitation. . . . Small American landing craft with their ramps down were literally scooping up bodies, driving them ashore, and dumping them on the beaches. . . . Of all those we took on board, there were only nine survivors."

The rescue effort had actually begun even before the two British ships arrived. *LST-507*'s Dale Rodman had managed to climb aboard the one lifeboat that had survived the destruction of his ship.

We pulled away from [our] sinking LST and began to pick up people from the water. I was startled to see scores of dead soldiers floating in the water with their packs and lifebelts on. The backpack and the lifebelt around their waists made them top heavy and they were lying on their backs with their heads underwater.

They had been knocked unconscious by the impact of hitting the water when they jumped overboard with their belts inflated, and they had drowned before they regained consciousness. Those of us on the lifeboat located what survivors we could in the darkness from the sound of their cries for help. Altogether there were between fifty and sixty survivors aboard when we were picked up by a British destroyer, HMS *Onslow*, at about 6:30 A.M. As I climbed to safety, I looked out over the water and saw hundreds of bodies still floating there.

Once it became clear that the E-boats had left the scene, the overall commander of the convoy had ordered all the surviving LSTs to head immediately for Slapton Sands. But Lieutenant John Doyle, captain of USS *LST-515*, could not bring himself to obey the order. How could he leave men from the other ships behind to die in the sea? Ignoring the consequences of disregarding a direct command, and with the overwhelming approval of those aboard *LST-515*, he began to search for survivors. Sadly, there were only a few who could be rescued, among them Ralph Bartholomay, a naval gunner on the stricken *LST-507*.

Describing what he experienced after he had been in the water for some time, Bartholomay later recalled,

> I spotted some wreckage with a few people hanging on so I swam over. There were the first live persons I had seen in a while and it was encouraging. We were holding on to a small piece of wreckage that wasn't too stable and one fellow was trying to sit up on it. Every time he tried, the object turned over and would spill us all into the water. It seemed almost like a game. No one became angry, we were all too tired. This is where I started to say the Lord's Prayer over and over. I was beginning to get drowsy, a bad sign in cold water, and praying supplied some hope. I was starting to slip in and out of reality, with the unreal parts getting longer, when I heard the faint sound of a boat engine with someone calling out. Maybe some day I will hear a more

welcome sound, but that night it sounded like the answer to a prayer. When the boat came close enough, I saw it was the *LST-515* come back to pick us up. I mustered what strength I had left and swam over. It was the longest ten yards I ever swam.

Bartholomay and several others owed their lives to Doyle's determination to follow his conscience and disobey a command. As for Doyle, he not only escaped reprimand, but was eventually officially commended for his actions.

According to the U.S. Department of Defense, 749 servicemen were killed during Exercise Tiger. Eventually, other reports placed the death toll considerably higher. Whatever the exact figure, this largest training disaster of the war was only the beginning of the Exercise Tiger story. For decades, the story of what had taken place at Lyme Bay was kept totally secret. The public was never told what had occurred. When relatives of those who had been killed tried to find out what happened to their loved ones, they were met with a wall of silence. Eisenhower, the man in charge of every aspect of the training exercise, never said a word about it in his best-selling memoirs.

The veil of secrecy began as early as mid-morning on April 28, 1944, when most of the surviving ships of the LST flotilla reached shore. "When we got closer to land," Corporal Eugene Carney of the 4th Infantry Division recalled, "we saw a long, sloping road leading down to the water. Ambulances were lined up bumper to bumper—a pitiful sight. We were unloaded from the ship and put into trucks before the dead and wounded were removed. We were told to keep our mouths shut and were taken to a camp where we were quarantined."

The secrecy continued when the wounded survivors of Exercise Tiger were taken to area hospitals. Captain Ralph Greene of the U.S. Army Medical Corps served in the laboratory of the 228th Station Hospital at Sherborne, Dorset. On the morning of April 28, he was going about his regular duties when an announcement was made that all personnel in the hospital were to assemble in the facility's recreation room, where they would be addressed by the hospital's commander, Colonel James Kendall.

What a tense Kendall had to say came as a complete surprise. He announced,

> We're in the war at last. In less than an hour we'll receive hundreds of emergency cases of shock due to immersion, compounded by explosion wounds. SHAEF [Supreme Headquarters, Allied Expeditionary Force] demands that we treat these soldiers as though we're veterinarians: you will ask no questions and take no histories. There will be no discussion. Follow standard procedures. Anyone who talks about these casualties, regardless of their severity, will be subject to court-martial. No one will be allowed to leave our perimeter until further orders.

It was an astounding announcement, and if Greene or any of his fellow hospital staff members had any doubts about the seriousness of the situation, they were removed once they looked out one of the hospital's windows. The entire compound had been surrounded by counterintelligence troops, each man carrying a bayoneted rifle.

About half an hour later, a host of ambulances and trucks began pulling up to the hospital. "They were filled," remembered Greene, "with wet, shivering, blue-skinned, blanketed, and bandaged young Army and Navy men." In the hours that followed, hundreds of men, many of them in great pain, were treated by the doctors, nurses, and orderlies without a single word being exchanged between them. Many of the patients responded quickly to the treatment. Many others required longer hospitalization. Others died.

A few days later, the bizarre episode ended as abruptly and as mysteriously as it had begun when all the remaining patients were suddenly removed from the hospital. Neither Greene nor any of his fellow personnel had any idea of where they had come from or where they were taken. The code of silence remained unbroken.

Unbeknownst to Greene, the same scenario had been played out in other hospitals and casualty stations throughout the southwestern corner of England. Wounded soldiers had suddenly arrived, hospital personnel were forbidden to talk with them, armed troops surrounded the hospital, and within days, whatever patients remained in the hospital were abruptly taken away.

So powerfully had the military authorities emblazoned the need for secrecy on the survivors of Exercise Tiger that for decades they did not discuss it publicly. In an interview he gave more than thirty years after the events at Lyme Bay, Crapanzano stated that in all the years following the disaster he never told anyone about it, not even his psychiatrist.

In 1974, many of the secrets of World War II became available through the passage of the Freedom of Information Act. By this time, the Exercise Tiger episode had been so long and so thoroughly buried that, despite the FOIA, it remained largely unreported. Greene, however, had never forgotten what he termed "that curious day" at the 228th Station Hospital. And in the early 1980s, while gathering material for a book he intended to write on the effects of malaria and hepatitis in World War II, he unexpectedly got the opportunity to try to satisfy a mystery that had perplexed him for more than forty years.

Stumbling upon previously unrevealed accounts of Exercise Tiger, he decided to put his book on hold while he attempted to contact survivors of the episode named in the documents he had encountered. What he discovered was that those who responded to him, including Eugene Carney, were enormously relieved to at last be able to relate their stories.

These initial accounts, when revealed, elicited a response from the British and American media that perhaps should have been expected. Typical of the statements included in newspaper reports and in a three-part report aired by a Washington, D.C., television station were such proclamations as: "It was a disaster which lay hidden from the world for forty years . . . an official American Army cover-up." "That a massive cover-up took place is beyond doubt. And that General Dwight D. Eisenhower authorized it is equally clear." "Generals Omar N. Bradley and Eisenhower watched the 'murderous chaos' and were horrified and determined that details of their own mistakes would be buried with the men." "Relatives of the dead men have been misinformed—and even lied to—by their government." "It was a story the government kept quiet . . . hushed up for decades . . . a dirty little secret of World War II."

Strong words—but was it really a cover-up? Or were there legitimate reasons why Exercise Tiger was cloaked in secrecy? In the 1980s, when more information about the ill-fated exercise became available, it became clear that there might well have been an important reason for strict suppression of information immediately following the disaster. Records revealed that among those aboard the eight LSTs were ten officers who had so-called Bigot-level clearance for the invasion of Normandy. That meant that they knew such vital details as the date and location of the assault. If, following the E-boat attacks, these men had been captured and made to reveal what they knew, it would have jeopardized the invasion.

In the days following the Exercise Tiger disaster, divers were sent to Lyme Bay to check the bodies lying at the bottom of the bay, in the wreckage of the sunken LSTs, and in the tanks and other vehicles that rested there. The divers removed the dog tags from every body they found. Remarkably, when these tags were checked against the roster of those who had been aboard, it was discovered that every one of the "Bigoted" officers had been killed and had taken the secrets of D-Day with them.

There could have also been other reasons for the suppression of information immediately following the disaster. The military may well have been determined to keep secret any clues that might link the rehearsals at Slapton Sands to the planned invasion of Utah Beach. But a giant question remains. Why the cloak of secrecy for the better part of forty years after World War II had ended? And why, in 1954, when the United States erected an obelisk to thank the people of Slapton Sands and its neighboring villages for leaving their homes, was there absolutely no mention of the hundreds of lives that had been lost?

Another mystery that remains is more macabre. What happened to the bodies of the men who sacrificed their lives in the D-Day rehearsal? According to Slapton Sands resident Ken Small, who in the early 1970s conducted an extensive search for records of their interment, the only thing that is known is that some of the remains were buried near Cambridge,

❖ A SHERMAN TANK stands as a memorial for Allied soldiers killed during Exercise Tiger at Slapton Sands, Devon. The tank was raised from the sea in 1984.

England, at a place called Madingley Hill. Other than that, according to Small, there are "virtually no records of the disposal of the bodies."

We do know, through accounts by survivors such as Eugene Carney, that immediately following the tragedy, scores of bodies were buried in temporary graves. And there is a seemingly reliable eyewitness account from a woman who swore that she saw a mass unmarked grave in a meadow close to Slapton Sands in which soldiers in American battle dress were buried. According to the woman, who visited the site often, the bodies were never exhumed. The U.S. Department of Defense, however, disputes that part of the woman's testimony. According to the Pentagon, approximately 450 bodies were never recovered and still lie on the bottom of Lyme Bay. The Department of Defense agreed that more than three hundred bodies were buried in that mass grave, but by 1956 all had been secretly transferred to various official cemeteries. Again, if true, why the need for secrecy?

What is unmistakable is that the operation known as Exercise Tiger was a major disaster from the very beginning. Even when the exercise was well over, the tragedy continued, as evidenced by the fate of Exercise Tiger's last casualty—Rear Admiral Don P. Moon. Moon, the officer in charge of the naval part of the invasion rehearsal, was severely reprimanded by his superior in the presence of his own officers and reduced to a lesser command. He never recovered. Months later he took his own life, the only high-ranking American officer to commit suicide during World War II.

The story of Exercise Tiger, deliberately hidden for so long and mostly forgotten today, is one that needs to be remembered. Out of the many tragic blunders that were committed came changes vital to D-Day's success. Radio frequencies were standardized to prevent the type of tragic errors in communication that had plagued the ill-fated rehearsals.

❖ ON JUNE 1, 1944, five days before the D-Day invasion, artillery equipment is loaded aboard LSTs at Brixham, England.

The conveyance of detailed instructions for the proper use of life belts was made mandatory on every type of naval vessel. New, more effective procedures for the rescue of survivors in the sea were created. All proved invaluable in the Normandy invasion. Most important, what must be recaptured from the lost pages of history is the story of the sacrifices made by so many who gave their lives to give their country and its allies their best chance of victory.

✈ ACKNOWLEDGMENTS ✦

The author is most indebted to Sterling editorial director Michael Fragnito for having suggested this book. Thanks are due also to Katherine Worten and Danielle Antosta for their valuable help. As always, Carol Sandler has been both a colleague and an inspiration.

As with my previous Sterling books, I am also indebted to a host of dedicated and accomplished professionals who made this book possible, including, at Sterling, publisher Jason Prince, Associate Art Director Christine Heun, and production editor Andrea Santoro. Special thanks to copyeditor Lori Paximadis and proofreader Loretta Mowat.

Finally, once again I have been blessed with having Barbara Berger as my editor. And again I find that there are no words adequate to express what Barbara's insights, editing skills, and work ethic have brought to this book. Barbara—you are the best and I am deeply grateful.

→ NOTES ←

Preface

IX "The only thing new in the world": Merle Miller, *Plain Speaking: An Oral Biography of Harry S Truman*. (New York: Berkley Publishing, 1974.)

IX "history can only live if one recovers": Russell Potter, foreword to *Resolute: The Epic Search for the Northwest Passage and John Franklin, and the Discovery of the Queen's Ghost Ship*, by Martin W. Sandler. (New York: Sterling Publishing Co., Inc., 2006.)

Chapter 1: Ziryab

1 "There never was, either before or after him": Ahmad ibn Muhammad al-Makkari, as quoted in Yusef Ali, "The Music of the Moors in Spain," in "Golden Age of the Moor," ed. Ivan Van Sertima, *Journal of African Civilizations* 11 (1991).

1 "undoubtedly one person alone cannot change": Henri Terrasse, *Islam d'Espagne: Une rencontre de l'Orient et de l'Occident* [Islamic Spain: A Meeting of East and West] (Paris: Plon, 1958).

2 Ziryab's rise from slavery to extraordinary fame: Jan Carew, "Moorish Culture-Bringers: Bearers of Enlightenment," in "Golden Age of the Moor," ed. Ivan Van Sertima, *Journal of African Civilizations* 11 (1991).

2 "A Black slave": Ibid.

2 "He is a freeman of thy family": Ahmad ibn Muhammad al-Makkari, as quoted in Yusef Ali, "The Music of the Moors in Spain," in "Golden Age of the Moor," ed. Ivan Van Sertima, *Journal of African Civilizations* 11 (1991).

3 "What difference is there": Ibid.

3 "By Allah! Were it not that I consider thee": Ibid.

3–4 "Envy is one of the basest vices": Ibid.

7 "He was deeply versed in every branch of art": Ibid.

7   "answered to the four elementary principles of the body": Titus Burckhardt, *Moorish Culture in Spain* (New York: McGraw-Hill, 1972).

8   "restore the equilibrium of the soul the same way that medicine restores the equilibrium of the body": Yusef Ali, "The Music of the Moors in Spain," in "Golden Age of the Moor," ed. Ivan Van Sertima, *Journal of African Civilizations* 11 (1991).

8   The lute before Ziryab represented these four humors: Julian Ribera, *Music in Ancient Arabia and Spain* (Stanford, Calif.: Stanford University Press, 1929; reprint: Whitefish, Mont.: Kessinger Publishing, 2007).

8   "by the soft down which covers the claw of that bird": Chris Lowney, *A Vanished World: Medieval Spain's Golden Age of Enlightenment* (New York: Free Press, 2005).

8   Some of these new instruments included the *carrizo*: Ivan Van Sertima, "The Moor in Europe: Influences and Contributions," in "Golden Age of the Moor," ed. Ivan Van Sertima, *Journal of African Civilizations* 11 (1991).

10   "a complete musical work, composed of various airs and melodies": George Dimitri Selim, "A Gift of Music," *Library of Congress Information Bulletin*, Vol. 55, No. 15 (1996).

11   Ziryab always began by testing a new pupil's voice: Ivan Van Sertima, "The Moor in Europe: Influences and Contributions," in "Golden Age of the Moor," ed. Ivan Van Sertima, *Journal of African Civilizations* 11 (1991).

11   "the founder of the musical traditions of Muslim Spain": Clifford E. Bosworth, *Encyclopedia of Islam* (Leiden, the Netherlands: Brill, 2004).

11   "Ziryab's music influenced all neighboring countries": G. Talebzadeh, "Zaryâb: A Genius Iranian Musician" (Fravahr.org, 2003).

11   "Andalusian music was advanced by Ziryab": Ibid.

11   "Even when the Moors had been defeated": Ivan Van Sertima, "The Moor in Europe: Influences and Contributions," in "Golden Age of the Moor," ed. Ivan Van Sertima, *Journal of African Civilizations* 11 (1991).

12   "The artistic Spain of olden times": Julian Ribera, *Music in Ancient Arabia and Spain* (Stanford, Calif: Stanford University Press, 1929; reprint: Whitefish, Mont: Kessinger Publishing, 2007).

12   "The tradition of changing clothes": Ahmad ibn Muhammad al-Makkari, as quoted in Yusef Ali, "The Music of the Moors in Spain," in "Golden Age of the Moor," ed. Ivan Van Sertima, *Journal of African Civilizations* 11 (1991).

12   "A vogue for brightly colored clothes": Jan Read, *The Moors in Spain and Portugal* (Totowa, NJ: Rowman and Littlefield, 1975).

13   "Both men and women wore the hair": Ahmad ibn Muhammad al-Makkari, as quoted in Yusef Ali, "The Music of the Moors in Spain," in "Golden Age of the Moor," ed. Ivan Van Sertima, *Journal of African Civilizations* 11 (1991).

13   "Bangs were out": Chris Lowney, *A Vanished World: Medieval Spain's Golden Age of Enlightenment* (New York: Free Press, 2005).

13   "the fetid smell of the armpits": Ahmad ibn Muhammad al-Makkari, as quoted in Yusef Ali, "The Music of the Moors in Spain," in "Golden Age of the Moor," ed. Ivan Van Sertima, *Journal of African Civilizations* 11 (1991).

14   a vast improvement over anything: Ivan Van Sertima, "The Moor in Europe: Influences and Contributions," in "Golden Age of the Moor," ed. Ivan Van Sertima, *Journal of African Civilizations* 11 (1991).

16–17   "[Ziryab] was fitted with so much penetration and wit": Ahmad ibn Muhammad al-Makkari, as quoted in Yusef Ali, "The Music of the Moors in Spain" in "Golden Age of the Moor," ed. Ivan Van Sertima, *Journal of African Civilizations* 11 (1991).

Chapter 2: Cahokia

19   "warfare that was insane, unending, continuously attritional": Alfred L. Kroeber, "Native American Population," *American Anthropologist* 36 (1934).

19–20   "For thousands of centuries—centuries in which human races were evolving": Alan Brinkley, *American History: A Survey* Vol. 1 (New York: McGraw-Hill, 2007).

20   "Native Americans transformed their land": Charles C. Mann, *1491: New Revelations of the Americas Before Columbus* (New York: Knopf, 2005).

20   "a thriving, stunningly diverse place": Ibid.

22   "From their central location, [the Cahokians] traveled vast distances": Claudia G. Mink, *Cahokia: City of the Sun* (Collinsville, Ill.: Cahokia Mounds Museum Society, 1992).

22–23   "As years passed, people learned to cultivate corn": Sidney G. Denny and Ernest Lester Schusky, *The Ancient Splendor of Prehistoric Cahokia* (Prairie Grove, Ark.: Ozark Publishing, 1997).

23   "When I reached the foot of the principal mound": Ibid.

23–24   "It is absurd to suppose a relationship of any kind": J. D. Baldwin, *Ancient America* (New York: Harper and Brothers, 1871).

24   "signalized by treachery and cruelty": J. W. Foster, *Pre-Historic Races of the United States of America* (London: S. C. Griggs and Co., 1887).

26   "This pharaonic enterprise required carrying 14,666,666 baskets": Sally A. Kitt Chappell, *Cahokia: Mirror of the Cosmos* (Chicago: University of Chicago Press, 2002).

27   beneath Mound 72 were found the remains of a man buried in about 1050: Including Biloine Whiting Young and Melvin Fowler, *Cahokia: The Great Native American Metropolis* (Champaign, Ill.: University of Illinois Press, 2000).

28   "Only a person of central importance": Thomas E. Emerson and R. Barry Lewis, *Cahokia and the Hinterlands: Middle Mississippian Cultures of the Midwest* (Champaign, Ill.: University of Illinois Press, 1999).

28   the four men were deliberately placed in graves: Rinita A. Dalan et al., *Envisioning Cahokia: A Landscape Perspective* (DeKalb, Ill.: Northern Illinois University Press, 2003).

29   a city aligned with the cosmos: Including Sally A. Kitt Chappell, *Cahokia: Mirror of the Cosmos* (Chicago, Ill.: University of Chicago Press, 2002).

30   "sacred geography": Sally A. Kitt Chappell, *Cahokia: Mirror of the Cosmos* (Chicago: University of Chicago Press, 2002).

31   "Situated upon a very beautiful plain": Biloine Whiting Young and Melvin Fowler, *Cahokia: The Great Native American Metropolis* (Champaign, Ill.: University of Illinois Press, 2000).

33   since his fellow archaeologist allowed no time for the planning: Ibid.

33   "Cahokia being the biggest city around": Charles C. Mann, *1491: New Revelations of the Americas Before Columbus* (New York: Knopf, 2005).

33   "evidence of Cahokia's response to its uneasy relations": Biloine Whiting Young and Melvin Fowler, *Cahokia: The Great Native American Metropolis* (Champaign, Ill.: University of Illinois Press, 2000).

33   "It surrounded the central core of the community": Ibid.

36   gambling was frequently associated with the game: Timothy Pauketat, *Ancient Cahokia and the Mississippians* (Cambridge, England: Cambridge University Press, 2004).

36 "the seat of the largest political chiefdom": Thomas E. Emerson and R. Barry Lewis, *Cahokia and the Hinterlands: Middle Mississippian Cultures of the Midwest* (Champaign, Ill.: University of Illinois Press, 1999).

36–37 "Cahokia is unique. . . . I still can't say it is a state": Biloine Whiting Young and Melvin Fowler, *Cahokia: The Great Native American Metropolis* (Champaign, Ill.: University of Illinois Press, 2000).

38–39 "The primary facts now seem to indicate": Thomas E. Emerson and R. Barry Lewis, *Cahokia and the Hinterlands: Middle Mississippian Cultures of the Midwest* (Champaign, Ill.: University of Illinois Press, 1999).

Chapter 3: Gil Eanes

42 "big and strong of limb, his hair": Gomes Eanes de Zurara, *Crónica dos Feitos da Guiné* [The Chronicle of the Discovery and Conquest of Guinea] (1453).

43 "bound to engage in great and noble conquests": Ibid.

44 "Beneath the huge red sandstone cliffs": Peter D. Jeans, *Seafaring Lore and Legend* (New York: McGraw-Hill, 2004).

45 "So the Infant [prince] . . . began to make ready": Gomes Eanes de Zurara, *Crónica dos Feitos da Guiné* [The Chronicle of the Discovery and Conquest of Guinea] (1453).

48 "Now the Infant always received home again": Ibid.

49 "probably sailed in a simple square-rigged": Hugh Thomas, *The Slave Trade: The Story of the Atlantic Slave Trade: 1440–1870* (New York: Simon and Schuster, 1997).

50 "The Infant made ready the same vessel": Gomes Eanes de Zurara, *Crónica dos Feitos da Guiné* [The Chronicle of the Discovery and Conquest of Guinea] (1453).

51 "and as he proposed, he performed": Ibid.

53 "This achievement of Gil Eanes marks an era": John Fiske, *The Discovery of America with Some Account of Ancient America and the Spanish Conquest* (Boston: Houghton, Mifflin and Company, 1892).

Chapter 4: Joseph Warren

58 "Awake! Awake, my countrymen": *Boston Gazette*, October 7, 1765.

61 "The former . . . was accomplished": John H. Cary, *Joseph Warren: Physician, Politician, Patriot* (Urbana, Ill.: University of Illinois Press, 1961).

61   "The colonies, until now": Richard Frothingham, *Life and Times of Joseph Warren* (Boston: Little, Brown and Company, 1865).

64   "The fatal fifth of March, 1770": John H. Cary, *Joseph Warren: Physician, Politician, Patriot* (Urbana, Ill.: University of Illinois Press, 1961).

65   Hutchinson's words proved prophetic: Richard Frothingham, *Life and Times of Joseph Warren* (Boston: Little, Brown and Company, 1865).

66   "Last night three cargoes of Bohea Tea": John Adams Diary 19, 16 December 1772–18 December 1773 [electronic edition], Adams Family Papers: An Electronic Archive, Massachusetts Historical Society, www.masshist.org/digitaladams/.

68   "The British people of the Atlantic": D. W. Meinig, *The Shaping of America: A Geographical Perspective on 500 Years of History*, Vol. 1: *Atlantic America* (New Haven, Conn.: Yale University Press, 1986).

70   "For solidity of reasoning, force of sagacity": *The Works and Correspondence of the Right Honourable Edmund Burke*, Vol. 3 (London: Francis and John Rivington, 1852).

72   "a few hisses from some of the officers": John H. Cary, *Joseph Warren: Physician, Politician, Patriot* (Urbana, Ill.: University of Illinois Press, 1961).

72   "The interest and safety of Britain": Ibid.

77   "We conjure you": Ibid.

77   George Washington donated: Benjamin Hart, *Faith and Freedom: The Christian Roots of American Liberty* (Carrollton, Tex.: Lewis and Stanley, 1988).

78–79   "I am here only as a volunteer": Oliver Clay, *Heroes of the American Revolution* (New York: Duffield and Company, 1916).

80   "It was a dear-bought victory": John Ferling, *Almost a Miracle: The American Victory in the War of Independence* (New York: Oxford University Press, 2007).

80   "the trials we have had": Ibid.

80   "Doctor Warren, president of the Provincial Congress": John H. Cary, *Joseph Warren: Physician, Politician, Patriot* (Urbana, Ill: University of Illinois Press, 1961).

81   "We mourn . . . for the citizen": Richard Frothingham, *Life and Times of Joseph Warren* (Boston: Little, Brown and Company, 1865).

81   "Our dear Warren has fallen": John H. Cary, *Joseph Warren: Physician, Politician, Patriot* (Urbana, Ill.: University of Illinois Press, 1961).

81   "if [Warren] had lived": Ibid.

81 "Neither resentment . . . nor interested views": Richard Frothingham, *Life and Times of Joseph Warren* (Boston: Little, Brown and Company, 1865).

81 "As he lived an ornament to his country": Ibid.

83 "The personal representative of those brave citizens": Ibid.

Chapter 5: Outdoing Revere

85 "If you mean to be a historical figure": Virginius Dabney, "Jack Jouett's Ride," *American Heritage* 13, No. 1 (1961).

86 "Upon his head a metallic cap sword-proof": James R. Case, *An Account of Tryon's Raid on Danbury in April, 1777* (Danbury, Conn.: Danbury Printing Co., 1927).

88 "As the British troops reached a point": James Montgomery Bailey, *History of Danbury, Conn., 1684–1896* (New York: Burr Printing House, 1896).

89 "The drunken men went up and down": James R. Case, *An Account of Tryon's Raid on Danbury in April, 1777* (Danbury, Conn.: Danbury Printing Co., 1927).

92 "The Colonel's most vigilant and watchful companion": Louis S. Patrick, "Secret Service of the American Revolution," *Connecticut Magazine* 11, No. 2 (1907): 265–274.

92–93 "These fearless girls, with guns in hand": Ibid.

94 "One who even now rides": Willis Fletcher Johnson, *Colonel Henry Ludington: A Memoir* (Whitefish, Mont.: Kessinger Publishing, 2007).

95 "Come on my boys! Never mind such random shots": Albert Van Dusen, *Connecticut: A Fully Illustrated History of the State from the Seventeenth Century to the Present.* (New York: Random House, 1961).

96 Arnold . . . . calmly replied: Ibid.

97 "Henry Wordsworth Longfellow, God rest his bones": Virginius Dabney, "Jack Jouett's Ride," *American Heritage* 13, No. 1 (1961).

100 "The unfrequented pathway over which this horseman": Virginius Dabney, "Jouett Outrides Tarleton," *Scribner's* (June 1928).

102 "had an eccentric custom of wearing such habiliments": Henry S. Randall, *The Life of Thomas Jefferson* (New York: Derby and Jackson, 1858).

102 when McLeod came into view on the approach: Ibid.

104 **they heard a woman's screams coming from an isolated cabin:** Virginius Dabney, "Jack Jouett's Ride," *American Heritage* 13, No. 1 (1961).

105 **"shared his grandfather's fate in being forgotten by history":** Ibid.

105 **"But for Captain Jack Jouett's heroic ride":** Stuart G. Gibbony, as quoted in "Jack Jouett of Virginia: The 'Other Ride,'" ed. Donald Norman Moran, reprint from *The Valley Compatriot* (February 1984), Americanrevolution.org.

Chapter 6: Elisha Kent Kane

110–111 **As historian Pierre Berton observed:** Pierre Berton, *The Arctic Grail: The Quest for the North West Passage and the North Pole, 1818–1909* (Toronto: Anchor Canada, 1988).

127 **whose summer hunting grounds were nearby:** Mark Horst Sawin, "Raising Kane: The Making of a Hero, the Marketing of a Celebrity," unpublished thesis, 1997, www.ekkane.org.

128 **"They are deserters, in act and in spirit":** Pierre Berton, *The Arctic Grail: The Quest for the North West Passage and the North Pole, 1818–1909* (Toronto: McClelland and Stewart, 1988).

132 **"humanized the Arctic":** Frank Rasky, *The North Pole or Bust* (n.p.: Book Sales, 1984).

Chapter 7: The *Sultana*

136 **"To become a prisoner in the Civil War":** Bruce Catton, *The American Heritage Short History of the Civil War* (New York: Dell Laurel Leaf, 1960).

137 **"Physically weakened as many of them were":** "Reminiscence of the War," *Wayne County Democrat*, April 28, 1880.

139 **"On every part of her the men seemed":** Records of the Inquiry Conducted by Gen. William Hoffman, Records of the Adjutant General's Office, Record Group 153, National Archives, Washington, D.C.

139 **"if we arrive safe at Cairo":** Gene Eric Salecker, *Disaster on the Mississippi: The Sultana Explosion, April 27, 1865* (Annapolis, Md.: Naval Institute Press, 1996).

140–141 **"I . . . mingled with the living skeletons":** Jerry O. Potter, *The Sultana Tragedy: America's Greatest Maritime Disaster* (Gretna, La.: Pelican, 1992).

142 **Hundreds of passengers:** *National Tribune*, March 10, 1900.

142 **"Oh the awful sight!":** Jerry O. Potter, *The Sultana Tragedy: America's Greatest Maritime Disaster* (Gretna, La.: Pelican, 1992).

144 **"Captain Mason rushed into the steam-filled main cabin":** *Argus* (Memphis), May 28, 1865.

144 **"I thought the sights on the battle-fields":** Jerry O. Potter, *The Sultana Tragedy: America's Greatest Maritime Disaster* (Gretna, La.: Pelican, 1992).

145 **Fortunately for the courageous woman:** Gene Eric Salecker, *Disaster on the Mississippi* (Annapolis, Md.: Naval Institute Press, 1996).

145 **they had been clinging to the same log:** Jerry O. Potter, *The Sultana Tragedy: America's Greatest Maritime Disaster* (Gretna, La.: Pelican, 1992).

145 **"Although I felt that I would not drown":** Chester Berry, *Loss of the Sultana and Reminiscences of Survivors* (Lansing, Mich.: Darius D. Thorp, 1892).

146 **"Minutes seemed hours":** Chester Berry, *Loss of the Sultana and Reminiscences of Survivors* (Lansing, Mich.: Darius D. Thorp, 1892).

146 **"The cries of sufferers had ceased":** Jerry O. Potter, *The Sultana Tragedy: America's Greatest Maritime Disaster* (Gretna, La.: Pelican, 1992).

147 **"Now, when I hear persons talking":** Chester Berry, *Loss of the Sultana and Reminiscences of Survivors* (Lansing, Mich.: Darius D. Thorp, 1892).

148 **"One poor boy clutched":** William H. C. Michael, "Explosion of the *Sultana*," *Civil War Sketches and Incidents* (Omaha, Neb.: Commandery of the State of Nebraska, Military Order of the Loyal Legion of the United States, *1902).*

148 **Frank Barton was also credited:** Jerry O. Potter, *The Sultana Tragedy: America's Greatest Maritime Disaster* (Gretna, La.: Pelican, 1992).

148–149 **"We are still in hopes":** Ibid.

150–151 **"We have, as a people":** *Argus* (Memphis), May 8, 1865.

151 **"No troops belonging to States":** *New York Times*, May 3, 1865.

Chapter 8: America's First Subway

153 **By the time this secret subway was built:** Ric Burns et al., *New York: An Illustrated History* (New York: Knopf, 2003).

154 **It was, in many ways:** Kenneth T. Jackson and David S. Dunbar, *Empire City: New York Through the Centuries* (New York: Columbia University Press, 2002).

155 **Several New York doctors speculated:** Edward Robb Ellis, *The Epic of New York City: A Narrative History* (New York: Kodansha America, 1997).

155–156 **"The driver swears at the passengers":** James Blaine Walker, *Fifty Years of Rapid Transit, 1864–1917* (New York: Arno Press, 1970).

159 **"The entire distance [of the tunnel]":** Alfred E. Beach, *The Pneumatic Dispatch* (New York: American News Company, 1868).

160 **"[It] is by far the largest machine":** Alfred E. Beach, *Illustrated Description of the Broadway Pneumatic Underground Railway with a Full Description of the Atmospheric Machinery and the Great Tunneling Machine* (New York: S. W. Green, 1870).

161 **"A tube, a car, a revolving fan":** Alfred E. Beach, *The Pneumatic Dispatch* (New York: American News Company, 1868).

163–164 **"It is . . . estimated":** Ibid.

165 **The building, which in 1858 was originally budgeted:** Kenneth Ackerman, *Boss Tweed: The Rise and Fall of the Corrupt Pol Who Conceived the Soul of Modern New York* (New York: Carroll & Graf, 2005).

165 **Among the possessions for which he was best known:** Ibid.

170 **"Our original intention was to construct":** "The Broadway Mystery," *New York Times,* January 8, 1870, www.nycsubway.org/articles/beach-1870-01-08.html.

170 **On February 26, Beach held his reception:** Alfred E. Beach, *Illustrated Description of the Broadway Pneumatic Underground Railway with a Full Description of the Atmospheric Machinery and the Great Tunneling Machine* (New York: S. W. Green, 1870).

172 **"The conductor touched a telegraph wire":** Ibid.

172 **"So the world goes on":** Helen C. Weeks, "What a Bore!" *Youth's Companion,* February 2, 1871, p. 40, www.merrycoz.org/yc/BORE.HTM.

173 **"The days of dusty horsecars and rumbling omnibuses":** Ibid.

174 **Unlike the subway extension proposal:** Alfred E. Beach, *Illustrated Description of the Broadway Pneumatic Underground Railway with a Full Description of the Atmospheric Machinery and the Great Tunneling Machine* (New York: S. W. Green, 1870).

174 **"It is only through an underground railway":** Joseph Brennan, *Beach Pneumatic,* 2004–2005, www.columbia.edu/~brennan/beach/.

177 **"Now is it likely I'm going to run away?":** Kenneth Ackerman, *Boss Tweed: The Rise and Fall of the Corrupt Pol Who Conceived the Soul of Modern New York* (New York: Carroll & Graf, 2005).

Chapter 9: Peshtigo

183 **By 1870, more than seven miles:** "Remembering the Peshtigo Fire," *Peshtigo Times*, October 7, 1998.

183 **Six miles northeast was Marinette:** Denise Gess and William Lutz, *Firestorm at Peshtigo: A Town, Its People, and the Deadliest Fire in American History* (New York: Henry Holt, 2002).

184–185 **"Farmers had profited":** Peter Pernin, "The Great Peshtigo Fire: An Eyewitness Account," *Wisconsin Magazine of History* 54, No. 4 (1971). Courtesy of the State Historical Society of Wisconsin, www.library.wisc.edu/etext/WIReader/WER2002-1.html.

186–187 **"On September 22":** Ibid.

187 **Father Pernin's narrow escape:** Peter Pernin, *The Great Peshtigo Fire: An Eyewitness Account* (Madison: Wisconsin Historical Society Press, 2nd ed., 1999).

188 **"I have . . . seen fires sweep":** Peter Pernin, "The Great Peshtigo Fire: An Eyewitness Account," *Wisconsin Magazine of History* 54, No. 4 (1971). Courtesy of the State Historical Society of Wisconsin, www.library.wisc.edu/etext/WIReader/WER2002-1.html.

188–189 **"Sunday evening, after church":** Elias Colbert and Everett Chamberlin, *Chicago and the Great Conflagration* (Cincinnati: C. F. Vent, 1872).

189 **"To reach the river":** Ibid.

192 **"Horses' manes and tails blowin' to the right":** Alice Behrend, *Burning Bush* (Peshtigo, Wis.: Peshtigo Times, 2002).

193 **"Scores failed to reach the river at all":** Franklin Tilton, *Sketch of the Great Fires in Wisconsin at Peshtigo . . . and Thrilling and Truthful Tales by Eye Witnesses* (Green Bay, Wis.: Robinson and Kustermann, 1871).

193 **"The bridge was thoroughly encumbered":** Peter Pernin, "The Great Peshtigo Fire: An Eyewitness Account," *Wisconsin Magazine of History* 54, No. 4 (1971). Courtesy of the State Historical Society of Wisconsin, www.library.wisc.edu/etext/WIReader/WER2002-1.html.

194 **"Standing in the cold water":** Ibid.

194 **"Ever'thin' was driftin' up against us":** Alice Behrend, *Burning Bush* (Peshtigo, Wis.: Peshtigo Times, 2002).

195 **"I looked up the street":** "Remembering the Peshtigo Fire," *Peshtigo Times*, October 7, 1998.

196 **Gradually, those who had managed:** Denise Gess and William Lutz, *Firestorm at Peshtigo: A Town, Its People, and the Deadliest Fire in American History* (New York: Henry Holt, 2002).

196 **"My father saved his orphaned children":** Alice Behrend, *Burning Bush* (Peshtigo, Wis.: Peshtigo Times, 2002).

196 **"At the boarding house":** Franklin Tilton, *Sketch of the Great Fires in Wisconsin at Peshtigo . . . and Thrilling and Truthful Tales by Eye Witnesses* (Green Bay, Wis.: Robinson and Kustermann, 1871).

197 **"Here lay a group":** Ibid.

197 **"Whilst wandering among the ruins":** Peter Pernin, "The Great Peshtigo Fire: An Eyewitness Account," *Wisconsin Magazine of History* 54, No. 4 (1971). Courtesy of the State Historical Society of Wisconsin, www.library.wisc.edu/etext/WIReader/WER2002-1.html.

197 **Like Frank Tilton, owner and editor Luther Noyes:** Denise Gess and William Lutz, *Firestorm at Peshtigo: A Town, Its People, and the Deadliest Fire in American History* (New York: Henry Holt, 2002).

198 **"Alas that I should have to record":** Peter Pernin, "The Great Peshtigo Fire: An Eyewitness Account," *Wisconsin Magazine of History* 54, No. 4 (1971). Courtesy of the State Historical Society of Wisconsin, www.library.wisc.edu/etext/WIReader/WER2002-1.html.

198–199 **"After daylight, stragglers began":** Franklin Tilton, *Sketch of the Great Fires in Wisconsin at Peshtigo . . . and Thrilling and Truthful Tales by Eye Witnesses* (Green Bay, Wis: Robinson and Kustermann, 1871).

200 **"In the entire Upper Bush country":** Elias Colbert and Everett Chamberlin, *Chicago and the Great Conflagration* (Cincinnati: C. F. Vent, 1872).

200 **"When I heard the roar of the approaching tornado":** Franklin Tilton, *Sketch of the Great Fires in Wisconsin at Peshtigo . . . and Thrilling and Truthful Tales by Eye Witnesses* (Green Bay, Wis.: Robinson and Kustermann, 1871).

201 **Frances Fairchild, the governor's wife:** Denise Gess and William Lutz, *Firestorm at Peshtigo: A Town, Its People, and the Deadliest Fire in American History* (New York: Henry Holt, 2002).

201 **Ogden, who had lost over $1 million in property:** Ibid.

203 **On February 24, 1872, in a tribute:** Denise Gess and William Lutz, *Firestorm at Peshtigo: A Town, Its People, and the Deadliest Fire in American History* (New York: Henry Holt, 2002).

203 **"The true total will never be known"**: Peter Pernin, "The Great Peshtigo Fire: An Eyewitness Account," *Wisconsin Magazine of History* 54, No. 4 (1971). Courtesy of the State Historical Society of Wisconsin, www.library.wisc.edu/etext/WIReader/WER2002-1.html.

204 **What *is* known is that for years after the fire**: Denise Gess and William Lutz, *Firestorm at Peshtigo: A Town, Its People, and the Deadliest Fire in American History* (New York: Henry Holt, 2002).

204–205 **"A prolonged drought, a rural agriculture"**: Stephen J. Payne's foreword to the reprint edition of Peter Perrin, *The Great Peshtigo Fire: An Eyewitness Account.* Madison: Wisconsin Historical Society Press, 1999.

Chapter 10: Gustave Whitehead

209 **"In approximately April or May 1899"**: G. K. Weissenborn, "Did Whitehead Fly?" *Air Enthusiast,* January 1988.

209 **"I recall that someone was"**: Ibid.

210–211 **"A novel flying machine"**: *Scientific American,* June 8, 1901.

212–213 **"When the power was shut"**: *Bridgeport Herald,* August 18, 1901.

214 **"Mr. Whitehead . . . last Tuesday night" these articles stated**: *New York Herald,* August 19, 1901; *Boston Transcript,* August 19, 1901.

214 **"It's a funny sensation to fly"**: *Bridgeport Herald,* August 18, 1901.

215 **"Not far ahead the long field ended"**: Ibid.

216 **"I did witness and was present"**: G. K. Weissenborn, "Did Whitehead Fly?" *Air Enthusiast,* January 1988.

217 **the Spanish-American War**: Frank Delear, "Gustave Whitehead and the First Flight Controversy," *Aviation History,* March 1996.

217 **"Whitehead in 1901 and Wright Brothers in 1903"**: Ibid.

221 **"Newspaper readers will remember"**: Megan Adam, "Gustave Whitehead's Flying Machine," www.deepsky.com/~firstflight/Pages/article4.html.

222 **Forced to take a job**: Frank Delear, "Gustave Whitehead and the First Flight Controversy," *Aviation History,* March 1996.

225 **"Weisskopf's excommunication from the halls"**: G. K. Weissenborn, "Did Whitehead Fly?" *Air Enthusiast,* January 1988.

225 **In what can only be regarded:** Thomas D. Crouch, *A Dream of Wings: Americans and the Airplane, 1875–1905* (New York: Norton, 1976).

227 **"The long-suffering ghost of Gustave Whitehead":** Frank Delear, "Gustave Whitehead and the First Flight Controversy," *Aviation History*, March 1996.

Chapter 11: Exercise Tiger

230–231 **"I am concerned over the absence":** Harry C. Butcher, *My Three Years with Eisenhower: The Personal Diary of Harry C. Butcher* (New York: Simon and Schuster, 1946).

232 **Under authority of the 1939 Compensation:** Ken Small, *The Forgotten Dead* (London: Bloomsbury, 1988).

234 **"NOTICE":** "The Evacuation of the South Hams by Jane Putt," www.bbc. co.uk/ww2peopleswar/stories/25/a8633225.shtml.

237 **Some were armed with either:** Ralph C. Greene and Oliver E. Allen, "What Happened Off Devon," *American Heritage*, February/March 1985.

238 **"We crossed the convoy route":** Ibid.

238 **"We all saw it":** Ibid.

239 **"[At 2:30 a.m.]":** Ibid.

239 **"General Quarters rudely aroused us":** Naval Historical Center, Oral Histories—Exercise Tiger, 28 April 1944, Recollections by Lt. Eugene E. Eckstam, MC, USNR (Ret.), adapted from "The Tragedy of Exercise Tiger," *Navy Medicine* 85, No. 3 (May–June 1994): 5–7.

240 **"There was a deafening roar":** Susan English and Aaron Elson, *A Mile in Their Shoes: Conversations with Veterans of World War II* (Maywood, NJ: Chi Chi Press, 1998).

240 **"Suddenly . . . there was [another] explosion":** Clifford M. Graves, *Front Line Surgeons: A History of the Third Auxiliary Surgery Group* (San Diego: Frye and Smith, 1950).

240 **"Trucks, men, and jeeps":** Ralph C. Greene and Oliver E. Allen, "What Happened off Devon," *American Heritage,* February/March 1985.

241 **"There were a lot of guys on the front end":** Susan English and Aaron Elson, *A Mile in Their Shoes: Conversations with Veterans of World War II* (Maywood, NJ: Chi Chi Press, 1998).

241 **"The worst memory I have"**: Paul Stokes, "Veterans Honour 749 Who Died in D-Day Rehearsal," *Daily Telegraph* (London), April 29, 1994.

243 **Although it took hours:** Ralph C. Greene and Oliver E. Allen, "What Happened Off Devon," *American Heritage*, February/March 1985.

243 **"The convoy was now broken up"**: Ken Small, *The Forgotten Dead* (London: Bloomsbury, 1988).

244 **"We arrived in the area at daybreak"**: Ralph C. Greene and Oliver E. Allen, "What Happened Off Devon," *American Heritage*, February/March 1985.

244–245 **"We pulled away from [our] sinking LST"**: Ken Small, *The Forgotten Dead* (London: Bloomsbury, 1988).

245–246 **"I spotted some wreckage"**: Ibid.

246 **"When we got closer to land"**: Ralph C. Greene and Oliver E. Allen, "What Happened Off Devon," *American Heritage*, February/March 1985.

247 **"We're in the war at last"**: Ibid.

247 **"They were filled"**: Ibid.

248 **Typical of the statements:** Charles H. MacDonald, "Slapton Sands: The Cover-up That Never Was," *Army* 38, No. 6 (June 1988).

250 **"virtually no records"**: Ken Small, *The Forgotten Dead* (London: Bloomsbury, 1988).

250 **The Department of Defense agreed:** Ralph C. Greene and Oliver E. Allen, "What Happened Off Devon," *American Heritage*, February/March 1985.

BIBLIOGRAPHY

Chapter 1: Ziryab

Ali, Yusef. "The Music of the Moors in Spain," in "Golden Age of the Moor," ed. Ivan Van Sertima, *Journal of African Civilizations* 11, 1991.

Bosworth, Clifford E. *Encyclopedia of Islam*. Leiden, the Netherlands: Brill, 2004.

Burckhardt, Titus. *Moorish Culture in Spain*. New York: McGraw Hill, 1972.

Carew, Jan. "Moorish Culture-Bringers: Bearers of Enlightenment," in "Golden Age of the Moor," ed. Ivan Van Sertima, *Journal of African Civilizations* 11, 1991.

DeGuyangos, Pascual, trans. *Ahmed Ibn Al–Makkari*. New York: Johnson Reprint Corp., 1964.

Lowney, Chris. *A Vanished World: Medieval Spain's Golden Age of Enlightenment*. New York: Free Press, 2005.

Morgan, Michael H. *Lost History. Enduring Legacy of Muslim Scientists, Thinkers, and Artists*. Washington, D.C.: National Geographic, 2007.

Read, Jan. *The Moors in Spain and Portugal*. Totowa, NJ: Rowman and Littlefield, 1975.

Ribera, Julian. *Music in Ancient Arabia and Spain*. Stanford, Calif.: Stanford University Press, 1929; reprint: Whitefish, Mont.: Kessinger Publishing, 2007.

Selim, George Dimitri. "A Gift of Music," *Library of Congress Information Bulletin*, Vol. 55, No. 15, 1996.

Stanley, Lane Poole. *The Story of the Moors in Spain*. New York: G. P. Putnam's, 1886.

Talebzadeh, G. "Zaryâb: A Genius Iranian Musician." Fravahr.org, 2003.

Terrasse, Henri. *Islam d'Espagne: Une rencontre de l'Orient et de l'Occident* [Islamic Spain: A Meeting of East and West]. Paris: Plon, 1958.

BIBLIOGRAPHY

Chapter 2: Cahokia

Baldwin, J. D. *Ancient America*. New York: Harper and Brothers, 1871.

Brinkley, Alan. *American History: A Survey* Vol. 1. New York: McGraw-Hill, 2007.

Chappell, Sally A. Kitt. *Cahokia: Mirror of the Cosmos*. Chicago: University of Chicago Press, 2002.

Dalan, Rinita. *Envisioning Cahokia: A Landscape Perspective*. DeKalb, Ill.: Northern Illinois University Press, 2003.

Denny, Sidney G., and Ernest Lester Schusky. *The Ancient Splendor of Prehistoric Cahokia*. Prairie Grove, Ark.: Ozark Publishing, 1997.

Emerson, Thomas E., and R. Barry Lewis. *Cahokia and the Hinterlands: Middle Mississippian Cultures of the Midwest*. Champaign, Ill.: University of Illinois Press, 1999.

Foster, J. W. *Pre-Historic Races of the United States of America*. London: S. C. Griggs and Co., 1887.

Fowler, Melvin L., and Biloine W. Young, *Cahokia: The Great Native American Metropolis*. Champaign, Ill.: University of Illinois Press. 2000.

Kroeber, Alfred L. "Native American Population," *American Anthropologist* 36, 1934.

Mann, Charles C. *1491: New Revelations of the Americas Before Columbus*. New York: Knopf, 2005.

Milner, George R. *The Cahokian Chiefdom: The Archaeology of a Mississippian Society*. Gainsville, Fla.: University Press of Florida, 2006.

Mink, Claudia G. *Cahokia: City of the Sun*. Collinsville, Ill.: Cahokia Mounds Museum Society, 1992.

Pauketat, Timothy. *Ancient Cahokia and the Mississippians*. Cambridge: Cambridge University Press, 2004.

Young, Biloine Whiting, Melvin Fowler, et al. *Cahokia: The Great Native American Metropolis*. Champaign, Ill.: University of Illinois Press, 2000.

Chapter 3: Gil Eanes

Boorstein, Daniel. *The Discoverers: A History of Man's Search to Know His World and Himself.* New York, Random House, 1985.

Fiske, John. *The Discovery of America with Some Accounts of Ancient America and the Spanish Conquest.* Boston: Houghton, Mifflin and Company, 1892.

Helps, Sir Arthur and Peter Russell. *Prince Henry the Navigator.* Yale University Press, 2001.

Jeans, Peter D. *Seafaring Lore and Legend.* New York: McGraw-Hill, 2004.

Thomas, Hugh. *The Slave Trade: The Story of the Atlantic Slave Trade: 1440–1870.* New York: Simon and Schuster, 1997.

Villers, Alan. *Men, Ships and the Sea.* Washington, D.C.: National Geographic, 1962.

Zurara, Gomes Eanes de. *Crónica dos Feitos da Guiné* [The Chronicle of the Discovery and Conquest of Guinea], 1453.

Chapter 4: Joseph Warren

Boston Gazette. October 7, 1765.

Cary, John H. *Joseph Warren: Physician, Politician, Patriot.* Urbana, Ill.: University of Illinois Press, 1961.

Clay, Oliver. *Heroes of the American Revolution.* New York: Duffield and Company, 1916.

Ferling, John. *Almost a Miracle: The American Victory in the War of Independence.* New York: Oxford University Press, 2007.

Frothingham, Richard. *Life and Times of Joseph Warren.* Boston: Little, Brown and Company, 1865.

Hart, Benjamin. *Faith and Freedom: The Christian Roots of American Liberty.* Carrollton, Tex.: Lewis and Stanley, 1988.

John Adams Diary 19, 16 December 1772–18 December 1773 [electronic edition], Adams Family Papers: An Electronic Archive, Massachusetts Historical Society, www.masshist.org/digitaladams/.

Langguth, A. J. *Patriots: The Men Who Started the American Revolution.* New York: Simon and Schuster, 1988.

Meinig, D. W. *The Shaping of America: A Geographical Perspective on 500 Years of History.* Vol. 1: *Atlantic America.* New Haven, Conn.: Yale University Press, 1986.

The Works and Correspondence of the Right Honourable Edmund Burke. Vol. 3. London: Francis and John Rivington, 1852.

Chapter 5: Outdoing Revere

Bailey, James Montgomery. *History of Danbury, Conn., 1684–1896*. New York: Burr Printing House, 1896.

Case, James R. *An Account of Tryon's Raid on Danbury in April, 1777*. Danbury, Conn.: Danbury Printing Co., 1927.

Dabney, Virginius. "Jack Jouett's Ride," *American Heritage* 13, No. 1, 1961.

———. "Jouett Outrides Tarleton," *Scribner's*, June 1928.

———. *Virginia: The New Dominion, A History from 1607 to the Present*. Charlottesville, Va.: University of Virginia Press, 1989.

Johnson, Willis Fletcher. *Colonel Henry Ludington: A Memoir*. Whitefish, Mont.: Kessinger Publishing, 2007.

Langguth, A. J. *Patriots: The Men Who Started the American Revolution*. New York: Simon and Schuster, 1988.

Moran, Donald Norman, ed. "Jack Jouett of Virginia: The 'Other Ride.'" Reprint from *The Valley Compatriot*, February 1984, Americanrevolution.org.

Patrick, Louis S. "Secret Service of the American Revolution." *Connecticut Magazine* 11, No. 2 (1907): 265–274.

Randall, Henry S. *The Life of Thomas Jefferson*. New York: Derby and Jackson, 1858.

Van Dusen, Albert. *Connecticut: A Fully Illustrated History of the State from the Seventeenth Century to the Present*. New York: Random House, 1961.

Chapter 6: Elisha Kent Kane

Berton, Pierre. *The Arctic Grail: The Quest for the North West Passage and the North Pole, 1818–1909*. Toronto: Anchor Canada, 1988.

Hendrik, Hans. *Memoirs of Hans Hendrik, the Arctic Traveller Serving Under Kane, Hayes, Hall, and Nares*. London: Trubner & Co., 1876.

Kane, Elisha Kent. *Arctic Explorations: The Second Grinnell Expedition in Search of Sir John Franklin, 1853, '54, '55*. Philadelphia: Childs & Peterson, 1856.

———. *The United States Grinnell Expedition in Search of Sir John Franklin: A Personal Narrative*. Philadelphia: Childs & Peterson, 1854.

Rasky, Frank. *The North Pole or Bust*. N.p.: Book Sales, 1984.

Sandler, Martin W. *Resolute: The Epic Search for the Northwest Passage and John Franklin, and the Discovery of the Queen's Ghost Ship.* New York: Sterling, 2005.

Sawin, Mark Horst. "Raising Kane: The Making of a Hero, the Marketing of a Celebrity." Unpublished thesis, 1997, www.ekkane.org.

Chapter 7: The *Sultana*

Argus (Memphis), May 28, 1865.

Berry, Chester. *Loss of the Sultana and Reminiscences of Survivors.* Lansing, Mich.: Darius D. Thorp, 1892.

Catton, Bruce. *The American Heritage Short History of the Civil War.* New York: Dell Laurel Leaf, 1960.

Hunter, Louis. *Steamboats on the Western Rivers.* New York: Octagon Books, 1969.

Michael, William H. C. "Explosion of the *Sultana*." *Civil War Sketches and Incidents.* Omaha, Neb.: Commandery of the State of Nebraska, Military Order of the Loyal Legion of the United States, 1902.

New York Times, May 3, 1865.

Potter, Jerry O. *The Sultana Tragedy: America's Greatest Maritime Disaster.* Gretna, La.: Pelican, 1992.

Records of the Inquiry Conducted by Gen. William Hoffman, Records of the Adjutant General's Office, Record Group 153, National Archives, Washington, D.C.

"Reminiscence of the War." *Wayne County Democrat*, April 28, 1880.

Salecker, Gene Eric. *Disaster on the Mississippi: The Sultana Explosion, April 27, 1865.* Annapolis, Md.: Naval Institute Press, 1996.

Chapter 8: America's First Subway

Ackerman, Kenneth. *Boss Tweed: The Rise and Fall of the Corrupt Pol Who Conceived the Soul of Modern New York.* New York: Carroll & Graf, 2005.

Beach, Alfred E. *Illustrated Description of the Broadway Pneumatic Underground Railway with a Full Description of the Atmospheric Machinery and the Great Tunneling Machine.* New York: S. W. Green, 1870.

———. *The Pneumatic Dispatch.* New York: American News Company, 1868.

Brennan, Joseph. *Beach Pneumatic.* 2004–2005, www.columbia.edu/~brennan/beach/.

"The Broadway Mystery." *New York Times,* January 8, 1870, www.nycsubway.org/articles/beach-1870-01-08.html.

Burns, Ric, James Sanders, et al. *New York: An Illustrated History.* New York: Knopf, 2003.

Ellis, Edward Robb. *The Epic of New York City: A Narrative History.* New York: Kodansha America, 1997.

Fischler, Stan. *Subways of the World.* Minneapolis: MBI, 2000.

Heller, Vivian, and the New York Transit Museum. *The City Beneath Us: Building the New York City Subways.* New York: W. W. Norton, 2004.

Jackson, Kenneth T. and David S. Dunbar. *Empire City: New York Through the Centuries.* New York: Columbia University Press, 2002.

Pflueger, Lina. *Thomas Nast, Political Cartoonist.* Berkeley Heights, NJ: Enslow, 2000.

Walker, James Blaine. *Fifty Years of Rapid Transit, 1864–1917.* New York: Arno Press, 1970.

Weeks, Helen C. "What a Bore!" *Youth's Companion.* February 2, 1871, p. 40, www.merrycoz.org/yc/BORE.HTM.

Chapter 9: Peshtigo

Behrend, Alice. *Burning Bush.* Peshtigo, Wis.: Peshtigo Times, 2002.

Colbert, Elias, and Everett Chamberlin. *Chicago and the Great Conflagration.* Cincinnati: C. F. Vent, 1872.

Gess, Denise, and William Lutz. *Firestorm at Peshtigo: A Town, Its People, and the Deadliest Fire in American History.* New York: Henry Holt, 2002.

Holbrook, Stuart. *Burning an Empire: The Story of American Forest Fires.* New York: Macmillan, 1943.

Pernin, Peter. "The Great Peshtigo Fire: An Eyewitness Account." *Wisconsin Magazine of History* 54, No. 4 (1971). Courtesy of the State Historical Society of Wisconsin, www.library.wisc.edu/etext/WIReader/WER2002-1.html.

"Remembering the Peshtigo Fire." *Peshtigo Times,* October 7, 1998.

Tilton, Franklin. *Sketch of the Great Fires in Wisconsin at Peshtigo . . . and Thrilling and Truthful Tales by Eye Witnesses.* Green Bay, Wis.: Robinson and Kustermann, 1871.

BIBLIOGRAPHY

Chapter 10: Gustave Whitehead

Adam, Megan. "Gustave Whitehead's Flying Machine." www.deepsky.com/~firstflight/Pages/article4.html.

Boston Transcript, August 19, 1901.

Bridgeport Herald, August 18, 1901.

Crouch, Thomas D., *The Bishop's Boys: A Life of Wilbur and Orville Wright*. New York: Norton, 2003.

———. *A Dream of Wings: Americans and the Airplane, 1875-1905*. New York: Norton, 1976.

Delear, Frank. "Gustave Whitehead and the First Flight Controversy." *Aviation History*, March 1996.

Josephy, Alvin. *The American Heritage History of Flight*. New York: American Heritage, 1962.

New York Herald, August 19, 1901.

O'Dwyer, William. *History by Contract: The Beginning of Motorized Aviation, August 14, 1901: Gustave Whitehead Fairfield, Conn*. New York: F. Majer, 1978.

Randolph, Stella. *Before the Wrights Flew: The Story of Gustave Whitehead*. New York: Putnam, 1966.

Scientific American, June 8, 1901.

Weissenborn, G. K. "Did Whitehead Fly?" *Air Enthusiast*, January 1988.

Zahn, Albert. *Early Powerplane Fathers*. New York: University Press, 1945.

Chapter 11: Exercise Tiger

Bolkoski, Joseph. *Utah Beach: The Amphibious Landing and Airborne Operations on D-Day, June 6, 1944*. Mechanicsburg, Pa.: Stackpole Books, 2006.

Butcher, Harry C. *My Three Years with Eisenhower: The Personal Diary of Harry C. Butcher*. New York: Simon and Schuster, 1946.

English, Susan, and Aaron Elson. *A Mile in Their Shoes: Conversations with Veterans of World War II*. Maywood, NJ: Chi Chi Press, 1998.

"The Evacuation of the South Hams by Jane Putt." www.bbc.co.uk/ww2peopleswar/stories/25/a8633225.shtml.

BIBLIOGRAPHY

Greene, Ralph C., and Oliver E. Allen. "What Happened Off Devon." *American Heritage;* February/March 1985.

Lewis, Nigel. *Exercise Tiger: The Dramatic Story of a Hidden Tragedy of World War II.* New York: Prentice Hall, 1990.

MacDonald, Charles H. "Slapton Sands: The Cover-up That Never Was." *Army* 38, No. 6, June 1988.

Naval Historical Center. Oral Histories—Exercise Tiger, 28 April 1944, Recollections by Lt. Eugene E. Eckstam, MC, USNR (Ret.), adapted from "The Tragedy of Exercise Tiger," *Navy Medicine* 85, no. 3 (May–June 1994): 5–7.

Small, Ken. *The Forgotten Dead.* London: Bloomsbury, 1988.

Stokes, Paul. "Veterans Honour 749 Who Died in D-Day Rehearsal." *Daily Telegraph* (London), April 29, 1994.

⇥ INDEX ⇤

Note: Page numbers in *italics* refer to illustrations and photographs/captions.

Index

INDEX

INDEX

✦ PHOTO CREDITS ✦

Courtesy Cahokia Mounds State Historic Site: 18, 24, 30

Courtesy of Geography & Map Division, Library of Congress: 87: g3784d ar102500; 183: g4124p pm010495

Courtesy Google Books: 118: *Arctic Explorations: The Second Grinnell Expedition in Search of Sir John Franklin, 1853, '54, '55,* by Elisha Kent Kane (1856)

Courtesy of Library of Congress American Memory: 82: Portfolio 38, Folder 18b/rbpe 0380180b; 182: DN-0058274, *Chicago Daily News* negatives collection, Chicago History Museum

Courtesy of Prints & Photographs Division, Library of Congress: ii: LC-DIG-highsm-02121; 57: LC-DIG-ppmsca-15713; 59: LC-USZ62-21637; 75: LC-DIG-ppmsca-05484; 78: LC-USZ62-45282; 112: LC-USZ62-95944; 134: LC-DIG-cwpb-01012; 137: (detail) LC-DIG-ppmsca-10762; 141: LC-USZ62-48778; 142: LC-USZ62-77201; 147: LC-USZ62-117669; 150: LC-USZC4-5341; 152: LC-DOG-pga-02127; 154: LC-USZ62-95636; 165: USZ62-22467; 167: LC-USZ62-73662; 168: LC-USZ62-73661; 171: LC-USZ62-73660; 175: LC-DIG-ppmsca-10607; 178: LC-USZ62-43668; 180: LC-USZ62-104898; 185: LC-USZ62-105558; 199: LC-USZ62-75221; 202: LC-USZ62-109591; 228: LC-USZ62-132795

Courtesy of Library of Congress Rare Book and Special Collections Division: 67: us0012_01

Courtesy of the National Oceanic & Atmospheric Administration (NOAA): 108: theb3498; 113: libr0568; 116: libr0562; 126: libr0559

Copyright by William J. O'Dwyer and Flughistorische Forschungsgemeinschaft Gustav Weisskopf: 206, 208, 210, 211, 216, 218–19, 226 (http://www.weisskopf.de)

Courtesy of Wikimedia Commons: xii: Fresco chehel sotoun 26; 6: Mosque Cordoba/Author: Timor Espallargas; 9: Mehmooni2/Photo by User Zereshk; 15: DeCessolis/Author: William Caxton (publisher); 38–39: Monk's mound panorama/Author: Tim Vickers; 40: Azulejos Parque Eduardo VII-1/Author: Alvesgaspar; 46–47: Africae tabula nova/Contributor: PALMM Project/Florida Map Collection Project; 52: GilEannes-Lagos/Author: Glen Bowman; 60: LC-DIG-ppmsca 15709;

63: LC-DIG-ppmsca-19159; 70: CongressJournal1774Cover/ http://diplomacy. state.gov/exhibitions/100935.htm; 79: WarrenPutnam/NYPL; 84: Paul Reveres Ride BAH-p-114/Montgomery's The Beginner's American History; 91: Riflemen at Saratoga/US Army Center of Military History/painting by Hugh Charles McBarron, Jr.; 96: Ludington statue 800/Author: Anthony22; 99: Jack jouett silhouette/http://www.history.org/Foundation/journal/Summer06/ride.cfml; 124: Life in the brig cropped/Arctic Explorations, by Elisha Kent Kane, published in Philadelphia in 1856/Engraving by J.M. Butler based on a sketch by Dr. Kane; 156: Alfred Ely Beach/http://fdelaitre.perso.sfr.fr/BeachPortrait.jpe; 157: *Scientific American*, volume 14, issue 32, page 257; 162–63: Pneumatic Dispatch—Figure 7/"The Pneumatic Dispatch" (pamphlet), by Alfred Ely Beach, American News Co. via Google Books; 204: PeshtigoFireCemetery; 230: D-Day allied assault routes/Source: Center for Military History/Author: Lhgodoy; 231: LST325-1044/ Source: http://www.lstmemorial.org/history/17d.jpg (USS LST Ship Memorial); 233: Slapton Sands 1; 237: Bundesarchiv Bild 101II-MW-1913-31, Schnellboot übernimmt Torpedos/Author: Vorländer; 250: Sherman tank at memorial for those killed in Operation Tiger/Author: Shahirshamsir; 251: SC206438/Source: http:// www.history.army.mil/reference/Normandy/Pictures.htm/Author: Nehez

Shutterstock: 54: © Shutterstock/Alex Neauville

State Historical Society of Wisconsin: 190–91

Courtesy of the US Navy Historical Center: 131: NH 59607; 236 and 242: The US Navy Historical Center/Exercise Tiger National Foundation

✦ A NOTE ON THE TYPE ✦

Lost to Time is composed largely in the classic font known as Adobe Caslon. Caslon was originally designed in 1725 by acclaimed English font designer William Caslon, for whom the font was named. Caslon's typefaces were among the most popular in the eighteenth century and were used for the first printings of the Declaration of Independence and the Constitution. Today's Adobe Caslon is a revival of the original type cut by Caslon; it was created by Adobe Systems Inc. in 1990 under the direction of Carol Twombly. The other font used is Trajan (1989), also designed by Carol Twombly, who was inspired by the inscription on the base of Trajan's Column in Rome.

Printed and bound by Maple-Vail in York, Pennsylvania.

Interior designed by Christine Heun.